Theorizing Muriel Spark

Also by Martin McQuillan

DECONSTRUCTION: A Reader

DECONSTRUCTING DISNEY (*with Eleanor Byrne*)

THE NARRATIVE READER

PAUL DE MAN

POST-THEORY: New Directions in Criticism (*co-editor*)

Theorizing Muriel Spark

Gender, Race, Deconstruction

Edited by

Martin McQuillan
Lecturer in Cultural Theory and Analysis
University of Leeds

First published 2002 by
PALGRAVE
Houndmills, Basingstoke, Hampshire RG21 6XS and
175 Fifth Avenue, New York, N. Y. 10010
Companies and representatives throughout the world

PALGRAVE is the new global academic imprint of
St. Martin's Press LLC Scholarly and Reference Division and
Palgrave Publishers Ltd (formerly Macmillan Press Ltd).

ISBN 0–333–79414–1

This book is printed on paper suitable for recycling and
made from fully managed and sustained forest sources.

A catalogue record for this book is available
from the British Library.

Library of Congress Cataloging-in-Publication Data
Theorizing Muriel Spark : gender, race, deconstruction / edited by
Martin McQuillan.
        p. cm.
    Includes bibliographical references and index.
    ISBN 0–333–79414–1
        1. Spark, Muriel—Criticism and interpretation. 2. Women and
literature—Great Britain—History—20th century. 3. Sex role in
literature. 4. Race in literature. 5. Deconstruction. I. McQuillan,
Martin.
    PR6037.P29 Z94 2001
    823'.914—dc21
                                                                2001036535

10   9   8   7   6   5   4   3   2   1
11   10   09   08   07   06   05   04   03   02

Printed and bound in Great Britain by
Antony Rowe Ltd, Chippenham, Wiltshire

Contents

v

Part III Deconstruction

Acknowledgements

It seems that I have been proselytizing about Muriel Spark for most of my adult life. Consequently I would like to thank all those who have been prepared to discuss her work with me over the years. In chronological order (I think) Paddy Lyons, Sandra Kemp, Drummond Bone, Patrick Reilly, Vassiliki Kolokotroni, John Coyle, Bob Maslen, Dorothy Macmillan, Philip Hobsbaum, Faith Pullen, Helen Boden, Brian Reid, Robin Purves, Graeme Macdonald, Stephen Thomson, Paul Wilson, Gun Orgun, Ellen Jackson, Claire Brennan, Megan Fowler, Jeremy Lane, Leslie Macdowell, Shona Allen, Mary Reilly, Janet Stewart, Damien Walsh, Donald MacLoed, Antony Roland, Angela Keane, Peter Buse, Nuria Triana-Toribio, Sharon Kivland, Scott McCracken, Robert Eaglestone, and Lucie Wenigerova. Special thanks go to all the contributors for their wisdom and support, Charmian Hearne, who first commissioned this book, and Eleanor Birne, who saw it through to the end. I would also like to thank the School of Humanities and Social Sciences at Staffordshire University which funded a visit to Tuscany, and Robin Smith of the National Library for Scotland whose help has been invaluable. I would like to single out Alan Taylor for very special thanks for all his encouragement and support since the beginnings of my research. Acknowledgements are also due to the publishers of Muriel Spark's work and other copyright material. This book is dedicated to Muriel Spark and Penelope Jardine in thanks for their kind hospitality.

MARTIN McQUILLAN

Abbreviations

References for quotations from the works of Muriel Spark will be given in the body of the text, with the following abbreviations:

A   *The Abbess of Crewe*
BA   *The Bachelors*
BP   *The Ballad of Peckham Rye*
CO   *The Comforters*
CS   *The Collected Stories of Muriel Spark*
CV   *Curriculum Vitae*
DA   'The Desegregation of Art'
DS   *The Driver's Seat*
G   *The Girls of Slender Means*
I   *The Public Image*
K   *A Far Cry From Kensington*
L   *Loitering with Intent*
MG   *The Mandlebaum Gate*
MM   *Memento Mori*
MS   *Mary Shelley: A Biography*, revised edition
N   *Not to Disturb*
O   *The Only Problem*
P   *The Prime of Miss Jean Brodie*
S   *Symposium*
TT   *The Takeover*
TR   *Territorial Rights*

Notes on the Contributors

Eleanor Byrne is Lecturer in English at Manchester Metropolitan University. She is the author (with Martin McQuillan) of *Deconstructing Disney* (1999). She has written on post-colonial literature and theory, film, and women's writing.

Bryan Cheyette is Professor of English and Judaic Studies at the University of Southampton. His publications include: *Constructions of 'the Jew' in English Literature and Society: Racial Representations, 1875–1945* (1995), *Muriel Spark* (2000), the edited volumes *Between 'Race' and Culture: Representations of 'the Jew' in English and American Literature* (1996), *Contemporary Jewish Writing in Britain and Ireland: An Anthology* (1998) and the co-edited volume *Modernity, Culture and 'the Jew'* (1998).

Hélène Cixous is Director of Studies at the Centre d'Études Féminines at the Université de Paris VIII. Her recent publications in English translation include *The Third Body* (1999), *First Days of the Year* (1998), *Stigmata* (1998), *Rootprints: Memory and Life Writing* (1997), *Manna, for the Mandelstams for the Mandelas* (1994), *Three Steps on the Ladder to Writing* (1993), *Readings, The Poetics of Blanchot, Joyce, Kafka, Lispector, Tsvetaeva* (1992), *'Coming to Writing' and Other Essays* (1991), *The Book of Promethea* (1991).

Patricia Duncker is Senior Lecturer in English at the University of Wales (Aberystwyth). Her publications include *Sisters and Strangers* (1992) and the acclaimed fictions *Hallucinating Foucault* (1996), *Monsieur Shoushana's Lemon Trees* (1998), and *Miranda James Barry* (2000).

Alan Freeman is Lecturer in British Literature and Literary Theory in Yeditepe University, Istanbul. He has written on women's writing, contemporary fiction, and Scottish literature.

Jeremy Idle is Lecturer in English at Nene University College. He has written on Georges Bataille, contemporary fiction, and Scottish literature.

Martin McQuillan is Lecturer in Cultural Theory and Analysis at the Centre for Cultural Studies, University of Leeds. His publications include *Deconstructing Disney* (1999) with Eleanor Byrne, the co-edited collection *Post-Theory: New Directions in Criticism* (1999), *The Narrative Reader* (2000), *Deconstruction: A Reader* (2000) and *Paul de Man* (2001).

Willy Maley is Professor of Renaissance Literature at the University of Glasgow. His publications include *Salvaging Spenser: Colonialism, Culture and Identity* (1997), *A View of the State of Ireland: From the First Published Edition* (1997), *A Spenser Chronology* (1994) and the co-edited volumes *Postcolonial Criticism* (1997), and *Representing Ireland: Literature and the Origins of Conflict, 1534–1660* (1993).

Judith Roof is Professor of English and Film Studies at Michigan State University. Her publications include *A Lure of Knowledge: Lesbian Sexuality and Theory* (1993), *Reproductions of Reproductions: Imaging Symbolic Change* (1996), *Come As You Are: Sexuality and Narrative* (1996), and the co-edited volumes *Who Can Speak? Authority and Critical Identity* (1995) and *Staging the Rage* (1998).

Nicholas Royle is Professor of English Literature at the University of Sussex. His publications include *Telepathy and Literature: Essays in the Reading Mind* (1991), *After Derrida* (1995), *E.M. Forster* (2000), *The Uncanny* (2000), the edited volumes *Afterwords* (1992) and *Deconstructions* (2000), and with Andrew Bennett *Elizabeth Bowen and the Dissolution of the Novel* (1994) and *An Introduction to Literature, Criticism, and Theory* (1999).

Susan Sellers is Professor of English Literature at the University of St. Andrews. Her publications include *Language and Sexual Difference* (1991), *Hélène Cixous: Authorship, Autobiography and Love* (1996), *Writing Differences: Readings from the Seminar of Hélène Cixous* (1998), *The Hélène Cixous Reader* (1994), *The Semi-Transparent Envelope* (1994) with Sue Roe, Nicole Ward Joue, and Michelle Roberts, and the co-edited volume *The Cambridge Companion to Virginia Woolf* (2000).

Julian Wolfreys is Associate Professor of English at the University of Florida. His publications include *Being English* (1994), *The Rhetoric of Affirmative Resistances* (1997), *Writing London* (1998), *Deconstruction – Derrida* (1998), *Readings* (2000), *The Derrida Reader: Writing Perfomances* (1998), *Literary Theories: A Reader and Guide* (1999) and the co-edited volumes *Victorian Identities: Social and Cultural Formations in Nineteenth-Century Literature* (1995), *Literary Theories: A Case Study in Critical Performance* (1996), *Applying: to Derrida* (1996), *Re: Joyce* (1998), *The French Connections of Jacques Derrida* (1999), *Victorian Gothic* (2000).

Introduction
'I Don't Know Anything about Freud': Muriel Spark Meets Contemporary Criticism

Martin McQuillan

> The world has surely become unhinged, and only violent movements can put it all back together. But it may be that among the instruments for doing so, there is one – tiny, fragile – which requires to be wielded delicately.
>
> Brecht[1]

> 'Fuck the general reader,' Solly said, 'because in fact the general reader doesn't exist.'
>
> *Loitering with Intent*

Religion within the limits of fiction alone

Muriel Spark is one of the most important novelists of the twentieth century. However, critical (as opposed to religious) orthodoxy declares that she 'is a Catholic writer'.[2] For some this may appear an unproblematic formulation but much will depend here upon what is meant by 'Catholic', 'writer' and – in the immortal words of William Jefferson Clinton – what the meaning of 'is' is. One does not need to go far to find testaments to this universal Catholic criticism. Malcolm Bradbury is perhaps the greatest sinner in this regard. In his oft-cited essay 'Muriel Spark's Fingernails' he writes that 'Mrs. Spark' can be compared to 'a number of our Catholic writers (who have contributed more than their proportionate share to aesthetic speculation in the English novel).'[3] It is not clear what one should be most surprised by here, the marginalizing gesture of fixing the marital status of a female author (what for heaven's sake is wrong with referring to her as plain 'Muriel Spark') or the quaint assumptions about Anglo-Protestant hegemony. Who are the collective 'we' implied by 'our Catholic

1

writers'? A phrase which is on a par with 'our best China' or 'our pet spaniels'. One can imagine the disquiet had Bradbury referred in such assured tones to 'our black writers' or 'our Jewish writers'.

What is this thing 'the English novel' to which these poor souls 'have contributed more than their proportionate share'? If it refers to novels produced by English people (and so apparently a predominantly Protestant affair), Muriel Spark is Scottish. The question of the 'Catholic contribution' to the Scottish novel would be a matter of an altogether different sectarian stripe. If it refers to the novel in English, then this worldwide phenomenon is surely more Catholic than it ever was Protestant: Joyce, Beckett, O'Brien, Ford, Conrad, McCarthy, O'Conner, Burgess, Hemingway, Fitzgerald, Dos Passos, and so on. One will never hear an Irish critic speak of 'our Catholic writers' or an American critic suggest that Catholics 'have contributed more than their proportionate share' to the novel. In fact the question of 'aesthetic speculation in the English novel' owes more to non-English, European or South American (Catholic) influences than to internal development: Zola, Proust, Bataille, Robbe-Grillet, Marquez, Eco, and so on. The idea of 'the Catholic writer', so complacently invoked in conjunction with Spark's name, depends upon a corresponding idea of 'the English novel' and English society which is equally fixed and equally unreal. Evelyn Waugh and Graham Greene might be thought of as Catholic writers (although none of their novels ever carried a papal imprimatur) but it is equally impossible to understand the work of James Joyce, Edna O'Brien, Neil Jordan, or Alan Bleasdale (whose confessions would all make interesting listening) outside of an idea of Catholicism. What is Shakespeare if not a Catholic writer? What is Pedro Almodovar if not a Catholic film-maker? As if the idea of 'Catholicism' could be prophylacticly sealed; as if 'converting' to Catholicism were the equivalent of a software upgrade. One wonders what 'the Protestant novel' or 'Protestant writing' might look like: Jeanette Winterson and John Milton make strange bedfellows.

Such divisive and rigid categorization (which takes little account of Spark's Scottish Presbyterian upbringing and entirely overlooks her avowed Jewish cultural history) leads to doctrinal criticism, which reads Spark's novels for moral and theological content, reading her texts like the penny catechism. For example, in his account of *The Driver's Seat* Bradbury writes:

> The casual relationships with strangers, the hints of sexual complicity, the passing claims of politics, the truth or otherwise of

revolutionary promise and of the substantial world of economic or material temptations: these are the things that make up the main substance of the story, diverse alternatives which are then put in their place by her [Lise's] own discounting of the contingent by the morally, philosophically, and theological artful use of her own mortality.

(p. 253)

In other words, everything which might be interesting about this book is squeezed out by Bradbury's reading, in the name of a Catholic doctrinal, orthodoxy which is nowhere present in the novel and is constantly subverted by Spark's other hybrid-convert characters, from Caroline Rose's antipathy towards her fellow Catholics in *The Comforters* onwards. If one takes 'the hints of sexual complicity', remotely serious in this novel, it becomes a thoroughly immoral read. The book ends with the 'clank' of the police typewriter ticking out an 'unnerving statement' by Lise's murderer in which he says 'she told me to kill her' (DS, p. 107). From here the whole of the novel, with its cool as marble depthlessness and its refusal to engage with the emotions or motivations of its characters, can be reread as an unnerving police report. Such self-referential endings are a common Sparkian conceit: *The Comforters* itself turns out to be the novel Caroline is writing, *The Abbess of Crewe* is revealed as the edited transcripts published by the Abbess. In *The Driver's Seat* this institutionally patriarchal report writes to type and blames the female victim (whose name is an anagram of 'lies') for being complicit in her own rape and murder. As readers we are encouraged by this reportage to confuse chronology with consequence [*post hoc ergo propter hoc*] and view Lise as a willing accomplice in her own death – she was asking for it. Far from being philosophically and theologically 'useful' her death is brutal and shocking. Given that the 'discounting of the contingent' in the name of an artful end is the very work of narrative itself, what does this novel have to say about the reporting of women's experience by men? Spark's use of the form of the 'anti-novel' allows her to invert the inequalities of narrative, which determine the history of 'the English novel'. As Jane Austen's character Anne Elliot notes early on in this history, men have always been in the driver's seat: '. . . no reference to examples in books. Men have had every advantage of us in telling their own story . . . the pen has been in their hands. I will not allow books to prove any thing.'[4]

Frank Kermode describes Spark as 'an unremittingly Catholic

novelist committed to immutable truths'.[5] Fiction would seem an odd career choice for someone 'committed to immutable truths'. However, for Kermode, 'like the wit of the seventeenth-century preacher, they are jokes for God's sake, [Spark's are] fictions which have to do with truth' (p. 273). The novelist, like the devil, is the father (or mother) of lies and as Shelley notes, all writers are of the devil's quarter. Spark writes fictions (for God's sake) not theological pamphlets. Incidentally, her 'theology', when it appears, is conveniently novelistic rather than rigorously orthodox. Graham Greene knew that the threat of eternal damnation was a useful narrative ploy, if not much cop for living one's life by. Kermode suggests that the interest of Spark 'for non-believers' is that even the pagans make plots and 'seek and accept images of order' (p. 274) so are well equipped to appreciate Spark's alleged absolute structures. This is an argument that seems to imply its own converse, namely that Spark's use of narrative is not necessarily any more Christian than it is pagan. If, as Kermode seems to assume, stories are everywhere and not only do we tell stories but stories tell us, then stories are always multiple (there is always more than one). Spark's novels and short stories always tell more than one story. More often than not the telling of her stories are always bound up with questions of power, authority, domination, and the proper (Jean Brodie, the Abbess of Crewe, Sir Quentin Oliver). Similarly, telling the story of Spark's critical reception would pass through these questions. The uncanny, 'experimental', or postmodern effects of her writing are continually reduced by the power and authority of English canonical criticism to the safe domain of the properly 'Catholic'. Even David Lodge, no stranger to the disruptive influence of 'modern criticism and theory', reads *The Prime of Miss Jean Brodie* (Spark's novel of Fascism and fascisms) as a contest 'between the Catholic God who allows free will and the Calvinistic one who doesn't'.[6] If only going to heaven were as simple as being the 'master' of a really good prolepsis.

My argument is not that Spark is not a writer who happens to be a Catholic (although Cardinal Winning might have got his cassock in a twist over what is promoted in Jean Brodie's classroom). Rather, if she is a 'Catholic', or 'religious', writer then this question of religion has yet to be thought. What does it mean to be a 'Catholic writer'? Surely, the term is an oxymoron. Writing is not a theological activity, it purposely undermines essential and stable meanings, which presuppose and seek a single and authoritative centre. Meaning is always plural, writing is always cut adrift from its source and origin. In this sense even the documents of the Catholic church are not Catholic, at least not Catholic in the sense that Bradbury and Kermode (two 'non-believers') suppose. Must one make reference to heaven, hell, death, and judgement (ideas not currently *en vogue* in the Catholic church) to be a 'Catholic writer'? In fact, in what way could a novelist writing in Europe in the last half of the twentieth century fail to be Catholic? Religion is everywhere, from the so-called rise of Islam to the American presidential hopefuls who pander to Midwest creationists, from the Irish peace process to the claims of European civilization employed to bomb Orthodox Serbia. The history of Europe (this includes America) is the history of the Christian (not to say Judeo–Christian) tradition. Islamaphobia has a history as long as the Crusades'. The Enlightenment and all that it implies (reason, science, philosophy, psychoanalysis, Marxism and so on) has a history at least as old as the Reformation, which in turn derives from a certain Catholic theological heritage. The current 'world war' between the West and its 'others' is a consequence of the history of Christian (undoubtedly Catholic) domination and colonization of the globe. Latin remains the world language through its cognate English, spoken by the assuredly Latin Americans. Globalization is, in Derrida's phrase, a project of 'globalatinization'.[7] Rome is both a site of the origins of European colonialism and Occidental onto-theology. The structure of our political experience remains messianic, from 'the promised land' of socialist utopia to 'the good news' of Francis Fukuyama's 'end of history'. In this sense the very idea of democracy as a universal value is a 'Catholic' one. It is impossible to be European today and not to be 'Catholic', it is impossible to live in the world today and not to be, in some way, 'Abrahamic'. No one is more 'Catholic' than Bradbury and Kermode who insist upon reading as a theological event, which finds fixed and authoritative meaning in the sense of an ending.

If Muriel Spark 'is a Catholic writer', then the 'is' here refers to the essence of Sparkness (she *is* Catholic, although her personal history encounters at least two of the Abrahamic religions). On the other hand, 'is' refers to the present indicative, she *is* today 'a Catholic'. Spark is a writer of the 'is', of the present. Her novels are a conductor for all the signs and meanings in circulation in the contemporary scene. Whether that scene is the decolonization of the fifties in her short stories, the feminist concerns of the sixties in *Jean Brodie*, the Eichmann trial in *The Mandlebaum Gate*, the early-seventies geo-political crisis of capital in *The Takeover*, the re-valuation of London in the eighties (*A Far Cry From Kensington*), or the question of redundancy in the nineties (*Reality and Dreams*). These texts are 'Catholic' in the sense that they treat the theological–political issues of the West over the course of the last five decades, which in so far as they are concerns for the West intrude upon the rest of the world and become 'universal' or 'catholic'. As texts, Spark's novels produce their own forms of knowledge, emerging from the historical conjunction in which they are rooted. Whether this knowledge is 'theologically' or 'philosophically' useful is yet to be determined. However, it is inextricably bound up with the conditions of postmodernity, which Spark's novels both record and define. Just as it would be difficult to read a renaissance play without some appreciation of renaissance history or renaissance cosmography, it is equally problematic to attempt to engage with postmodern literature (if that is what Spark's metafictions are) without reading them through postmodern forms of knowledge. This book brings together a collection of essays which attempts to read Spark's fiction through the philosophy and theory of the contemporary scene (feminism, postcolonialism, Marxism, psychoanalysis, deconstruction) and so takes an alternative view of Spark than the one offered by canonical criticism. This no more turns Spark into a 'theorist', a feminist, a Marxist, or a 'deconstructionist', than reading Shakespeare with a knowledge of Ptolemy's model of the universe turns Shakespeare into an astronomer. As Spark disarmingly states in the interview which concludes this book 'I don't know anything about Freud', this does not stop her writing being a source of the uncanny. As the Danish critic Bent Nordhjem writes:

> Muriel Spark's novels in their way incorporate all the fashionable isms of the modern scene: surrealism, existentialism, absurdism, structuralism, feminism, etc. They do not expound them but take them as read. The Spark world is made up of what little the storm has left. The novels focus on the fragments scattered by the trends.[8]

The most 'deconstructive' of literature can take place in the absence of knowledge of Derrida, while even an explicit disavowal of feminism does not stop Spark being a female writer in a man's world (even if that man is God).

It remains one of the curiosities of English Studies that while most of the canonical texts of English literature and all of the period specializations which make up the discipline have been thoroughly worked over by 'literary theory', contemporary writing (the writing contemporaneous with theory) remains more or less the preserve of the humanist criticism expelled from other areas. This is certainly true of critical accounts of Spark, from Bradbury and Kermode's admittedly 'dated' essays to more recent incursions by the likes of Judy Sproxton and Norman Page.[9] There remains a need to read contemporary writing (post-colonial criticism of course does justice to post-colonial literatures) in a theoretical mode. The persistent absence of such readings is particularly odd given that contemporary writing seems at pains to engage with theoretical ideas and postmodern epistemology. One might think of the proliferation of women's writing and women's presses which dovetailed with the ubiquity of academic feminism in the 1980s, or, of the visibility of post-colonial literature which accompanied the academic ascendancy of post-colonial theory in the 1990s. The history of Spark's writing is the history of post-War literature in English; it is indissociable from the history of post-War thought and the 'postmodern' opening. The task of 'theorizing Muriel Spark' (one might say the task of allowing 'Muriel Spark' to be thought) is long overdue.

Committed writers

How does one write today?

The mediatic and tele-technological conditions of social interaction and representation that shape the world today do not easily accommodate thought. The contemporary mediatic and political space is definingly marked by the absence of the intellectual. This is not to say that there are no intellectuals left or that they no longer have anything to say. Indeed, the opposite is true. The pertinence of quality thinking about our world has never been quite so evident, nor has the work been undertaken with such rigour and in such depth. The silence of the intellectual should not be confused with the death of the intellectual. Rather, another set of questions has to be asked: if the intellectual is not dead, and the terms of his/her analysis are more relevant than ever, why do they remain silent? What is it about the spaces of the social, politics and the media which renders them silent?[10]

Jacques Derrida suggests that intellectuals, reduced to silence by the banality and reductiveness of the media, 'need a bit more time, and are not prepared to adapt the complexity of their analysis to the conditions under which they would be permitted to speak.'[11] If the nightly news or the newspaper column is an inadequate and/or inappropriate space in which to provide a complex and complicating analysis of the social it does not mean that this interpretation is not taking place. That would be to mistake the thinking that must take place with what can be seen on television or read in newspapers. One must know then how to read the contemporary (the 'is'). One must be aware of the work that is taking place elsewhere, away from the cameras and the noise of pseudo-actuality which imposes silence on everything which is not on the same mediatic wavelength of pseudo-politics and bogus-journalism. The difficulty in reading what is being written can make the contemporary a disturbing, 'illegible', place. However, the fact of this writing leaves hope for the future, for what Derrida calls the 'reckoning with the untimely' and with 'the political virtue of the contretemps'.[12] The contretemps is an anachronistic virtue. Not only does it speak against the grain of the present moment but it disrupts the very pertinence of the now. The contretemps is at odds with the present and the idea of the present as the arbiter of truth, such as the homogenizing effects of mediatic discourse today. It is a voice that cries in the wilderness and in this way it is messianic without necessarily invoking a messiah. The contretemps calls for the arrival of another way of thinking, of a thought that cannot be recognized in advance but which in the event arrives.

The current space of the market-led media does not allow for the rigorous writing of critique, or for the rigorous critique of writing. Even today, more than thirty years after Roland Barthes proposed a new way of reading, 'the image of literature to be found in ordinary culture is [still] tyrannically centred on the author, his person, his life, his tastes, his passions'.[13] It is not so much that criticism continues to insist that 'Baudelaire's work is the failure of Baudelaire the man', but that our journalism persists in the belief that Martin Amis' teeth are of greater significance than his novels and that the periodic assertion of Muriel Spark's Catholicism is an adequate substitute for an account of her latest novel. The logic of the market is, as Baudrillard would say, 'all that is singular and irreducible must be reduced and absorbed.'[14] However, if we have long since given up hope of finding anything like 'reading' in our media, the question should be raised, how far is it possible to write a rigorous critique *per se*? It is no longer possible to be Zola, just as it is no longer possible to be Wilde, or Yeats, or Woolf, or Sartre. Wilde, Yeats, Woolf, and Sartre are not out of date: rather it is the form and space in which they wrote that are dated. For an artist in this age of tele-communication it is no longer enough to entrust the message (however revolutionary it might be) to the medium without questioning and transforming the forms of involvement open to the sender and the means by which any message might be sent.[15] This is part of the work which has to be done today to transform the public space which silences thought and action. It is not possible for remotely serious thinking to be heard above the din of today's mediatic pseudo-actuality, but even if one were able to be heard it would first be necessary to transform (as a condition of being allowed to speak) the means by which one speaks. A transformation is necessary to avoid even the most potent of thought being reduced and banalized by the media which relays it.

Following Hölderlin's elegy 'Bread and Wine' Heidegger asks, 'What are poets for in a destitute time?'[16] He answers himself by suggesting that the use of certain poets is that 'they dare the precinct of Being. They dare language' (p. 132). Heidegger continues: 'the mark of these poets is that to them the nature of poetry becomes worthy of questioning, because they are poetically on the track of that which, for them, is what must be said' (p. 141). For the writer in a destitute time – is today a destitute time? – commitment cannot be judged or expressed at the level of content. It is necessary to question the form of critique open to the writer: what Stephen Heath calls, 'an activity of reflection on this general writing, on the forms of intelligibility it sustains.'[17] As a condition of writing the contemporary at all, it is necessary, for the writer who thinks about what she is doing, to question the form of that writing. The way in which this questioning manifests itself – the form of the writing – represents a process of critique. Heath writes of the *nouveau roman*:

> The commitment of the *nouveau roman* lies here, then, in its reading of the formation of the 'Balzacian' novel and in its insistence on a work of research exploration, on understanding the foundations of intelligibility (of ourselves, of our world) in a presentation to the reader of possibilities of reading in the realisation of which he [sic] may read himself in his construction.
>
> (p. 33)

This does not just come down to the pat formulation that the writers of the *nouveau roman* (and the whole field of literature which follows from it, including Muriel Spark) were responding to the impossibility of continuing with the form of the 'Realist' novel in a new mediatic space. Rather, it implies that these writers were aware of the fact that it is narratives and signs (social and literary) which construct identity. Any disruption of the presentation of narrative forms would have consequences for the reader, who is constructed in the reading process and by signification in general.

The *nouveau roman*, and all that it means for the writing that follows it, is not an escape from narrative but a redistribution of narrative possibilities. It is a reaction to a certain use of narrative form in the novel, associated with the power of the middle class, and certain ideo-logically charged conceptions of the self and world. In as much as narrative is the mode by which we understand the world, to disrupt the hegemony of a certain narrative form is to introduce the possibility of a different way of understanding. The *nouveaux romanistes* (and those like Spark who cite them as an influence) thus question the forms of intelligibility and knowledge open to themselves, and present the reader with a different possibility of reading, 'in the realisation of which s/he may read [them]self in their construction.' Robbe-Grillet has said:

> Let us, then, restore to the notion of commitment the only meaning it can have for us. Instead of being of a political nature, commitment is, for the writer, the full awareness of the present problems of his own language, the conviction of their extreme importance, the desire to solve them *from within*. Here, for him, is the only chance of remaining an artist and, doubtless too, by means of an obscure and remote consequence, of some day serving some-thing – perhaps even the Revolution.[18]

That is to say, the poet in the destitute time can offer a radical commit-ment to reading and writing the contemporary by daring language, and so eschew a 'radical' political content in their writing.

Stephen Heath comments:

> Criticisms of the supposed non-commitment of the *nouveau roman* are based on the idea that commitment can be judged at the level of *content* and that what is to be challenged, therefore, is not the mode of writing, which is to be retained, but traditional realms of content which are to be replaced, this being the area of radical literary *engagement*. Nothing can be further from the truth in our contemporary society.
>
> (p. 32)

This writing only acts in the present through its untimely relation to the processes of reading open to the contemporary reader. If as

Wittgenstein states, 'the limits of my language are the limits of my world', then the task of understanding that world comes down to the problems of language.[19] This is not to renounce taking ethical and political positions: on the contrary it is to question the complacent belief that taking such positions is in itself adequate to understand the nature of the ethical or political. In this way contemporary literature shares the concerns of the critical thinking which is gathered together under the term 'literary theory'. Both literature and theory breathe 'the same informed air', as Muriel Spark puts it in the interview which concludes this volume: the deconstruction of the Subject, the decidability of History and Truth, suspicion of political commitment within the current mediatic space, and so on.

Ex cathedra

Spark's novels, from her early success as an 'experimental' novelist to her highly stylized novellas in the sixties and seventies and her increasingly rare and increasingly satiric offerings, are untimely because they come before their 'proper' or 'natural' time. They are 'premature' in their experimentation with novelistic form. Experimentation is a complex term that is often used to imply that writers who predicate the progress of the novel are extraneous rather than central to that tradition. Flaubert, Proust, Faulkner, Joyce, Stein, Beckett and Robbe-Grillet have all, at various times, been marginalized as 'experimental' novelists. Spark's novels are untimely because they represent the political value of the contretemps. They are unseasonable, inopportune, ill-timed, always unorthodox, constantly misread. In her geographical location (writing in Italy and France), her nationality (Scottish), her gender, her race ('part-Jewish') and her creed (Roman Catholic), she is decidedly in a relation of otherness to the tradition of English Literature. Her work eloquently expands this tradition but is seemingly determined not to come to terms with it. It is a peculiar paradox that the tradition of English writing and British academic criticism which recognized Spark's potential contribution to the novel in English, and which set the parameters for her literary reputation (Graham Greene, Evelyn Waugh, Frank Kermode, Malcolm Bradbury, David Lodge) seems so ill-equipped to deal with her postmodern poesis.

In her 1970 essay 'The Desegregation of Art' Spark identifies her own writing with a worrying-through of the problems of commitment, the conditions of identity and the un/decidability of the representation of history and truth (Willy Maley provides an alternative reading of this essay in his contribution to this volume). She recognizes the need to question the forms of intelligibility open to the writer and reader in 'Realist' art and offers a redistribution of novelistic possibilities with a view to bringing the reader to an awareness of their own 'construction'. She writes:

> We have in this century a marvellous tradition of socially-conscious art. And especially now in the arts of drama and the novel we see and hear everywhere the representation of the victim against the oppressor, we have a literature and an artistic culture, one might almost say a civilisation, of depicted suffering, whether in social life or in family life. We have representations of the victim-oppressor complex, for instance, in the dramatic portrayal of the gross racial injustices of our world, or in the exposure of the tyrannies of family life on the individual. As art this can be badly done, it can be brilliantly done. But I am going to suggest that it isn't achieving its end or illuminating our lives any more, and that a more effective technique can and should be cultivated.
>
> (DA, p. 23)

Just as the *nouveau roman* attempted to redistribute the possibilities of narrative production within the form of the novel, Spark shares these concerns and makes an identical call for the evolution of artistic practice. In particular she highlights the difficulty of achieving a radical political effect in art. She argues that the inadequacy of the forms of intelligibility open to the 'Realist' novel are depoliticizing, 'the art of pathos is pathetic, simply; and it has reached a point of exhaustion, a point where not the subject matter but the art form itself is crying for vengeance' (DA, p. 26). For Spark this need to rework the forms of the novel – to dare language and create a new space of intelligibility – is connected to the difficulty of providing an effective political commitment in the techno-medio-military-economic culture of late capitalism. She writes:

> I'm sure you all remember the silly old saying 'The pen is mightier than the sword.' Perhaps when swords were the weapons in current use, there was some point in the proverb. Anyway, in our time, the least of our problems is swords.
>
> But the power and influence of the creative arts is not to be belittled. I only say that the art and literature of sentiment and emotion,

however beautiful in itself, however striking in its depiction of actuality, has to go. It cheats us into a sense of involvement with life and society, but in reality it is a segregated activity. In its place I advocate the arts of satire and of ridicule. And I see no other living art form for the future.

   Ridicule is the only honourable weapon we have left.

(DA, p. 24)

Spark suggests that the mere production of a political content in a novel, the depiction of racial injustice for example, does not (or at least no longer) constitutes an engagement on the part of the writer. It is, on the contrary, a depoliticizing gesture which re-establishes the powerfully inertial set of inequalities which were responsible for the original injustice through their graphic representation. At the very least, such a critique only manages to swap one set of inequalities for another.

   In reaction to this exhausted art form, and as a commitment to writing, Spark suggests the subversive potential of ridicule (something more committed than irony, something more cutting than satire). By redistributing the possibilities of narrative production within the novel, offering ridicule as form, the reader is presented with, as Heath might say, 'possibilities of reading in the realisation of which s/he may read [them]self in their construction.' Spark says this is because, 'we should all be conditioned and educated to regard violence in any form as something to be ruthlessly mocked' (DA, p. 24). Spark offers mockery as more than genre (mere 'comedy'), as a mode of intelligibility by which a writer might offer an account of the political. A mode that will certainly be 'funny peculiar' if not necessarily 'funny ha-ha'. As in the case of the *nouveau roman*, Spark's concern is with the forms of thinking sustained by the mode of writing, in order to constitute a political engagement, and not the realm of novelistic content. Ridicule, as form, is Spark's considered response to the noise of mediatic pseudo-actuality:

We have come to a moment in history when we are surrounded on all sides and oppressed by the absurd. And I think that even the simplest, the least sophisticated and uneducated mind is aware of this fact. I should think there is hardly an illiterate peasant in the world who doesn't know it. The art of ridicule is an art that everyone can share in some degree, given the world that we have.

(DA, p. 26)

In this essay (if we are prepared to accept it as a 'ridiculous manifesto' for Spark's novelistic experimentation) there is a desire to offer an engagement with the political in her writing. There is also a desire to provide, through the redistribution of the possibilities of narrative production, a form of intelligibility whereby the subject in general may think and act in a politically effective way:

> I would like to see in all forms of art and letters, ranging from the most sophisticated and high achievements to the placards that the students carry about the street, a less impulsive generosity, a less indignant representation of social injustice, and a more deliberate cunning, a more derisive undermining of what is wrong. I would like to see less emotion and more intelligence in these efforts to impress our minds and hearts.
>
> (DA, p. 25)

Just as this manifesto is assuredly dissimilar to the 'seeming' voice and 'ostensible' concerns of Spark's svelte novellas and short stories, it is assuredly similar to the concerns of a theoretical avant-garde. Muriel Spark, through her novelistic experimentation, wishes 'to bring about a mental environment of honesty and self-knowledge, a sense of the absurd and a general looking-lively to defend ourselves from the ridiculous oppressions of our time' (DA, pp. 26–7). She is aware of the various writerly and political impasses of her aporetic condition. So, the question which must be addressed is, how does she produce a textual practice which responds to and works through these positions of aporia? I would like to suggest that she attempts this through the use of narrative contrapuntality to offer an untimely relation between her writing and the world it confronts and constitutes.

So, if Spark's political commitment does not necessarily manifest itself at the level of content in what way does she choose to 'dare the precinct of being'? How does she produce a method of representation by 'daring language' at the level of novelistic form? The form pioneered by Spark through the sixties, seventies and eighties has, amongst other 'innovations' (one might think here of her experiments with narrative tense, see Judith Roof's essay in this volume), increasingly questioned the constraining novelistic necessity of the narratorial anecdote. Robbe-Grillet wrote in 1957: 'the demands of the anecdote are doubtless less constraining for Proust than for Flaubert, for Faulkner than for Proust, for Beckett than for Faulkner ... Henceforth, the issue is elsewhere; to tell a story has become strictly impossible.'[20] Similarly for Spark the issues in writing 'lie elsewhere' and her novels demonstrate that telling a story *per se* has 'become strictly impossible.' Or, at least, to say what has to be said by means of the story, or by means of the story alone, has become for Spark strictly impossible. It is not necessarily the anecdote which is absent in Spark's novels but rather what Robbe-Grillet calls 'its character of certainty, its tranquillity, its innocence' (p. 33). In Spark's novels the untroubled tranquillity and certainty of the anecdote has been systematically deconstructed and has had its underlying metaphysical principles put on display and challenged by the distribution of narrative possibility within her texts. Spark's novels engage with the concerns of the theoretical avant-garde then, not necessarily at the level of anecdote, but in her attention to the forms of intelligibility. As Stephen Heath says of the *nouveau roman*, 'in the writing of the novel which, transgressed, is no longer repetition and self-effacement but work and self-presentation as text' (p. 22). Some examples may be necessary.

Operation Spark

If, as Derrida suggests, 'any coherent deconstruction is about singularity, about events, and what is ultimately irreducible in them,' then Spark's 1976 novel *The Takeover* offers a suitable example of her concern for both the aporetic conditions of the political and narrative.[21] Ostensibly a story of the vacuous Tuscan super-rich expatriate community, the novel is focused through the experience of the 'heroine' Maggie as she attempts to avoid being burgled and having her house sold from under her. It has been variously read by critics as a morality tale about spirituality versus materialism, or as an autobiographical account of how the author achieved fame and fortune and subsequently (because it is nearly 300 pages long and twice the usual length of a Spark novel) how this affected her ability to write. The novel is generally considered as an artistic failure. However, such opinions are suggestive of misreading. The very fact that Spark chooses to deviate from the shorter fiction she writes both prior to this novel (*The Public Image, The Driver's Seat, Not to Disturb, The Abbess of Crewe*) and subsequently (*Territorial Rights, Loitering with Intent*) must surely command the attention of the alert reader. The fact that the characters, including Maggie, are so terribly vacuous and the supposed anecdote of the novel so very tedious suggests one of two things. Firstly, a deliberate attempt to stretch the possibilities of character and anecdote so that the reader might begin to question the very categories of character and anecdote and the forms of intelligibility they offer in the form of the novel as a whole. Secondly a mid-career blip not suggested by the quality of Spark's novels which chronologically surround *The Takeover.*

Bearing in mind the possibility of the latter, it may be more productive to consider the former suggestion. There is a remarkable passage almost exactly half way through the novel – the rest of the text framing this singular event – that speaks contrapuntally in relation to the anecdote which before and after treats the venality of the characters. A group is sitting down to dinner:

It was not in their minds at the time that this last quarter of the year they had entered, that of 1973, was in fact the beginning of something new in their world; a change in the meaning of property and money. They all understood these were changing in value, and they talked from time to time of recession and inflation, of losses on the stock-market, failures in business, bargains in real-estate; they habitually bandied the phrases of the newspaper economists and unquestioningly used the newspaper writers' figures of speech. They talked of hedges against inflation, as if mathematics could contain actual air and some row of hawthorn could stop an army of numbers from marching over it. They spoke of the mood of the stock-market, the health of the economy as if these were living creatures with moods and blood. And thus they personalized and demonologized the Abstractions of their lives, believing them to be fundamentally real, indeed changeless. But it did not occur to one of those spirited and in various ways intelligent people round Berto's table that a complete mutation of our means of nourishment had already come into being where the concept of money and property were concerned, a complete mutation not merely to be defined as a collapse of the capitalist system, or a global recession, but such a sea-change in the nature of reality as could not have been envisaged by Karl Marx or Sigmund Freud. Such a mutation that what were assets were to be liabilities and no armed guards could be found and fed sufficient to guard those armed guards who failed to protect the properties they guarded, whether hoarded in banks or built on confined territories, whether they were priceless works of art, or merely hieroglyphics registered in the computers. Innocent of all this future they sat round the table and, since all were attached to Nemi, talked of Hubert. Maggie had him very much on her mind and the wormwood of her attention focused on him as the battle in the Middle East hiccuped to a pause in the warm late October of 1973.

(TT, pp. 126–8)

The narrative suddenly breaks from a close-up representation of the sexual and material excesses of an insular, bourgeois, Western community, panning out to consider the global setting. This setting is specifically pinned down to October 1973, the date of the fourth Arab–Israeli war, the OPEC oil embargo and the geo-politics of the energy crisis.

In this passage Spark offers a counternarrative to the narratorial anecdote and sets in play the conditions of contrapuntality as a formal aspect of her novel. The behaviour of her characters prior to this has been presented to the reader without guidance, or any indication to the contrary, in the accurate 'Realist' manner of a textual world for the purposes of entertainment, self-recognition, and pathetic engagement. However, their behaviour is suddenly and unexpectedly brought into sharp contrast with this untimely textual moment, which is both out of place and out of keeping with the tone and tropes of narrative editing and selection used hitherto. After this singular textual moment not only does the alert reader begin to question the absurdity of the bourgeois characters' lives but also the absurdity of the very categories of character and anecdote as they are associated with the bourgeois novel. This manoeuvre works through one set of aporetic conditions in order to reproduce another. A political consideration is offered, only to be subverted by the self-referentiality of the novel's own status as a suspended relation to reference and meaning.

On the one hand, this is a textual joke (President Sadat named his war plan 'Operation Spark') but on the other hand, the whole novel – especially the title, *The Takeover* – begins to produce a series of highly suggestive meanings when considered in light of this seemingly incongruent, formal aside. Rather than being a novel about secular Europe's thirst for spirituality, it reads as a critique of the bankruptcy of Late Capitalism and fictions of exchange value. The burglary of Maggie's jewels and her trouble with property are notable examples of this. Such a use of contrapuntality allows Spark to identify in 1976, what Derrida calls in 1994, the 'appropriation of Jerusalem.' He belatedly comments in *Spectres of Marx*, 'the war for the "appropriation of Jerusalem" is today the world war' (p. 58). The event which both writers describe is a figure in which, according to Derrida:

> Messianic eschatologies [the Abrahamic religions] mobilise there all the forces of the world and the whole 'world order' in the ruthless war they are waging against each other, directly or indirectly; they mobilise simultaneously, in order to put them to work or to the test, the old concepts of State and nation-State, of international law, of tele-techno-medio-economic and scientifico-military forces, in other words, the most archaic and most modern spectral forces.
>
> (p. 58)

The use of contrapuntality allows Spark to make a political intervention in and through her novel. In particular she is concerned with the aporetic conditions of speech in the mediatic space of late capitalism and the theological structure of political messianism. Spark, in 1976, is in fact recognizing the importance of 1973 to the 'cultural logic of late capitalism.' 1973 is the date which both Jameson and Harvey give as constitutive of certain postmodern discourses in art and society.[22] She is similarly alert to the position of the writer and intellectual immanent within that culture and bound by that logic.

The manner in which the events of 1973 affected both systems of multinational capitalism and the conditions of intelligibility for subjective experience (and their importance to Spark's writing) had been previously demonstrated in the 1974 novel *The Abbess of Crewe*. This satire on the 1973 Watergate scandal offers a political engagement through the form of intelligibility Spark termed 'ridicule'. However, it also contains another incongruent formal aside, which produces a counternarrative in relation to the narrative anecdote. The Abbess, titular head of another enclosed community, tells Sisters Walburga and Mildred:

> The motorway from London to Crewe is jammed with reporters, according to the news. The A51 is a solid mass of vehicles. In the midst of the strikes and the oil crises.
>
> (A, p. 18)

The use of the insular community as a setting for the novel allows Spark to comment on the inadequacies of closure as a totalizing trope in literary and social narrative. It is also, of course, a comment on the insularity of the United States as it is introspectively scandalized by human behaviour while ignoring its own international scandals. However, a detailed consideration of Spark's political opinion is not necessarily the issue at the moment. For the purposes of this introduction it is enough to demonstrate that she shares the same writerly concerns with the theoretical avant-garde regarding how best to speak of the reductionism of mediatic conditions without being caught up in the process of reduction. What is currently at issue, however, is Spark's use of contrapuntality as a redistribution of narrative possibility within the form of the novel.

One might look with advantage at Spark's peculiar interest in manifestations of political protest such as the student riots of 1968 or the Red Brigades. Both of these examples work as *leitmotifs* in her novels during the seventies and early eighties. They act as a paradoxical emblem, for the futility of revolutionary violence (something to be ruthlessly mocked) and her admiration of a resistance to the compromised politics of social democracy. These 'guest/ghost appearances' by students and terrorists (two powerful cultural icons of a historically specific moment) are introduced, like the above passages, seemingly out of context and in an incongruous relation to anecdotes of bourgeois intransigence. This allows Spark to offer a critique of the simulacra of media representation and of fictions of legality and legitimation. In the 1970 novel *The Driver's Seat* the narrative is claustrophobically focused on the seemingly sex and death obsessed Lise, who visits an unnamed southern city (probably Rome perhaps Athens, either way the onto-theological significance is acute) allegedly to plan her own rape and murder. In a contrapuntal moment, the student riots, and all the cultural and ideological baggage they carry with them, intrude upon this enclosed world. Lise and an elderly companion are visiting an archaeological site when:

Suddenly round the corner comes a stampede. Lise and Mrs. Fiedke are swept apart and jostled in all directions by a large crowd composed mainly of young men, with a few smaller, older and grimmer men, and here and there a young girl, all yelling together and making rapidly for something else. 'Tear-Gas!' someone shouts and then a lot of people are calling out, 'Tear-Gas!' A shutter on a shop-front near Lise comes down with a hasty clatter, then the other shops start closing for the day. Lise falls and is hauled to her feet by a tough man who leaves her and runs on.

Just before it reaches the end of the street which joins the circular intersection the crowd stops. A band of grey-clad policemen come running towards them, in formation, bearing tear-gas satchels and with their gas-masks at the ready. The traffic on the circular intersection has stopped. Lise swerves with her crowd into a garage where some mechanics in their overalls crouch behind the cars and others take refuge underneath a car which is raised on a cradle in the process of repair.

(DS, p. 74)

After shouting at Lise and trying to make her leave the garage the head mechanic, 'finally tells her she is a student' (DS, p. 75). Each of these examples of the use of contrapuntality have shown, not only Spark's interest in the political but also, her concern at the inability of the form of intelligibility offered by the narratorial anecdote to provide an adequate space in which to discuss the complexities of its condition. Spark only feels able to offer a political reflection through the use of contrapuntality. It allows her narrative to accede to the wider socio-political concerns which undoubtedly inform her work. It is through contrapuntality as a formal device that Spark is able to connect the feminist concerns of *The Driver's Seat* to the struggle of the students. Spark wants the students' own narrative (their, 'forms of art and letters ... the placards that the students carry about the street') to be cunning enough to 'defend ourselves from the ridiculous oppressions of our time.' For Spark even the space of the novel is an inadequate form of intelligibility when confronted with the 'ridiculous nature of the reality before us', as she wrote in 'The Desegragation of Art' in the same year as *The Driver's Seat*. Spark's politics take place away from the pseudo-actuality of mediatic noise (hidden in the margins of her own novels): in a space which offers an untimely relation to the forms of intelligibility open to the reader of novels at a historically specific moment, and seemingly lost on the journalism which claims to 'read' her. This space also reproduces the same aporetic impasses it works through. This working through of the process of critique and the medium of commitment is the impossible invention which is the condition of responsibility and commitment.

Such passages remain opaque, they say what they say and no more, they remain as secrets in Spark's text.[23] Secrecy is the very condition of responsibility for the writer. The formulation of a response to the urgency of today requires that this response be thought through in all its infinite complexity and singularity. In the event, however, the writer must write and so cut short the process of formulating a response. Their response will always be inadequate, compromised, not thought enough, and so be irresponsible. A truly responsible response must remain in thinking: undecidable, unknowable and thus a secret. As a secret, responsibility cannot respond and so fails to act responsibly. Responsibility finds the conditions of its own impossibility in religion and fiction. The Latin *'respondere'* has its root in the 'answering back' of liturgical responses, responsibility as an 'answering back' is a religious activity and like the Latin *'religio'* it is a binding obligation. However, *'spondere'* means to promise and fiction will always be a question of the promise – of the contract between author and reader, of the promise of fiction as such. Fiction depends upon the promise of its own fictionality; it can be no more than fiction and is only allowed to say what it says because it is fiction. A writer can only be political because she is in the first instance fictional. Accordingly, responsibility must always fail because it can be no more than fictional, just as fiction must fail because it aspires to be responsible.

However, by the time Spark came to write her 1984 novel *The Only Problem* a new arrival had taken place in the state of politics and the forms of intelligibility open to the novelist. The students had departed the stage and instead the good news of neo-liberalism became the new orthodoxy. Few thinkers, except for the most unreconstructed, did not set about the introspective task of rethinking the terms of their understanding of the political: responding to new technology, a redistribution of the class struggle, and the developments within the global economy. Throughout this period any commentary or engagement still had to take place surrounded by the pseudo-actuality of a media culture. In 1981 Spark retreated to the London of 1949, in *Loitering with Intent*, before allowing herself to speak about her then present conditions (her mature reflection on the craft of fiction). She went into retreat again in 1984, sending Harvey Gotham (one of her few leading males) on retreat to the Vosges in *The Only Problem*. There, Harvey, a millionaire (the nature of his business is never revealed), contemplates the question of suffering while writing a monograph on *The Book of Job*. Harvey argues with his wife, Effie, over the theft of a bar of chocolate – she says, 'Why shouldn't we help ourselves? These multinationals and monopolies are capitalising on us, and two-thirds of the world is suffering' (O, p. 15). Effie disappears, only to re-emerge as the leader of the *'Front de la Libération de l'Europe'* (O, p. 80). In this role she commits various acts of terrorism around the Vosges region and eventual shoots a policeman in Paris. In a parallel to the story of Job, Harvey is consoled by a selection of comforters (from friends and family to the police). The echo here between Harvey/Job and the title of Spark's first novel, *The Comforters*, published in 1956, is no accident. When a re-examination is necessary where else does one start but at the beginning?[24]

The use of contrapuntality (the mode by which Spark feels able to offer a political consideration) changes in this novel just as the requirements of political engagement changed. There is still an instance of the narrative acceding to the political through a moment of counternarrative. Hopes are raised that Effie is not a terrorist when she is allegedly spotted on an American television programme in an alternative commune in California. Again Spark connects her enclosed narrative to wider concerns by linking Harvey's cloistered life to youth rebellion and the counter-culture, and all that this implies. However, in this novel Spark also deems it necessary, and possible, to move the discussion of the political from the margins of the narrative to the centre of the text. She presents the story of Effie as a counternarrative which constitutes the conditions of possibility for Harvey's own narrative. It is more than mere plot and sub-plot (one running parallel to the other); rather, the action of Effie's narrative (her movements and humiliation of Harvey) makes Harvey's narrative possible. Similarly, Harvey's narrative (his money and intransigence) make Effie's narrative of terrorist intervention possible. The exemplary value of this novel is not just that it shows Spark's use of contrapuntality but that, in so doing, Spark makes explicit connections between the conditions of writing (contrapuntality) and the conditions of political commentary at a particular historical conjunction. While the time of the action is undated the activities of the *FLE* are suggestive of the Red Brigades. The intrusion of the Californian counter-culture is also suggestive of a similar date.

Whatever the chronological placing of the story, it is an experience of re-assessment in 1984 which informs Spark's novel. She says of the manifesto issued by the *FLE*:

> It was much the same as every other terrorist announcement Harvey had ever read. 'The multinationals and the forces of the reactionary imperialist powers ...' It was like an alarm clock that ceases to wake the sleeper who, having heard it morning after morning, simply puts out a hand and switches it off without opening his eyes.
>
> (O, p. 104)

Ineffective as the announcement may be it is still intended as an 'alarm'. As Spark notes in 'The Desegragation of Art', 'ineffective literature must go' when it reaches 'a point where not the subject matter but the art form itself is crying to heaven for vengeance.' If the form of intelligibility offered by the revolutionary manifesto, or revolutionary act, is inadequate or reductive then, as a condition of commitment, it is necessary to transform the apparatus by which the message is sent. Just as Spark no longer feels able to trust her message to the form of contrapuntality she adopted in the seventies, so too the meaning of revolution can no longer be trusted to the apparatus of the revolutionary.

The Red Brigades, Umberto Eco suggests, shared cognitive affinities with the theoretical avant-garde. The Brigade's own announcements before the death of Aldo Moro offered, says Eco:

> A thesis which has been widely taken up in Europe and America for some time, whether by the students of '68, by the theoreticians of *Monthly Review*, or by the Left political parties ... [The difference lying] not in the premises but ... in the practical conclusions drawn from them.[25]

What this political thesis, and form of engagement in revolutionary acts, failed to come to terms with, was the immanence of the subject within the capitalist system. This aporetic impasse was the explicit concern of those writers who re-examined the political conditions at the start of the 1980s. Baudrillard concludes of revolutionary violence:

> One knows nothing about terrorism if one does not see that it is not a question of real violence, nor of opposing one violence to another (which, owing to their disproportion, is absurd, and besides, all *real* violence, like real order in general, is always on the side of power), but to oppose to the *full* violence and the *full* order a clearly superior model of extermination and virulence operating through emptiness.[26]

Here Baudrillard highlights the reproduction of oppressive conditions within the terrorist act and the simulacra of signification associated with that act. Both Baudrillard's and Spark's thinking about terrorism seems to cast an eye to the global media event of the Maze Prison hunger strikes in 1981. Mediatic simulacra was an issue which came to fore in British politics at this time not only in Ulster but during the Falklands War and the Conservative Party's election campaign of 1983. Spark and Baudrillard are concerned with the disjunction between the moral condemnation of the media and the sanctioned fascination of a mediatic simulacra which constitutes the terrorist act.

In *The Only Problem* Harvey Gotham convenes a press conference to deny any involvement in terrorism only to find his denial used against him in several pages of manufactured non-news. In a separate incident the police manage to convince Harvey of Effie's guilt when they show him a photograph of her. It later transpires that this photograph was taken from Harvey's own home.

Eco comments that, 'terrorism is not the enemy of the great systems. On the contrary it is their natural, accepted, taken-for-granted counterpart' (p. 179). This is because, 'terrorism provides a justification for disciplinary interventions in circumstances where an excess of democracy is making a situation ungovernable' (p. 180). Similarly, the narrative of the millionaire Harvey is the necessary counterpart to the narrative of the terrorist Effie. Eco concludes that the real concern of the system of global multinationalism:

> Is that party political control would interfere with a form of power management which is impatient of any process of mass consultation.
> Terrorism on the other hand is much less of a worry, because it is a natural biological consequence of the multinationals' rule, just as a day of feverishness is a reasonable price to pay for an effective vaccine.
>
> (p. 181)

Terrorism, as a form of action open to the revolutionary in the medio-techno-economic culture of Late Capitalism, is – as a consequence of the conditions of implication – merely a reproduction of another set of oppressive circumstances which justifies and constitutes the original oppression. Terrorism, for Spark, is an allegory of contrapuntality. In terrorism the narrative and counternarrative do not represent a binary opposition but have a differential relation in which both constitute the conditions of possibility for the other. Recognizing these conditions is the first stage in the production of a narrative apparatus which writes through the conditions of aporia. Spark hints at the ridiculous nature of immanence when Harvey – undecided with regards to his wife's guilt – tells Inspector Chatelian, 'a bar of chocolate isn't a dead policeman' (O, p. 164). The Inspector replies, 'we are looking for a political fanatic, not a bar of chocolate' (O, p. 167). Just as *The Abbess of Crewe* ridicules Watergate, by reducing it allegorically to a squabble over a nun's thimble, so *The Only Problem* ridicules the oppression of terrorism, and the disciplinary interventions it justifies, by comparing them to shop-lifting. However, what this novel really demonstrates, is the continual necessity to rework the forms of intelligibility open to the political thinker as the very condition of a continued and effective thought.[27]

In light of all that I have said above concerning Muriel Spark, one question remains. Why is she continually misread by critics? As Heidegger says of Hölderlin:

> It would ... be mistaken to believe that Hölderlin's time will come only on that day when 'everyman' will understand his poetry. It will never arrive in such a misshapen way; for it is its own destitution that endows the era with forces by which, unaware of what it is doing, it keeps Hölderlin's poetry from becoming timely.
>
> (p. 142)

Similarly, it is the very destitution of the time which Spark describes – the silence imposed upon the committed intellectual by a reductive mediatic space – which makes the contrapuntal strategy Spark adopts untimely and therefore valuable. Her novels have endured, and constitute a sustained consideration of the (theo-)political over five decades, precisely because of their untimeliness, 'Where there is danger, there grows/ Also what saves', says Hölderlin.

The order of this collection might have been otherwise. There is little here which might not be characterized as deconstruction (Judith Roof's elegant queering of the Sparkian text, Bryan Cheyette's consideration of cultural hybridity). Similarly, in one way or another, all of the essays are bound up with the questions of gender (Julian Wolfrey's account of *Mary Shelley*, Eleanor Byrne's reading of Spark's colonial women) or race (wherever the issue of religion is raised – Nicholas Royle, Willy Maley – the formulation Judeo-Christian rather than plain Christian seems more suited to the complexity of Spark's writing). In the end, the categories adopted by the book seem the least arbitrary and the most economic in relation to our analysis of Spark's oeuvre.

In Chapter 1, '*Tales of Love*: Narcissism and Idealization in *The Public Image*', Susan Sellers reads Spark's tale of 'crossed-star' lovers through Kristeva's psychoanalytic account of love. Kristeva, a novelist like Spark, knows something about Freud but Sellers uses *The Public Image* to interrogate Kristeva's formulation of the story of Narcissus as an empowering paradigm for women. While Kristeva proposes Narcissus as a positive model for confronting the emptiness of individuation, the narcissism of Annabel and Frederick in Spark's novel leads to the drowning of the individual in their own media image. For Sellers, the prognosis for Annabel and her baby at the end of this novel is not good. Judith Roof continues the psychoanalytic encounter with Spark in 'The Future Perfect's Perfect Future: Spark's and Duras's Narrative Drive' (Chapter 2). Roof begins the serious task of thinking through Spark's relation to the *nouveau roman* (a relation nodded to but seldom elaborated by Spark criticism) in a reading of *The Driver's Seat* and Marguerite Duras's *The Ravishing of Lol V. Stein*. Roof looks to Freud's theory of drives to explain the conjunction of death and desire in both texts, while recognizing that these writers exceed the psychoanalytic model with their own employment of specifically narrative drives, comprised of the interrelation between knowledge of the story's resolution and sexuality. In part Roof's essay is a reflection on the curious fact that Duras is taken seriously as a writer by feminist and psychoanalytic critics while Spark's reception to date has remained firmly rooted in an English humanist tradition unable to appreciate her work fully.

Patricia Duncker follows Roof's consideration of Spark and sexuality in 'The Suggestive Spectacle: Queer Passions in Brontë's *Villette* and *The Prime of Miss Jean Brodie*' (Chapter 3). Duncker offers a refreshing account of Spark's best-seller by mapping the libidinal economy of each novel (Spark having cited reading *Villette* as a formative experience, see also her comments on *Villette* in the interview which concludes this volume). The essay argues for a queer reading of the all-female classroom in *Jean Brodie*, and again finds a feminist interest in the Sparkian text. In Duncker's words 'men have key sexual roles to play, but these are essentially walk-on and lie-back parts'. Patricia Duncker has the sensibility of a novelist and finds in Jean Brodie herself an example of the writerly practise of elaboration from a biographical source. In Chapter 4, 'In Bed with Muriel Spark: Mourning, Metonymy and Autobiography', my own essay examines four different texts which revisit a singular biographical experience. This essay reads Spark's accounts of a night she spent in the house of the poet Louis MacNeice during the war, in fiction and non-fiction. While Spark argues for this 'fetish like experience' as the origin of her writing career, my essay suggests that her writerly origins are more complex and that this incident should be read as a metonymic concentration of those experiences.

Bryan Cheyette provides a long overdue account of Spark's hybrid cultural identity in 'Writing against Conversion: Muriel Spark the Gentile Jewess' (Chapter 5). He argues that Spark's writing both acknowledges her Jewishness and also keeps open other personal histories and identities. Cheyette suggests that one should not think of her writing as fully determined either by Jewishness or Catholicism because this would of necessity exclude and diminish possible futures for the reading of Spark. The essay rigorously critiques both the idea that Spark has ever attempted to erase her Jewishness, and the idea that 'Jewishness' itself is fixed. In 'Muriel Spark Shot in Africa' (Chapter 6) Eleanor Byrne reads Spark's (post)colonial short stories 'Bang, Bang You're Dead' and 'The Curtain Blown by the Breeze'. Again, this critical encounter between Spark's African fiction and post-colonial theory is long overdue. Byrne reads these stories in relation to questions of whiteness and gender, of racial difference, desire and miscegenation. As with previous essays, Byrne finds it possible to read Spark's fiction in terms of a complex relation to biographical material. However, Byrne asserts that the importance of these stories lies not in another attempt to read a female writer through her biography but in the political commentary they provide on decolonization written in the fifties and sixties, even if their subject matter is the thirties and forties. Alan Freeman's essay 'A Bit of the Other: *Symposium*, Futility and Scotland' (Chapter 7) concludes Part II of the collection. While the identification of Scotland with race, suggested by this placing, might be open to question, Freeman uses post-colonial theory to discuss Scottish identity within the 'New Europe'. He argues that in *Symposium* Spark restates Socrates' refusal of simple national and conceptual demarcations while revisiting the clichés of her native culture. For Freeman the novel performs the aporia common to Spark's writing and literary theory, namely the attempt to negotiate otherness and transcendentality.

Part III of the collection provides accounts of deconstruction in and of the Sparkian text. Jeremy Idle's essay 'Muriel Spark's Uselessness' (Chapter 8) reads Spark's oeuvre alongside the work of Georges Bataille. He argues for compatibility between Spark's fictional treatments of utility and Bataille's notions of economy and use-value. The essay opens with a useful account of Bataille's theory of uselessness and goes on to offer a wide-ranging examination of Spark's novels in relation to it, from *The Comforters* to *A Far Cry from Kensington*. Idle argues that Spark is a poet of excess, her fictions contain an abundance of actions which lead to nothing and cancel moments of excessive expenditure. However, Idle is at least as interested in the possibility of a Sparkian reading of Bataille as he is of a Bataillean reading of Spark. Julian Wolfreys is also interested in the possibility of a Sparkian reading in his essay 'Muriel Spark's *Mary Shelley*: A Gothic and Liminal

Life' (Chapter 9). Wolfreys reads Spark's biography of Mary Shelley according to a double strand, the liminal and the gothic. He argues that these two aspects are mutually interdependent. Mary Shelley's apparent marginality in her own life (the wife of a famous poet, the daughter of famous parents) and the role she is made to play in the subsequent retelling of it by Spark is inescapably informed by gothic details, as emphasized by her biographer. Wolfreys's reading of the gothic as the mode of Spark's critical biography has significant consequences for an appreciation of Spark's own uncanny fiction.

In 'Not to Deconstruct? Righting and Deference in *Not to Disturb*' (Chapter 10) Willy Maley argues for a Derridean reading of Spark's fiction. He suggests that Spark's writing is affirmative, open, playful and materialistic. The absence of a theoretical account of Spark has, says Maley, served to neutralize her radicalism and allowed her work to be characterized as conservative. He reads *Not to Disturb* as 'a dark tale of class and revolution' which is concerned with the deconstructive effects of marginal voices. In this novel, Maley argues, Spark's formal radicalism is matched by political concerns, which leads to 'textual disturbance'. Maley also provides us with a fascinating critique of Spark criticism, exposing its own conservative agenda. Nicholas Royle's bravura performance in his text 'Memento Mori' (Chapter 11) provides another deconstruction of Spark. Royle reads Spark's novel as a meditation upon telepathy, telephones, death, religion, and teleculture. In this way, he leaves a trace in the text he reads, following the contours of Spark's novel (even adopting its title for his own) and through the proximity of his reading reveals the alogic which structures the novel. Royle does not take Spark's text apart (it is not an operation in this sense), rather he shows the absence of a fixed ground or centre within Spark's 'religious' novel. For Royle, theology is indissociable from teletechnology: both are conspicuous components of the modern scene.

The final section of the book contains: two previously untranslated texts by Hélène Cixous, an interview with Muriel Spark (in which she responds to thematic concerns raised by this collection), and a bibliography of primary and secondary sources. Cixous' two reviews of Spark first appeared in *Le Monde* in 1968. They may well be the first attempts to 'theorize' Muriel Spark. However, the two texts, 'Grimacing Catholicism: Muriel Spark's Macabre Farce' and 'Muriel Spark's Latest Novel: *The Public Image*', come from the prehistory of Cixous' own more celebrated studies of *l'écriture féminine* and should not be thought of as examples of Cixous' mature work. Nevertheless, they remain of interest to both the Spark and Cixous scholar. These texts were written by one of Europe's (Cixous is of course Algerian) leading intellectuals at a time of political turmoil, and in the same year as the thirty-year old Cixous wrote her Prix Medicis winning novel *Dedans* [*Inside*]. To the scholar such an interstice is not insignificant.

This book was to have been called *Muriel Spark meets Contemporary Criticism*: criticism of the contemporary or criticism that takes place today in the fifth decade of Spark's writing career. However, in the sense that this phrase has been used throughout this introduction, it also means that mode of criticism which is the primary form of analysis in the academy today, namely literary theory. As such, this encounter might be a strange meeting. One that is long overdue but one hedged around by unfamiliarity and mutual incomprehension. A meeting which might be more accurately described as a juxtaposition or an intersection – a brief encounter if you will – in which both parties talk a different language. There is no intrinsic reason why theorists and writers should be foreign to one another; quite deliberately this volume includes contributions from critics who are also practising artists (Hélène Cixous, Patricia Duncker, Willy Maley). However, in the case of Spark and Theory, there remains, at least, a difference of vocabulary and the need for translation. The interview that concludes this book is, on occasion, marked by this disjunction between Muriel Spark and the 'contemporary criticism' which solicits her to speak. All interviews are necessarily edited, amended and rewritten, but in preparing this particular interview for publication I did not wish to iron out all of the discontinuities and interruptions which for me, during the course of editing this volume, have come to define the relation between Spark and Theory. It is only in the gap between Muriel Spark and contemporary criticism that this relation has a chance of being thought. The interview was based upon the premise of not discussing Spark's biography; in the end we talked of little else. The return of this particular repressed, which writes itself all over the interview, may tell us more about the hidden desires of literary theory than it does about Muriel Spark. Accordingly, theory is marked by its encounter with Spark, just as much as theory leaves a trace in the text of Spark.

Notes

1. Bertolt Brecht quoted by Roland Barthes, 'Program for an Avant-Garde', in *Roland Barthes*, trans. Richard Howard (London and Basingstoke: Macmillan, 1977), p. 107.

2. The titles of critical texts on Spark usually indicate their orientation, for example: Ruth Whittaker, *The Faith and Fiction of Muriel Spark* (London: Macmillan, 1982); Rodney Stenning Edgecombe, *Vocation and Identity in the Fiction of Muriel Spark* (London: University of Missouri Press, 1990); Jennifer Lynn Randsi, *On Her Way Rejoicing: the Fiction of Muriel Spark* (Washington DC: The Catholic University of America Press, 1991) .

3. Malcolm Bradbury, 'Muriel Spark's Fingernails', *Possibilities: Essays on the State of the Novel* (Oxford: Oxford University Press, 1973), p. 247.

4. Jane Austen, *Persuasion* (London: Penguin, 1965 [1818]), p. 237.

5. Frank Kermode, 'Muriel Spark', *Modern Essays* (London: Fontana, 1990), p. 268.

6. David Lodge, 'Time-Shift', *The Art of Fiction* (Hammondsworth: Penguin, 1992), p. 76.

7. Jacques Derrida, 'Faith and Knowledge: The Two Sources of "Religion" at the Limits of Reason Alone', *Religion*, ed. Jacques Derrida and Gianni Vattimo (Cambridge: Polity, 1998), p. 29.

8. Bent Nordhjem, *What Fiction Means* (Copenhagen: Atheneum Distributor, 1987), p. 140.

9. Judy Sproxton, *The Women of Muriel Spark* (London: Constable, 1992); Norman Page, *Muriel Spark* (London: Macmillan, 1990).

10. A fuller discussion of the position of the intellectual during this historically specific moment can be found in: J-F Lyotard, 'The Tomb of the Intellectual', *Political Writings*, trans. B. Readings and K. P. Geiman (London: UCL Press, 1993) and Maurice Blanchot, 'Intellectuals Under Scrutiny: an Outline for Thought', *The Blanchot Reader*, ed. M. Holland (Oxford: Blackwell, 1995).

11. Jacques Derrida, 'The Deconstruction of Actuality', *Radical Philosophy*, (68), Autumn, 1994, p. 30. The following discussion is indebted to the arguments Derrida makes in this text.

12. Jacques Derrida, *Spectres of Marx: The State of the Debt, the Work of Mourning, and the New International*, trans. Peggy Kamuf (London and New York: Routledge, 1994), p. 88.

13. Roland Barthes, 'The Death of the Author', trans. Stephen Heath, in David Lodge and Nigel Wood, eds *Modern Criticism and Theory: A Reader, second edition* (Harlow, Essex: Longman, 2000), p. 147.

14. Jean Baudrillard, *The Gulf War did not Take Place*, trans. Paul Patton (Sydney: Power Publications, 1995), p. 26.

15. Derrida has much to say on the forms and space of commitment open to Zola and Sartre and which are no longer open to the intellectual of today, in 'The Deconstruction of Actuality', pp. 38–40.

16. Martin Heidegger, 'What are Poets for?', *Poetry, Language, Thought* , trans. A. Hofstader (New York: Harper & Row, 1975), p. 91.

17. Stephen Heath, *The Nouveau Roman: A Study in the Practice of Writing* (London: Elek Books, 1972), p. 32.

18. Alain Robbe-Grillet, 'On Several Obsolete Notions', in *For a New Novel: Essays on Fiction*, trans. Richard Howard (Illinois: Northwestern University Press, 1989), p. 41.

19. Ludwig Wittgenstein, *Philosophical Investigations*, trans. G.E.M Anscombe (Oxford: Blackwell, 1979).

20. Alain Robbe-Grillet, 'On Several Obsolete Notions', p. 33.

21. Jacques Derrida, 'The Deconstruction of Actuality', p. 29.

22. Fredric Jameson in *Postmodernism, or, the Cultural Logic of Late Capitalism* (London: Verso, 1991) and David Harvey in *The Condition of Postmodernity* (Oxford: Blackwell, 1992) identify 1973 as a defining moment in the history of postmodernism when the proximity of several examples of global upheaval helped to focus the attention of writers and critics on the cultural changes that had taken place over the preceding two decades.

23. On secrets and responsibility see Jacques Derrida, *The Gift of Death*, trans. David Wills (Chicago: University of Chicago Press, 1995).

24. Spark's first novel is characterized by an engagement with C J Jung's reading of the Job story in *Answer to Job*. Spark discusses Jung's reading in 'The Mystery of Job's Suffering: Jung's New Interpretation Examined', *The Church of England Newspaper*, 15 April 1955, p. 7.

25. Umberto Eco, 'Striking at the Heart of the State?', *Apocalypse Postponed*, ed. R. Lumley (Bloomington: Indiana University Press, 1994), p. 177.

26. Jean Baudrillard, *In the Shadow of the Silent Majorities*, trans. P. Foss *et al.* (New York: Semiotexte, 1983), p. 119.

27. For a fuller account of my use of the term 'contrapuntal' see my 'Aporias of Writing: Narrative and Subjectivity' in *The Narrative Reader*, ed. Martin McQuillan (London: Routledge, 2000) pp. 1–33.

Part I
Gender

'How wonderful it feels to be an artist and a woman in the twentieth century.'

Loitering with Intent

1

Tales of Love: Narcissism and Idealization in *The Public Image*

Susan Sellers

In the opening essay of her *Tales of Love*, Julia Kristeva stresses the intrinsic incompatibility of the loving couple. Since each love is individual it is incommensurable with the love of the other, and the only possibility of the two loves meeting is through a third party: an 'ideal, god, hallowed group'.[1] In Muriel Spark's *The Public Image*, Frederick and Annabel's ideal marriage as created by the media offers the otherwise indifferent lovers such a meeting. The opening sections of the novel, which involve a flashback to the early marriage prior to Annabel's stardom, emphasize the pair's apathy. Not even Annabel's bored infidelity with Frederick's best friend Billy provokes a response. On finding them together, Frederick merely repeats a condensed version of the lecture he gives daily to his students (I, p. 7). The mood of these early stages is very different to the extreme emotions that govern the marriage towards its close, where dependency, obsession and hatred motivate Frederick's suicide as well as Annabel's attempt to appropriate it for her own ends. Love, Kristeva writes, 'reigns between the two borders of narcissism and idealization' (TOL, p. 6). The ego either projects and glorifies itself or else is shattered and engulfed in the mirror of the idealized other/lover. The way through lies in transference love or the rerouting of desire into a symbolic form, positively located in Kristeva's account in the exchanges between analyst and analysand and perversely undertaken in *The Public Image* by the mass media.

It is significant that Spark's novel opens in a series of empty rooms. Annabel, now a successful actress, has rented a flat in Rome for herself, Frederick and their baby while she completes a film. The emptiness is conveyed through a detailed description of how the rooms will be filled: the text lists the days on which the furniture will be delivered and even gives the precise itinerary for the arriving housemaid. This paradoxical depiction is then followed by an account of how, because the flat is empty, workmen, delivery men, neighbours and friends treat it as a public space (I, p. 6). That the flat is a metaphor for Annabel is underscored by Billy's question to her 'Is this all in aid of your public image?', and by the insistence that her renting of it constitutes an unprecedented move away from the subservient position she has hitherto adopted in relation to Frederick (I, p. 7). She has acted not as Mrs. Frederick Christopher, her private self 'unaccustomed to organize anything', but as Annabel Christopher the public star (I, p. 5). In this light it is appropriate that later in the novel the flat becomes the setting for the orgy planned by Frederick to destroy his wife, as well as the location for the crucial press conference during which Annabel successfully stage-manages her public image.[2]

In *Tales of Love* Kristeva defines narcissism, in a formulation which recalls the opening of Spark's novel, as 'a screen over *emptiness*' (TOL, p. 23, Kristeva's italics). She draws on the work of psychoanalyst André Green to argue that an infant's mimetic play involves identifications which are premature, since they do not depend on a subject but derive from the chaotic, undifferentiated pre-Oedipal state. Kristeva suggests that the primary narcissism experienced in the mother/child dyad is crucial to the developing infant since it provides a basis from which to distinguish between self and other, the symbolic and the real. Narcissism, according to Kristeva's account, is thus a defence against what would otherwise be the emptiness of separation, its weapons the multifarious identifications, projections and representations that finally constitute subjectivity. The mythical Narcissus is consequently a heroic figure, as he braves emptiness and endeavours to become equal with the shimmering idealizations he sees mirrored in the maternal water.

Kristeva argues that although there is a link between the identifications that occur in the first, oral phase of human development, where incorporation and becoming correspond, and those that occur in the subsequent love relation, there is nevertheless a vital difference since what takes place in the love relation is not identification with an object but with 'what offers itself to me as a *model*' (TOL, p. 25, Kristeva's italics). This model is the idealized other who returns the lover's own ideal image. The choice of lover depends, Kristeva suggests, either on personal narcissistic reward (Narcissus as subject) or narcissistic delegation (Narcissus as other). Since there is no object in the identification but only an image, the subject-in-love becomes the hypnotized slave of the ideal they serve to create.

This formulation provides a useful frame from which to consider the development, apotheosis and final breakdown of the Christophers' marriage in *The Public Image*. In the initial stages of their relationship, it is Frederick who plays Narcissus as Annabel offers a familiar mirror in which his endeavours to construct and glorify himself go undisturbed. She does not contradict him even when his efforts at self-justification constitute a direct attack, while her money makes it possible for him to maintain the dream that he is destined for greatness. This pattern is reversed with Annabel's fame, since her success largely depends on a carefully orchestrated public image in which Frederick plays an important but supporting role.

It is striking, in terms of Kristeva's adoption of Narcissus as an emblem for what occurs in the love relation, that Frederick's attacks on Annabel concern acting. Acting is, after all, a consummate example of the narcissistic exchange. For Frederick, the actor's task is to become the character the script presents, and he despises Annabel's style of acting which consists in 'playing herself' in different situations (I, p. 10). Annabel initially agrees with Frederick's condemnation partly because she believes his insistence that she is stupid and 'it is the deep core of stupidity that it thrives on the absence of a looking-glass' (I. p. 9). Annabel's role as Frederick's mirror and her own lack of narcissistic support during this phase of the marriage could not be more emphatically underscored.

Annabel's method of playing herself is nevertheless as much a construction as Frederick's apparently superior art. Kristeva stresses the importance of narcissism in subject formation since it initiates self-other relations and forms the basis for healthy self-esteem, and this is echoed in *The Public Image* by Annabel's increasing autonomy as her success provides her with narcissistically sustaining self-images and models. She can now defend herself against Frederick when he criticizes her, and her growing bank balance is an obvious indication of her ability to function as an independent subject. With the help of the film director Luigi Leopardi, Annabel's sense of self is refined and honed until it is the easily graspable construct of the English Tiger-Lady.[3] Over time Annabel becomes an expert at this self both on and off screen, it is as if 'her face had changed . . . by action of many famous cameras, into a mould of her public figuration' (I, p. 35). It is noteworthy in this context that Leopardi refuses to recognize any discrepancy between Annabel's private and public self; personality, he insists, is simply 'the effect one has on others' (I, p. 34).[4] The choice of acting as the arena for Spark's novel also highlights the difficulties inherent in playing oneself. Unlike Frederick, whose talent is untested and who can therefore indulge in the fantasy of myriad possibilities, Annabel's success depends on her conforming repeatedly to the same image.

The course of Annabel and Frederick's marriage is carefully charted in the novel. Annabel initially mirrors Frederick, whose self-presentations become increasingly illusory as he withdraws from the theatre to contemplate the characters he might play. A first turning-point occurs when Frederick interferes directly with the career Annabel is beginning to build. Frederick insults a film director Annabel has complained about in private, and his attempt to intervene in her public persona frightens her. It is indicative of Frederick's continuing desire to dominate the marriage that at this point he writes a film-script with a role in it for Annabel. The film is not a success, however, and Frederick blames his wife for ignoring his script and playing her part in accordance with her public image. The division between the couple is underscored by Frederick's growing condemnation of Annabel's public image and her firm defence of it contained in her question 'What's wrong with a public image?' (I, p. 21).[5] The narrative makes it plain that at this juncture the pair might have separated. Annabel has ceased to function as the mirroring other for Frederick and he is not yet indispensable to her public image.

All this changes with Annabel's first big success, the release of the film that enshrines her as the English Tiger-Lady. The publicity that surrounds this film, and particularly the press secretary Francesca's skillful handling of it, turns Frederick and Annabel's marriage into a legend, with fixed characters and an unvarying plot. Their private lives are now public, and as Annabel gains in confidence through the images of their ideal marriage reflected in the press, she becomes paradoxically dependent on Frederick's acquiescence. It is a telling indication of the fact that it is not Frederick that Annabel requires but an image of him, that her concern to discover the identity of the woman he is having an affair with is motivated by her desire to ascertain whether or not she is the type to disrupt their public marriage. Interestingly, the press secretary Francesca's decision to make Frederick a vital part of Annabel's image is a consequence of her own sacrifice of him as lover. Although Frederick despises the new mirror, it nonetheless achieves a continuation of the Christopher marriage. Annabel now needs Frederick in his role as husband so that the public image responsible for her newly-acquired sense of self can be maintained, while Frederick is 'pacified' by the adulation he too receives (I, p. 31).[6]

Evoking the media's role in shoring up the Christopher marriage, Kristeva argues that the key to Narcissus' recognition lies in the intervention of a third party since it is only with the aid of an exterior view that he is able to interpret what he sees.[7] Crucially in terms of the terrain of *The Public Image*, she suggests that Narcissus' trajectory depends on a *specular* seduction, which is then transformed through external agency into comprehensible signs and meanings. Kristeva unpacks this point in *Tales of Love* in an essay specifically entitled 'Narcissus: The New Insanity'. Here she suggests that what Narcissus falls in love with is not an object but a 'mirage' – a 'product of the eye's mistake' (TOL, p. 104). Her statement can be productively linked to Spark's novel. There is insistence throughout the text that Annabel's role as the English Tiger-Lady depends on the latent passion detectable in her eyes. Yet this expression is a mirage, constructed by cinematic techniques and by Leopardi's direction. We are told repeatedly that the size of Annabel's eyes is magnified on screen, and that her naturally 'sickly' expression is transformed 'by the best colour methods of the cinema' and by a quality of the screen's texture to a look that is 'fiery and marvellous' (I, p. 16). Her eyes, already a product of cinematic effect, are then interpreted for the public by Leopardi and Francesca's press releases.

Kristeva suggests that for the love relation to work, the lover must be able to imagine that they are similar to and even indistinguishable from their ideal lover/other. Love, she insists, does not derive from a recognition and respect for difference but on merging and appropriation. Here too her account is borne out by Frederick and Annabel's marriage. Frederick refuses to believe any of the compliments about his wife's acting because his identity depends on perceiving her as a 'cheat': whenever anyone praises Annabel he 'silently nurtured the atrocity', reminding himself that 'nobody but he could know how shallow she really was. I know her, he thought, inside out. They don't' (I, p. 17). Later in the novel, as the power balance shifts, it is Annabel who claims to know the truth about her husband as she reiterates his role in her public image and denies his suicide.

Kristeva makes a further point concerning the story of Narcissus which is relevant to a reading of *The Public Image*. Narcissus' tragedy, she writes, does not stem from his realization that he is in love with an image but from his discovery that the image can desert him. Ovid, Kristeva's source for the myth, suggests that Narcissus would have been content with eternal contemplation, yet this is denied him as his own actions cause the reflection to vanish.[8] This recalls the stories of

Annabel and Frederick. What prompts Frederick's desertion of Annabel is not his realization that she will never fulfill his ideal but his fear that she cannot be trusted. Frederick's increasing financial dependence on Annabel finally forces him to acknowledge that 'at any moment she could change her mind. She could turn' (I, p. 22). For Annabel, Frederick's suicide is filtered through her anxiety that her public image will be destroyed. All she can think of is the headlines in the newspapers. Even years later, we are told, she can barely comprehend Frederick's death except in terms of how it has affected her (I, p. 58). It is noteworthy that immediately after hearing of her husband's suicide Annabel imagines she is taking part in a film. Her public and private worlds have become one. She manages the remainder of her affairs as if they are a film, albeit one she is now in control of. Annabel takes over the duties of her press secretary and even the skillfully manipulative Leopardi worries that she is treating the inquest as if it is a film.[9] Interestingly, the script she is engaged in learning provides welcome relief from these public performances. Annabel draws on her former typecasting as a 'frail, small, slip of a thing' to serve her in this guise, a further indication of the merging of her public and private selves (I, p. 62). She gathers her neighbours round her so that it is impossible for the press to ask any difficult or leading questions, handles Frederick's girlfriend, and even squashes the incriminating fact of Danya's overdose in her flat. In this way she prevents the disintegration of her image and preserves her identity. The boundaries between truth and mirage ultimately collapse as Annabel begins to believe the version she herself has given the papers.

Kristeva stresses that the narcissistic identifications that take place in the mother/infant dyad do not depend on the intervention of the Father which triggers the Oedipal process, but derive instead from the anterior presence of Freud's 'father of individual prehistory'. She defines this figure as an amalgam of both parents, totalizing and powerful as it satisfies both immediate existential and psychic needs. It is this 'archaic vortex of idealization' that opens up the arena of maternal plenitude and prepares us to love (TOL, p. 33). Significantly in terms of Spark's novel, Kristeva links the secondary identifications that occur through Oedipalization to the functioning of discourse itself, since their non-objectal forms resemble those of language. The Christophers' various endeavours to construct signifying images for themselves and each other in *The Public Image* can be profitably viewed in this light. I have already referred to Frederick's attempt to script a role for Annabel and Annabel's corroboration of the image the press presents of Frederick. In both cases the novel illustrates how the media as metonym for the symbolic order works to fashion the human subject in its own image. These examples are surpassed, however, by Frederick's bid to ruin his wife in his suicide letters and by Annabel's retaliation in the stories she feeds to the papers. Frederick's suicide letters are carefully crafted to manipulate their public. They exploit the Italian love of scandal and chauvinistic attitude to women. The letters – which are virtually identical – emphasize Annabel's neglect of her wifely and motherly duties; they include a letter to Frederick's own mother addressed to her as 'Mamma' although she is dead and he never called her Mamma while she was alive (I, p. 82). Even Annabel is impressed by how cleverly he has scripted her demise. Her response is equally adroit. She defies her doctor by insisting on a press conference in order to control the stories of the critical first releases, and Leopardi himself is struck by her sophisticated handling of the media. Annabel's final denouncement of Frederick at the inquest can also be interpreted in this context. Her decision to reveal the letters is based partly on her appraisal of Marina's reaction to them as symptoms of madness, a decision reinforced by her statement to the court that 'he was insane' (I, p. 123). Annabel may well risk her public image in the process, but the narrative makes it clear that if she does so it is because she now wishes to be released from it.[10]

Kristeva makes two further points which are relevant to the novel. First, while she believes that the ego's defences offer protection, she stresses that they cannot hide the fragility of the narcissistic elaboration or the fact that it is composed of imaginary recognitions and formations. As *The Public Image* demonstrates, for instance in the extraordinary scene where Billy takes fright at a balloon that suddenly appears at the hotel window as he gives Annabel the letters, any crack in our elaboration exposes the negative of the image to others. It is striking in this respect that when Annabel turns in Frederick's letters at the inquest her triumph is in seeing an identical expression on Billy's face: 'he was staring at the letters as he had stared at the white balloon at her hotel window' (I, p. 122). Secondly, Kristeva insists that since the mother as primary object of need must be narcissistically absorbed, the object of love is never the original but only its replica. As the original object is forever lost, what takes its place cannot fully be the object of desire. This provides an interesting gloss on the endless substitutions that permeate the Christophers' marriage. Both partners are unfaithful, and Annabel's focus on her baby is an obvious attempt to fill the lack of her marriage. It is even possible to view

Frederick's suicide in this light, since his strategy indicates that it is directed at Annabel in a final effort to possess her.

Kristeva's analysis in *Tales of Love* can be productively linked in terms of a reading of *The Public Image* to the work of two further writers on narcissism – Christopher Lasch and Joel Kovel. Lasch's *The Culture of Narcissism* and *The Minimal Self* offer interesting parallels with Kristeva's account of the agency of a third party in subject formation and, significantly in the context of the dominant role of the media in Spark's novel, interpret this agency with reference to contemporary culture.[11] For Lasch, mass communications and globalization have resulted in a hostile and incomprehensible environment in which identity and meaning are determined by market forces, and he suggests that one of the ways the individual endeavours to deal with this threatening social order is to block it out. This recalls Frederick's immersion in literature at the beginning of *The Public Image*, as well as the lure of the contrived escapism of the cinema and glossy magazines. Lasch argues that this constant denial exacerbates the rage which he believes accompanies narcissistic organization. We are estranged and disconnected through our bombardment by mass-produced commodity images, which foster an insatiable appetite for admiration even while we despise those we seek to impress. It is striking that Lasch highlights the fantasy worlds conjured by the media as especially influential here. As a result of their unprecedented technological mastery, the media produce a panoply of fleeting images which pervert identity formation and blur the boundaries of what is real. Developing Winnicott's notion of transitional space, Lasch maintains that this illusory array deceives the self into accepting it as its ideal, reflecting images which both flatter our desire for omnipotence and paradoxically reveal our insubstantiality. Instead of providing a productive intermediate realm, in which meaningful relations can be explored and established, it remains radically divorced from the self, proffering a mirage of apparently gratifying images based on calculations of profit and promise.[12] In this light, the closing sections of Spark's novel can be seen as a battle between two public images as Annabel and Frederick vie with each other to implant their own preferred ideal. Frederick's staging of his suicide through his letters, through the party he organizes, and through his choice of location at the site of the martyrdom of St Paul, are matched by Annabel's setting of her press conference, her careful choice of flowers and dress for the hospital, and above all her manipulative statements to the press. Lasch's interpretations also underscore Annabel's understanding that it does not matter that Frederick's mother is dead: his suicide letter to her will hit home with the Italian public so that even exposing it as a lie would not prevent it from achieving its effect.

Lasch's work on the negative emotions that accompany subject formation also presents a fertile context in which to read *The Public Image*. For Lasch, a deep undercurrent of hatred underpins narcissistic organization, since it involves an over-idealization of the object as a defence against infantile rage. This rage derives from the individual's failure to accept reality, and is accompanied by grandiose dreams of omnipotence in the yearning to return to an imaginary state of self-unity. Such fantasies are doomed to fail, so that desires for grandiosity alternate with feelings of emptiness and inferiority. Idealization, in Lasch's account, is thus the corollary of hatred, as the individual veers between illusions of omnipotence and furious disillusion.

This insistence on the negative underside to self/other relations is similarly a theme of Joel Kovel's work.[13] Returning to Freud, Kovel identifies anger and loathing as the products of an imperfect transition from primary to secondary narcissism. He suggests that the infant's necessary expulsion from the realm of narcissistic self-unity and plenitude is painful, and involves acute feelings of loss. While secondary narcissism builds on primary narcissism, it depends on the individual's insertion into a network of relations that are socially determined and which entail sacrifices as well as gains. The problem, Kovel writes, occurs wherever the evolution goes awry; when this happens the individual retains raw and destructive delusions of grandeur. Lacking connection with others, the individual lives in a state where persons and objects are split off, either powerfully idealized or arrogantly reviled. Kovel insists that such grandiosity hides anxieties of worthlessness and inadequacy, and that the narcissist's continual search for approval and paradoxical absorption in superficial pursuits is in fact a defence against a painfully fragile sense of self. The flip-side of the narcissist's superior pretensions is thus a 'ravenous rage' which constantly threatens to destroy them.[14] Cut off from social interaction, and consumed by intense feelings of powerlessness and inadequacy, the narcissist can only cope with reality through sadistic attempts at manipulation, control, and self-aggrandisement.[15] Taken in conjunction with Lasch's work, Kovel's analysis sheds an interesting light on Frederick's behaviour in *The Public Image* since it offers an explanation as to why his arrogant belief in his own talents is accompanied by his waste of them, and reveals his loathing and attempts to diminish Annabel as the corollary of his inability to leave her. It similarly provides an answer to the enigma of Frederick's suicide that haunts Spark's novel. If we examine Annabel from this perspective, her grandiose efforts to manipulate public opinion appear as a shield for her fragility, while her abdication at the novel's close becomes a deluded endeavour to renounce social ties. Kovel's account also elucidates Billy's highly puzzling actions, since it suggests that his callous ploy to make money from Frederick's suicide is a consequence of his inability to form relationships with others.[16]

To return to the work of Kristeva, it is striking that she too identifies hatred as an inextricable component of the love relation. She argues that this is most obviously the case for the individual for whom there has been no third party intervention and for whom the mother is the primary focus of narcissistic identification. Such an individual remains undifferentiated, and Kristeva stresses that their pleasure is consequently autoerotic and enjoyed with polymorphous perversity. If love appears they either accept it as a substitute maternal wrapping for their own gratification, or else hate the threat it poses to their (non)formation. More significantly, in terms of Frederick's suicide in *The Public Image*, Kristeva also links the negative emotions that haunt the love relation to death itself. She quotes Freud's work in *Beyond the Pleasure Principle* to suggest that of all the drives, the death drive is the most urgent. If this is left to itself, she writes, without the narcissistic prop of projection onto another, then the ego becomes its own target for aggression and murder. Narcissus in love thus reroutes his suicidal urge, and love 'is no more than a chancy stasis of hatred' (TOL, p. 124).

Kristeva suggests a further interpretation of Narcissus' death that elucidates Annabel's manipulation and final abandonment of the media and Frederick's suicide. She states that Narcissus' desire is to turn sight into origin; his search for the other opposite himself leads to his discovery that the reflection is no other but his own representation. This discovery of the alienation that constitutes his own self-image provokes first his sorrow and finally his death: 'deprived of the One', Kristeva writes, 'he has no salvation' (TOL, p. 121). Thus Frederick's suicide and Annabel's relinquishing of her public image at the end of the novel can be seen as the negative products of growth. For Kristeva a way out of the impasse would be for Narcissus to recognize that the object of his love is a fantasy and to play with its fiction. This last assertion casts a fascinating light on Frederick's suicide letters, which are a doubly perverse use of his obvious creative talents since they not only orchestrate his death but also attempt Annabel's ruin.[17] Significantly in terms of Frederick's condemnation of Annabel as a cheat, Kristeva suggests that one way of interpreting Narcissus' suicide is to connect it to his discovery that he is in love with a fake. She argues that such a situation arises where there has been no initial third party intervention and consequently no establishment of an Ego Ideal. This rules out the possibility of identification and the creation of its equal as a love-object or work of art, and reduces the other to an ersatz.[18]

For Kristeva, narcissism is not, then, an originary state but one dependent on a third party to supplement the autoeroticism of the mother/infant dyad. While this intervention precedes that which causes the formation of the oedipal ego, it nonetheless provides crucial preparation for later development. This last point is important since it suggests how the media function as an anticipatory mirror for Annabel, promoting her autonomy.[19] Her decision to reveal Frederick's letters at the inquest and thereby release herself from the media's thrall can from this point of view be seen as progressive actions.

There are, nevertheless elements of Kristeva's analysis that disturb such a positive interpretation. For Kristeva, the mother's role in loving her child in relation to a third party is vital: without this the bodily exchange becomes one of abjection or devouring against which the infant's only defence is hatred. As it is depicted in the novel, Annabel's love for her baby denies such a relation. The text stresses her delight in being on her own with her baby, informs us that he is 'the only reality of her life', and explains her refusal to allow him to be photographed by the press as a fear that 'this deep and complete satisfaction might be disfigured or melted away by some public image' (I, p. 35).[20] Even more significantly in terms of Kristeva's analysis, the text suggests that what the baby gives her is a 'sense of being permanently secured to the world' which she has not experienced since childhood (I, p. 65). Annabel's apparently courageous decision to reject her public image in order to be with her baby consequently has ominous undertones. At the end of the novel, as she waits at the airport, she feels as if she is still pregnant: as if the baby is 'perpetually within her' (I, p. 125). In a formulation which recalls Kristeva's definition of narcissism, Frederick accuses Annabel in his suicide letter to her of being an empty shell, and in the final lines of *The Public Image* this metaphor is reinvoked with the assertion that this emptiness is now filled by the baby. It is striking that the only reason Annabel gives for her action is a declaration to her lawyer that she wants 'to be free like my baby' (I, p. 123). This excessive focus on the baby is augmented by her unwillingness to communicate with him. While she feeds, bathes and changes him, the text suggests that she is too 'enamoured' to echo him with 'baby-babble' (I, p. 35). In the light of Kristeva's work on the importance of the mother's role in initiating external relationships, the prognostications for the future well-being of Annabel and her baby are perturbing.[21]

When Kristeva cites the priest and analyst as viable third-party agencies, she calls on figures who are guided by a sense of ethical responsibility. If, as Lasch suggests, the media have replaced religion, community and meaningful social interaction as formational powers, then what we have in Spark's novel is a cogent warning against the times.[22] Annabel's public image might initially increase her autonomy, but in contrast to the altruism of priest or analyst the more glamorous mirror through which she perceives herself depends on illusion and greed. Like Narcissus gazing into his pool, the images it offers are remote and treacherous since there is no possibility of exchange or even inventive play. It is a telling indictment of the media's stranglehold that it forces both Annabel and Frederick into strategies of denial: the Christophers' idolized marriage ends with Annabel seeking escape into maternal plenitude and Frederick committing suicide. While Narcissus' story can for Kristeva and others present a positive model for confronting the emptiness of individuation, the shadow he casts in Spark's novel is more sinister, as the media's dazzling idealizations drown the very individuals they appear to promote.

Notes

1. Julia Kristeva, *Tales of Love* (1983), translated by Leon S. Roudiez (New York: Columbia University Press, 1987), p. 3. Hereafter referred to in the text as TOL.
2. It is also significant in the light of what follows that the text highlights the fragility of the arrangements Annabel has made, some of which are bound to 'start moving anticlockwise', ibid.
3. It is noteworthy that the text repeats the details of Annabel's image a number of times, as if the reader too must be continually reminded of how to interpret it.
4. This point is reiterated in the manner in which Annabel speaks Italian. We are told that she does this exactly as if she were acting a part in Italian, yet the apparent pretence not only enables her to successfully hire a lawyer and rent a flat at a reasonable price in Rome, it also prompts her to think like an Italian.
5. Annabel later goes a stage further, following her question 'What's wrong with my public image?' with the statement 'It's a good one' (I, p. 30). Annabel's increasing predominance in the relation can be seen both in her

appropriation of 'my' public image and in her defence of it.

6. There is also an actual moment of reunion when Annabel takes fright at the new mythology surrounding their marriage and turns to Frederick. Their son is conceived during this reconciliation.

7. It is noteworthy in this context that the narration offers an exterior view of the Christophers' marriage, selecting, arranging and commenting on the material presented. Examples are Frederick's insistence that he is destined for great things and the narration's judgement and elucidation of this, ibid. p. 10; and the introduction of a future time-frame as Annabel reminisces about her life, ibid. p. 15. It is possible in the light of Kristeva's comments to argue that the narration functions for the reader as a third party in the recounting of the Christopher marriage.

8. 'Let me but gaze on what I may not touch', Ovid, *Metamorphoses*, translated by A. D. Melville (Oxford: Oxford University Press, 1987), p. 65, Book III, line 480. Narcissus' tears disturb the surface of the water and his reflection consequently disappears.

9. Luigi accuses Annabel of 'making a movie script of it in your mind' (I, p. 97).

10. Leopardi tells Annabel's lawyer that unless she avoids a scandal and maintains her public image her career in films is over (I, p. 122).

11. This is also the purpose of Catherine Belsey's reading of Jean Laplanche in her fascinating study *Desire: Love Stories in Western Culture* (Oxford: Blackwell, 1994). Following Laplanche, Belsey argues that sexuality does not exist in a pure state prior to the meanings and fantasies with which it is invested by a child's carers. Although sexual excitation is involved in the necessary processes of caring for the child, it is understood only retrospectively at puberty through the investments and prohibitions its carers have already imposed. Human sexuality is, then, inextricably tied to representation and Belsey suggests that the third party can consequently be identified as culture itself. Although Kristeva does not explicitly link the interventions of a third party to culture, she does argue that the role of Freud's 'father of individual prehistory' can be undertaken by the community at large. She gives the specific examples of a priest and an analyst but insists that the crucial component of this ideal is that it is an irrefutable power. Her quotation of Freud's analysis of the collective hysteria that causes crowds to abdicate their judgement presents a striking parallel with the way public opinion is directed in Spark's novel. The two texts referred to by Lasch are *The Culture of Narcissism* (London: Abacus, 1979) and *The Minimal Self: Psychic Survival in Troubled Times* (New York: Norton, 1984). I am indebted to Anthony Elliott's clear and comprehensive *Psychoanalytic Theory* (Oxford: Blackwell, 1994), for introducing this work to me.

12. Lasch's work can also be fruitfully read alongside Lacan's study of Freud. For Lacan, the mirror phase is a narcissistic process of imaginary misrecognition which 'situates ... the ego, before its social determination, in a fictional direction' – Jacques Lacan, *Ecrits: A Selection* (London: Tavistock Press, 1977), p. 2. This imaginary misrecognition of self-unity subsequently informs our self-perceptions as well as our relations with others. Lacan's analysis underscores the seductive power of the media to feed in and refashion these illusory images.

13. My source here is his essay 'Narcissism and the Family' (1980) quoted in *Psychoanalytic Theory*, pp. 55–7.
14. Ibid. p. 56.
15. For Catherine Belsey, hatred is a corollary of even healthy separation from the mother. She quotes Freud's analysis of the 'fort/da' game played by his nephew, where Freud stresses that by throwing away the cotton reel the child enacts emblematic revenge on the mother who has abandoned him. It is, Belsey suggests, an act of hostility, a dismissal of the loved object, a murder. Belsey also explores hatred in the mature love relation, citing Lacan's readings of Freud to argue that love confers on the Other the power to fulfill as well as to withhold satisfaction. Since the Other cannot fulfill this role it becomes an object of hate and love – *Desire: Love Stories in Western Culture*, pp. 58–9.
16. This is borne out in the novel by the absence of any but the most acrid, suspicious and deceitful exchanges between Billy and Annabel, and by the account of Billy's tenuous friendships in Rome (I, p. 38). There is no recorded exchange between Billy and Frederick.
17. Billy's evocative phrase to describe the letters is 'a dead man's deadly poison' (I, p. 80).
18. It is noteworthy in this context that the narration offers an exterior, third-party view. It is significant, in terms of this debasement of the other, that what Frederick endeavours to destroy in his story of orgies is Annabel's propriety. As she tells Leopardi: 'I don't like fun, quite honestly ... I don't like tiger-sex. I like to have my sexual life under the bedclothes, in the dark, on a Saturday night' (I, p. 101).
19. It is interesting that the man Annabel sees from her hotel window towards the close of the novel offers a different self-image, one which causes her 'despair' because he has mistakenly perceived her as 'an ordinary woman, free to come down and enjoy herself' (I, p. 76).
20. It is significant that she uses the baby at her press conference however, holding it in her arms as if it is a 'triumphant shield' (I, p. 65).
21. Although I do not have the space to discuss this here, it is noteworthy that in *Tales of Love* Kristeva discusses the institution of the Virgin and Child as the pinnacle of narcissistic love in the West, p. 60.
22. It is significant in this context that the Christophers' reception by the Pope is reduced in the novel to a series of photo-opportunities (see I, p. 33).

2
The Future Perfect's Perfect Future: Spark's and Duras's Narrative Drive

Judith Roof

> What fascinates Lol is the end.
>
> *The Ravishment of Lol V. Stein*

By the end of Muriel Spark's *The Driver's Seat* and Marguerite Duras's *The Ravishing of Lol V. Stein* readers will have traversed their histories of inevitable destinies; readers and characters will have returned to a rest which will have always seemed to have been the goal of the narratives' trajectories.[1] Focused on solitary and enigmatic female protagonists, the narratives reproduce the story of each woman's life (and vice versa) as if the story were already known. The novels' snug connection between the destinies of their central protagonists and the dynamic of their narratives seems curiously at odds with the stories' feeling of distance, a theatricalization that erodes intimacy in the telling and seduces not only through the mastery that might be appended to intimate foreknowledge, but also through the objectification, limited point of view, and proleptic hints that force the narratives to spiral through time and around and through perspectives at varying distances from the plotted action. The clash between familiar destiny and coiled distanciation in both novels sparks ruminations on the nature of narrative; it also draws attention to a drive which is neither Freud's 'death drive' nor the 'pleasure principle,' but a specifically narrative drive dependent upon knowledge of the story. This narrative drive, comprised of the dynamic interrelation between epistemology and sexuality, characterizes the seductive power of Lise and Lol as they transform activity into passivity and nothingness into desire.

Fashioning destiny

The Driver's Seat and *The Ravishing of Lol V. Stein* are, of course, quite different from one another, though both focus on a female protagonist and reflect such aspects of the *nouveau roman* as the absence of elaborate plot, linear chronology, heavily psychologized characters, and the conventions of certainty, and a focus on writing itself. *The Driver's Seat* (1970) tracks protagonist Lise, an exacting thin-lipped employee in an accountant's office, who carefully plans to be brutally murdered. Narrated by a third-person narrator whose knowledge is limited to surface facts, Lise's death appears to be the product of Lise's foreknowledge of her own fate, which she seems to hurry along by taking a vacation, purchasing the necessary accoutrements (scimitar paper knife, ties, and scarves), and finally trapping an unprepossessing (and reluctant) psychopath into doing the deed. The novel's intrusive sense of destiny is produced not only by Lise's deliberately eccentric behaviours – buying a dress and coat in shockingly loud and clashing colours, complaining vociferously about various minor matters in her hotel, hiding her passport in the seat of a taxi, making sure she is noticed at every turn – but also by the narrator's use of prolepsis.[2] Establishing in the second chapter that Lise will end up involved in a crime ('Her nose is short and wider than it will look in the likeness constructed partly by the methods of identikit, partly by actual photography, soon to be published in the newspapers of four languages' [p. 26]), the narrator drops hints in the future and future perfect tenses that make it apparent that Lise's present actions are part of a plan whose fulfillment will correspond to the end of the novel ('She lays the trail, presently to be followed by Interpol and elaborated upon with due art by the journalists of Europe for the few days it takes for her identity to be established' [p. 75]; 'The policeman is still finding words when she drives off, and in the mirror she can see him looking at the retreating car, probably noting the number. Which in fact he is doing, so that, on the afternoon of the following day, when he has been shown her body, he says, "Yes, that's her. I recognise the face"' [p. 12]). Leaping into the future gives the present a design, while the present, which already seems to belong to a future perfect, defines a future whose possible failure of fulfillment produces tension.

Duras's novel, published in 1964, is a character study of Lol, a woman who had been abandoned by her fiancé for another woman at a dance in a resort casino. The novel presents the narration of Lol's life from the point of view of a future lover, Jack Hold, whose narrative of

Lol becomes the story of his own desire.³ Hold's fascination with Lol lies in her inaccessibility, her strange unknowability. 'To know nothing about Lol Stein was already to know her,' Hold observes. As Jack Hold describes first what he imagines about the traumatic night of Lol's abandonment as she stands by the cluster of green plants with her friend Tatiana and afterward as she struggles through sickness, marries the undemanding John Bedford, moves to another town, and returns finally with husband and children to her family's home in South Tahla, what Hold narrates is not only important as the traumatic background that might explain Lol's behaviour, but also as the events that lead up to his meeting her. Lol spends her time walking through the town, one day compelled by some familiar quality in Hold to follow him until he ends up at the hotel of illicit love affairs where Lol had had trysts with her fiancé. After witnessing Hold and Tatiana in the hotel room, Lol finds where her old friend Tatiana lives and visits her. From the point when Lol rediscovers Tatiana, Lol's inevitable meeting with Jack Hold becomes retrospectively the entire point of Hold telling Lol's story, a narrative that deploys Lol – she who already stands for nothing – as the lure for a telling that situates narrative as the necessary appendage to a desire that cannot know its object. The unknowable object nonetheless has a destiny fashioned by the narrative and fixed at the point of the narrator's desire – the fate of becoming not only the object of the tale, but the epitome of an inexplicable desire that drives the desire to tell. Although Lol eventually accompanies Hold to the beach resort where her fiancé had abandoned her and goes to bed with him, she ultimately evades Hold, acquiescing to their affair as if it would always have been, but preferring to lie asleep in the rye field in sight of the hotel room where Jack and Tatiana will continue their fading affair.

On one level, the novels' distancing devices objectify the female protagonists and suggest that there is something in their behaviour that requires explanation. Like Teresa de Lauretis's ploy of 'Oedipus with a vengeance' where a narrative is so obviously Oedipal that Oedipal desire is made visible, both novels offer a plethora of possible interpretations whose very number exposes our (and the narratives') investment in figuring these characters out.⁴ The narrator's careful tracking of Lise's actions portrays her as an obsessive–compulsive whose need to control every aspect of her environment points to repressed sexuality, sado-masochism, and suicidal tendencies. Lol's abandonment suggests a traumatic basis for her behaviour; her compulsive neatness and walking imply neuroses; her relations to her husband and children hint at an existential dysphoria. Each of these behaviours in turn might also be a symptom for something else, some lack in being or hypersensitivity to gender politics. There are too many possibilities for both Lise and Lol, yet none suffices as explanation either for the character or for what happens to her.

Seeming in this way to provide an exploration of character motivation, underlying pathologies, and their various causes, the novels present themselves as if they were aestheticized case studies. Like case studies, both novels employ a distanced, observing narrator, who, detached from the protagonist, describes her actions as if they are at the same time familiar and alien. The provision of this kind of narrator, whether it be the deliberately bland but expert voice of Lise's documentarist or the first person witness whose descriptions say more about him than about Lol, produces a distance within the novels among the somewhat disparate agendas of a consciousness of perceiving others, the perception of another as an enigma, and understanding that enigma. These different levels of consciousness not only produce an analytical space, they also provide the distance necessary both to the illusion that the female protagonist is indeed the focus of the story and to fetishism. Lise and Lol are fetishes, but not because they provide a presence that both masks and points to an absence or function as sites of disavowal, but because they negotiate the complex ambivalences of the acts of telling and reading.

This notion of the fetish as negotiating ambivalence, delineated by E. L. McCallum, suggests that Freud's fetish is less a phallic substitute standing in for absence and more a tool for managing differences.[5] The enigmatic Lise and Lol serve as foci that negotiate narratorial ambivalence – an ambivalence constructed as a part of the problem of the sufficiency of telling as a mode of understanding. Because narrating (even narrating ignorance) implies a mastery, the act of telling is often situated as a revelation – as a filling in of the unknown. What *The Driver's Seat* and *The Ravishing of Lol V. Stein* make apparent is that narrative is not mastery at all, but is instead a questing that attempts to match the known with an unknown, an effect with a cause, or events with the proper narrative. Since, in the cases of Lise and Lol, narrating does not align the story with any definite understanding and thus exposes narrative's failure of insight, Lise and Lol become the figures whose inexplicability accounts for narrative's futility. They are the fetishes that both displace and obscure narrative's inadequacy while seeming to fill its space. This is not because these characters are merely present or centred (which would make them simple subjects whose acts are described and would suggest that all protagonists are fetishes), but because both novels make the act of narrating a conscious project. The fetish and ambivalence are linked to a consciousness of narrating, where an acknowledgement of having knowledge is manifested in the future perfect, the use of prolepsis, and frank expressions of certainty or ignorance that litter the texts. This doubled consciousness – a consciousness of telling a story and a consciousness of the story's shape – makes telling itself the subject of the novel, while the ambiguous female figures who preoccupy the tellers are the props of the tale, the symptoms of an uncertainty that lies not in Lise or Lol, but in the character of the narration itself.

Narrative's ambiguity exists both in the gaps between telling and understanding and also in its own inevitable and inescapable temporal paradox – that the end is known in the beginning and yet we tell the story anyway, a paradox which also produces a paradox of desire. Why do we want to know something (the end) we already apparently know? This temporal paradox engenders ambivalence between our knowledge of the story's plot and ending and disavowing such knowledge so that the story can continue. The novels' use of prolepsis also creates ambivalence between the novel's suggested knowledge (death, isolation) and the readers' projections. While readers may know the protagonists' fates and resist that knowledge, they might at the same time desire such fates, both for the characters and themselves. They both may and may not wish Lise dead, may or may not desire to see Lol regress (or advance) to peaceful, yet watchful slumber. Ambivalence also arises from the prolepsis' implication that there is some definitive end while the narratives move towards an increasing perplexity and failure of knowledge. The meshing of the end for which we have been long prepared and the uncertainty that actually attends the end produces an ambivalence negotiated by the figures who take the blame not only for narrative's incapacities, but for all the other temporal and libidinal ambivalences as well.

This narrative ambivalence and its fetishistic fixation on enigmatic female characters is paralleled by the relations among the characters described in the plots. In *The Ravishing of Lol V. Stein*, Lol serves as the third term in a perpetual ritual of triangulation, quite literally negotiating differences in gender, class, and nation or ethnicity among the characters. Her history (as told by Hold) begins with the trio of Lol, Tatiana, and Lol's wealthy fiancé Michael Richardson. This triangle shifts when Richardson is helplessly attracted to visiting colonial, Anne-Marie Stretter, for whom he abandons Lol. Incapacitated by this defection, Lol is the remainder, the supplement that attests to the rejoinder of continent and colonial and of young and older. The slowly recovering Lol marries John Bedford who likes her because she negotiates his pedophilia: 'She aroused in him his special penchant for young girls, girls not completely grown into adults, for pensive, impertinent, inarticulate, young girls' (p. 20). Bedford moves Lol to the English-inflected Uxbridge where her life is governed by a compulsive neatness. When Lol, Bedford, and their two daughters return to South Tahla, Lol wanders the streets and becomes fixed to a position outside of the window of a hotel where lovers meet – outside the room where she and her fiancé had met and where now Jack Hold and her old friend Tatiana meet. She becomes the third party in their affair, stealing Jack from Tatiana as Stretter had stolen Richardson from her, but remaining outside (both physically and emotionally) arrested in the position of watching the others in attitudes of love and rejection.

Lol's triangulations are a displaced configuration of the triangulation necessary to narrating an other as self – of using the narrative of another as a way to come back to self. As a narrator, Jack projects his own pleasure in voyeurism – the observation of Lol – onto Lol, and his pleasure in exhibitionism – in being seen as a lover – onto Lol's position as watcher. At the same time, the act of narrating makes him both voyeur and exhibitionist, a position displaced onto Lol as the ostensible subject of the story. In this way Jack enacts the perversity of narration – its deviations, side-tracks – while displacing its impetus toward completion onto Lol whom he presents as someone who unconsciously pursues an inevitable track. *Lol V. Stein's* connections between seeing and telling also suggest the theatrical qualities of this kind of framed narrative, performing both physical and temporal distance so that what is narrated comes back as if from another place. Duras's novel's emphasis on the position of a watcher who is distanced encapsulates the theatrical nature of a narration that uses a distanced object to deflect attention from its own process of narrating so that it can appear, via the object, to control precisely what it seeks to understand – the cause of the effects it describes, the destiny it seems to map out as inevitable. This narrating is thus ambivalent in another way: at any time, what is narrated is about both the narrator and the narrated, in two places at once, both watcher and watched. This ambivalence is also arbitrated by the third party object, represented by Lol in the novel, but also represented by the novel's reader who negotiates the layers of watching by watching and seeming to be in a position sufficiently distanced to judge, situated in alignment with both Hold and the inaccessible Lol.

The Driver's Seat seems less complicated than *Lol*, since it does not avail itself of the first-person narrator and thus it is less immediately evident how narrating the history of Lise can be the displacement of the fixations of another. But while it is less clear that Lise works as a third-term fetish to negotiate the differences among characters, it is more clear that Lise negotiates narrating's ambivalence between the violence of voyeurism and the empathy of identification as well as the ambivalence produced by narrative's temporal paradox. Theatricalized like *Lol*, *The Driver's Seat* focuses on a protagonist who transforms herself from a quiet and unprepossessing clerk with a compulsively neat apartment to a character who feigns loudness in dress and manner so as to attract attention. Lise does not seem interested in presenting the performance of an intrinsically flamboyant persona, but rather works to perform someone who is annoying, rude, and tasteless. Her selection of an orange and purple dress worn with a red and white striped coat suggests the deliberate production of a brashness so pronounced that witnesses will remember little else. Her sartorial offence accompanied by the ostentatious proclamation of various tastes and her aggressive pursuit of an unprepossessing man who tries to avoid her create the portrait of an insensitive and slightly hysterical middle-aged woman whose vacation to the south appears to be a desperate opportunity for belated love affairs.

Buying garish clothes, stridently checking in at the airport, annoyingly accosting an apparently innocent businessman, aggressively waylaying an obviously nervous gentleman, teasing along a macrobiotic devotee who had made clear his interest in her, shopping with the elderly Mrs. Fiedke whom she makes certain sees all of her purchases, stealing a car from a lecherous garage owner, and finally encountering the quiet businessman she had originally selected as seat partner on the plane, Lise leaves an unmistakable and very duplicitous trail to her own violent demise. Lise's performance dramatizes the making of a narrative from the inside out as she manufactures clues, but the clues she concocts are already seen simultaneously from two different perspectives depending upon one's temporal relation to Lise's construction. From the perspective of the proleptic's future perfect, Lise's actions represent the well-planned marking of a trail, each ostentatious gesture, each seemingly innocent purchase meaningful in a retrospect that inflects the present with the future. From the vantage of a disingenuous present marked by a certain dissimulation (or 'willing suspension of disbelief'), all of Lise's actions seem to be the perplexing vacation behaviour of a repressed woman, each purchase and action eccentric, but innocent in itself until it gains significance in relation to the end.

The narrator's use of prolepsis brings present and future perfect perspectives together as coexisting possibilities and the narrative oscillates between present and future perfect, producing a temporal ambivalence that distances our reading and makes evident a reliance upon the knowledge of an outcome as the way to make sense of competing possibilities. Even without the prolepses, it is likely that readers would anticipate Lise's demise before the end of the story. *The Driver's Seat* is no 'Purloined Letter;' the clues are so obvious that one suspects they are misleading. The novel's provision of proleptic hints produces a profound sense of wisdom and mastery accompanied by suspicion; all anticipations are still undone by the novel's violent end which somehow exceeds expectations while fulfilling them. Producing multiple coexisting temporalities through the interference of proleptic reminders, *The Driver's Seat* situates Lise and her motives as the figure that negotiates both temporal and epistemological ambivalence. But instead of being clearly the projection of the frame narrator, the fetish Lise becomes the projection of the reader – or perhaps more accurately – the projection of an act of reading that exposes readerly investment in watching the inevitable violence toward which Lise stalwartly heads. Our knowledge of the outcome, hinted at broadly in the narrator's many proleptic comments, makes our continued reading a fascinated voyeurism, while our denial of this knowledge – our reading as if the end is unsure – enables our perplexed identification with a figure whose actions seem the incomprehensible pieces of a puzzle offered for solution. As victim and enigma, Lise waivers between destiny and control. Like Lol, she seems to know what the end will be; like Lol she seems to cooperate with the forces that produce that end, wielding them herself when they don't seem to behave according to plan. Both protagonists seem simultaneously to be in total control of a story they have known all along – they are themselves narrators – and acquiescent objects of narration who function as sites of projection, displacement, and negotiation.

'*Wo es war, soll Ich werden*'

Even if (or because) Lise and Lol are fetishes that distract us from and draw our attention to the processes and investments of narrative, their enigmatic psychology seems to hold the key to the stories' dynamics in their push towards a seemingly ineffable and obvious end which arrives but does not provide definitive knowledge or closure. In this context, psychology refers to whatever 'inner' cause would justify the narrated actions. Since both novels focus on characters whose motivations are inaccessible and mysterious, and since those motivations seem (through the sleight of hand that substitutes the female figure for the desires of the narrator) to be the engines or lures that drive the narrative, reading is equated with analysing Lise and Lol to determine what odd trauma or quirk accounts for their actions. *The Ravishing of Lol V. Stein* seems to provide the answer to this question in Lol's having been jilted, and certainly one might explain her actions as a species of repetition compulsion as she seeks from that point on to repeat her position as watcher. But even if her abandonment by Richardson accounts for her obsessive neatness, compulsive walking, and distanced voyeurism, it doesn't account for why Lol responds in these ways in the first place: for why she has a nervous breakdown, becomes nearly catatonic, and seeks repetition. Like Lise, Lol seems driven by some knowledge that would have already determined that Richardson would leave her just as Lise seems uncannily certain of the manner of her own demise.

Focusing on character psychology seems to be giving in to the novels' provision of a distracting but engrossing focal point. But the sense of destiny exhibited by both characters correlates with the sense of narrative mastery produced through both novels' use of prolepsis and distanciation. The sense of destiny may provide a clue to what drives the engagement with narratives defined by a consciousness of their own shape not only as part of a formal understanding of narrative, but as a part of understanding evasive character psychology. The fact that both characters end up in the places that they seem to have known all along they would end up in suggests that both Lise and Lol are obeying some internal drive that has predetermined their fate – some drive appended to their own sense of a fitting end. It may well be that both novels illustrate Freud's outline of the drives in *Beyond the Pleasure Principle*, but it might also be that both novels perform a drive different from those outlined by Freud, linked to narrative and to their qualities of already having been where they are going.

The complex dynamic of the drives as outlined by Freud in *Beyond the Pleasure Principle* and adapted by Peter Brooks to narrative in 'Freud's Masterplot' pits the pleasure principle and the death drive against the reality principle and Eros in a battle to die at the right or appropriate time.[6] Freud's very narrative idea of the pleasure principle is 'that the course of those events is invariably set in motion by an unpleasurable tension, and that it takes a direction such that its final outcome coincides with a lowering of that tension' (p. 1). This pleasure principle which would seem in itself to stop any story short is offset by what Freud terms '"the reality principle," which demands and carries into effect the postponement of satisfaction and the temporary toleration of unpleasure as a step on the long indirect road to pleasure' (p. 4). Freud links the pleasure principle's lowering of tension to an innate death drive where death represents the ultimate lowering of tensions and return to an originary quiescence. He characterizes the reality principle and its instincts towards self-preservation and mastery as detours 'whose function it is to assure that the organism shall follow its own path to death and to ward off any possible ways of returning to inorganic existence other than those which are immanent in the organism itself' (p. 33).

Peter Brooks demonstrates how Freud's schema, which is quite obviously a narrative of life, is also a narrative of narrative, showing how 'plot' 'is stimulated from quiescence into a state of narratability, into a tension, a kind of irritation, which demands narration' (p. 291). Narrative, whose end, as Brooks notes, is already in its beginning, maintains itself as narrative through 'deviance, *détour*, an intention which is irritation' 'in the drive of desire towards meaning in time' (p. 292, p. 293). As Brooks concludes, 'we emerge from reading *Beyond the Pleasure Principle* with a dynamic model which effectively structures ends (death, quiescence, non-narratability) against beginnings (Eros, stimulation into tension, the desire of narrative) in a manner that necessitates the middle as *détour*, as struggle toward the end under the compulsion of imposed delay, as arabesque in the dilatory space of the text' (p. 295).

I cite Freud and Brooks at length between their descriptions of life as narrative and the narrative of life seem particularly apropos to both *The Driver's Seat* and *The Ravishing of Lol V. Stein*. Both narratives are fairly transparent examples of these tensions, played out both in the lives of the focal characters and in the manner by which those lives are narrated. Lise and Lol drive toward a quiescence, Lise in death and Lol in her foetal rest in the rye field. Both narratives consist of a series of delays and '*détours*' that perpetuate the narratives' tension. Both characters are the 'irritation' 'which demands narration' according to Brooks, their apparently irrational behaviour spurring a desire for meaning.

But more than simply exempla of the canny insight of Freud and

Brooks, these two novels perform yet another kind of a drive, linked less to desire than to mastery. If they merely comply with the dynamics outlined by Freud and Brooks, why do their endings not fulfill their promise? Why would we seem to know less at the end than at the beginning? Why would the stories end with an exposure of narrative's desire for a mastery which turns out not to have been the point at all? Something is awry in *The Driver's Seat* and *The Ravishing of Lol V. Stein* where the end turns out to have been more of a deviance than any of the middle's deviance, yet where the end was known from the beginning.

Both *The Driver's Seat* and *The Ravishing of Lol V. Stein* have an overly present, over-determined end, marked throughout the narrative through uses of the future perfect, intimations of narrative foreknowledge, and references to the action as being past events narrated from a future vantage point. Their omnipresent ends exceed the paradoxical temporal dynamic that Brooks discusses as narrative's 'double operation upon time' where 'it puts time into motion and suspends it' (p. 282, p. 281), and where 'the sense of beginning, then, is determined by the sense of an ending' (p. 283), and 'the very possibility of meaning plotted through time depends on the anticipated structuring force of the ending' (p. 283). In *The Driver's Seat* and *The Ravishing of Lol V. Stein* the end is more than a structuring force, it fronts a dynamic in which the end *becomes* the beginning, *is* the irritation inciting both narration and the characters' actions. The drive in these novels is, thus, not a drive to end at the end, as it would be in flashback narratives or histories, but rather a drive to narrate – to inhabit the point of tension, the middle, the *détour*, the deviance. This marks these narratives as perverse in the sense that their desire for the end is secondary because the sense of an end is already so prominent. The omnipresent consciousness of an ending and of narrating disallows any seductiveness or desire for the end or drive toward it. Instead, the end, as in *Oedipus Rex*, permeates the narratives as destiny, as the ineffable fact that produces tension only in its slow arrival. This slowness, the luxuriant pace of getting where we know we will end up, displaces end pleasure into the middle, into the getting instead of the there. Even though we know the ends, neither end seems proper to the action or rational in terms of human psychology. Like Freud's perverts, these stories delight in not ending properly; when they get to the end, the characters turn out to have had the wrong aim or have chosen the wrong object, ending, as does Lise, prematurely, or like Lol in a species of somnambulant voyeurism.[7]

This pleasure in the middle would seem to comply with Brooks' understanding of narrative as the middle, as the process initiated by an irritation that disturbs quiescent peace. Brooks, however, emphasizes the importance of the end; 'the passion' of narrating and reading, he exclaims, citing Roland Barthes, 'appears to be finally a desire for the end' – an end that in retrospect illuminates all (p. 282). This suggests that the passion for the end is a quest for knowledge, mastery, illumination. But if the end is already known, what kind of desire can the end inspire except the desire for mere fulfillment, a repetition of a story that is already known? The key in narratives such as *The Driver's Seat* and *The Ravishing of Lol V. Stein* is knowledge, which, omnipresent, produces not a desire for the end as revelation, but a desire that the story follow its proper course, much like the organism who follows 'its own path to death.' This shifts the site of meaning from the end as the significant point of register to the middle – to the telling itself – as a site of both a constant tension that the story will not proceed properly and meaning that makes sense out of the end we know is coming.

The desire for the story to follow its proper course is certainly the anxiety manifested by Lise throughout *The Driver's Seat* as she struggles to comply with her sense of the story. For example, as she anxiously seeks her murderer, she explains to Mrs. Fiedke how she will know when she finds the proper man:

> 'I wouldn't know till I'd seen him. Myself, I think he's around the corner somewhere, now, any time.'
> 'Which corner?' The old lady looks up and down the street which runs below them at the bottom of the steps.
> 'Any corner. Any old corner.'
> 'Will you feel a presence? Is that how you'll know?'
> 'Not really a presence,' Lise says. 'The lack of an absence, that's what it is. I know I'll find it. I keep on making mistakes, though.' She starts to cry, very slightly sniffing, weeping ...
>
> (pp. 104–5)

With the 'lack of an absence' the story is filled in. The question is not what Lise will know but how; she knows the story but does not know its details. She fears that her life will not comply with the story, that she will make mistakes; she does not fear or question the violent death toward which the story goes. Lise's desire is to conform to the story; the end will come of itself. While her demise is an end for Lise, it in turn sparks the narrative, which is itself a repetition of the events that lead up to the end we suspect is coming. This sense of narrative as the repetition of a story long known permeates Spark's other contemporaneous novels: *The Hothouse by the East River* (1973) is about a narrative continued after its end (the death of the characters), and *Not to Disturb* (1971) follows the scripted actions of a group of servants.

The end, at least according to Jack Hold, seems to have a different valence for Lol, who seeks each day to reproduce the traumatic moment of the end of the ball:

> I know Lol Stein in the only way I can; through love. It is because of this knowledge that I have come to this conclusion: among the many aspects of the Town Beach ball, what fascinates Lol is the end. It is the precise moment when it comes to an end, when dawn arrives with incredible cruelty and separates her from the couple formed by Michael Richardson and Anne-Marie Stretter, forever, forever. Each day Lol goes ahead with the task of reconstructing that moment. She even manages to seize a little of its lightening-like rapidity, to spread it out and pinpoint each second, arrest its movement, an immobility which is extremely precarious but, for her, infinitely graceful. (pp. 36–7)

In her daily repetitions of the trauma, Lol is riveted by the end, or so Hold believes. But the very fact of her repetitions and her ability to molecularize the moments that lead up to the end suggest a desire for the middle, for the events and feelings that accompany the getting there: anxiety, uncertainty, tension, hope. Repeating the drama is not simply a quest to re-experience the final moment which has no meaning or impact without the torture that accompanies it, but is rather a savouring of the middle, of the point before all becomes definitive, the point where multiple and conflicting emotions – a kind of pleasurable if terrible foreplay – produce feeling. Spreading out the rapidity of the night is a way to re-experience hope and terror by forestalling the inevitable, which for Lol leads to catatonia. It enables Lol to play through the more satisfying middle moments of the old familiar story by focusing on those points of uncertainty on the way to the end, not for the sake of the end, but for the sake of the story as an epistemological structure, as a way of making present the absence that Lol has become.

Lol's repetitions suggest the traumatic nightmares that produced Freud's dilemma in *Beyond the Pleasure Principle*: why, Freud wonders, if dreams are wish fulfillment, do dreamers revisit traumas? Lol seems to exemplify Freud's solution as well – that repetition enables mastery. But when a character such as Lol is conscious of the story and of its retelling, repetition may not be so much an unconscious attempt at mastery as a conscious attempt to relish the pathos and tension intrinsic to narrating a story whose end is all too well known. Lol's repetitions are less the playing out of *fort/da* and more a pleasure in simply *fort*. This pleasure in *fort* can be read in Lol's walking, which, like narrating, is done for its own sake rather than to get someplace. Her desire to take up with Tatiana again is another repetition in the restaging of triangulated scenes of desire that provide variations of Lol's essential theme of abandonment: Lol could abandon John Bedford, Peter Beugner could abandon Tatiana, Jack Hold could abandon Tatiana, Lol could abandon Jack Hold. The opening out of these variations on the story provide infinite possibility for narrating. Lol gives herself to Hold just enough to produce the maximal narrative complications. Lol's and the novel's conclusion, that 'Lol was asleep in the field of rye, worn out, worn out by our trip' (p. 181) implies that Lol's sleep is not only a repetition of post-traumatic catatonia or a return to quiescence in a very literal pleasure principle, but also that it is simply a pause in the narrating that wears her out.

The actions of Lise and Lol suggest that neither character is driven by a desire to end, but by a desire to live the story properly, to repeat a story by living it as a way to play out a knowledge each already had. Neither the dynamic nor the narratives of their lives is governed entirely by the combination of a death drive (or pleasure principle) and a reality principle (or Eros) that delays the end for the purposes of self-conservation. Rather, they both manifest a drive to narrate as an excess to the dynamic, a drive to repeat the middle properly. This narrative drive is reiterated by the novels themselves – in fact, characterizes the particularly self-conscious modes of narrating presented in both. Each novel is a repetition of a structure already known, retold not for the sake of finding meaning in the end, or meaning in the analyses of the events that lead up to it, but for the pleasure afforded by the act of telling and repeating. The juxtaposition of prolepses with speculation suggests that these novelistic repetitions are about the relation between knowing, telling, and repeating which embody a tension around the story itself as a story. Like Lol, narrators and readers replay the pattern to savour the desire and angst of the middle, the point before the end, not because such points exist in suspense, but because they are already too well known.

This narrative drive also characterizes the actions of the novels' protagonists. Lise, who seems to know the story, sets out to enact it. Sorting around with a level of uncertainty about details (This dress or that dress? This man or that man?) Lise is anxious that the events of her life comply with a story she already knows. Her 'vacation' is a repetition during which she writes the story with her life. This would seem to be the reverse of what is normally thought of as the relation between life as narrative (narrative follows life), bringing to the fore how much lives already do follow prescribed stories. Lol's repetitions, seen by the narrator as repetitions of her traumatic abandonment, might also be seen as the fine art of savouring each moment of the story, of making the story relive with a new cast of characters. In both cases, the drive to narrate is a particular way of taking control, of each protagonist putting herself in the position of narrator – in the driver's seat – controlling her own narrative.

That both protagonists are women suggests a relation in these novels between coming to control narratives/lives and the drive to narrate. While Freud's drives are not gendered and while this narrative drive need not necessarily be female, both novels enact the results of a shift from the woman as object of the narrative (as illustrated in *Lol V. Stein*) to the subject who operates it. Both novels play out a tussle between the narrator and the protagonist over control of the story. In *The Driver's Seat* Lise struggles to comply with the narrative as a way to take over her life even though her story enacts the violent relation between death and desire. In *Lol V. Stein* Lol controls her narrative despite Jack Hold's attempts to understand (and perhaps control her) through his narrative about her. In both cases narrating becomes a way to defeat objectification while playing the upper hand (or trying to) in a gender conflict.

By the end of Muriel Spark's *The Driver's Seat* and Marguerite Duras's *The Ravishing of Lol V. Stein* readers will have traversed their histories of inevitable destinies; readers and characters will have returned to a rest which will have always seemed to have been the goal of the narratives' trajectories. Focused on solitary and enigmatic female protagonists, the narratives reproduce the story of each woman's life (and vice versa) as if the story were already known. The novels' snug connection between the destinies of their central protagonists and the dynamic of their narratives seems curiously at odds with the stories' feeling of distance, a theatricalization that erodes intimacy in the telling and seduces not only through the mastery that might be appended to intimate foreknowledge, but also through the objectification, limited point of view, and proleptic hints that force the narratives to spiral through time and around and through perspectives at varying distances from the plotted action. The clash between intimate brooding destiny and coiled distanciation in both novels sparks ruminations on the nature of narrative as well as drawing attention to a drive which is neither Freud's 'death drive' nor the 'pleasure principle,' but a specifically narrative drive dependent upon knowledge of the story. This narrative drive, comprised of the dynamic interrelation between epistemology and sexuality, characterizes the seductive power of Lise and Lol as they transform activity into passivity and nothingness into desire.

Postscript

'Marguerite Duras s'avère savoir sans moi ce que j'enseigne'

In his 'Hommage fait à Marguerite Duras du ravissment de Lol V. Stein' Jacques Lacan credits Duras with already knowing what he teaches without him.[8] In other words, somehow Duras is already there. Both Duras and Spark play out the temporal paradoxes of being there before being there, of being already where one will soon be. The particular seductiveness of Duras's prose and insights situate her as a writer who indeed knows; her texts, then, become constant performances of this knowing where the narration is not only a repetition, but also pleasurable in itself. The drive to read Duras's work is another instance of a narrative drive where we read for the middle, for the pleasure of the telling rather than for the mastery of the end.

Duras's reputation as a 'knower' is far more widespread than Muriel Spark's reputation as a writer. Part of this is no doubt cultural; Duras wrote works of serious mien within a tradition that venerates authors, while Spark's superficially more whimsical offerings landed in English-speaking populations less interested in the idiosyncratic experiments of an expatriate Scot. Duras's work stimulates criticism that takes her textuality seriously and that doesn't rely on biographical evidence to explain either method or meaning. Spark's critics often resort to biography, using Spark's varied and mobile life to explain her shifts in style and theme. As an example of what is seen as Spark's 'literary-theological imagination,' *The Driver's Seat* is a 'tragic conflict between free will and determinism'.[9]

Duras's magical insight has also made her an author whose writings about gender are seen as complex and sophisticated. Part of this comes from Duras's own willingness to discuss issues of writing, genre, and gender openly in such conversations as *Les Parleuses* (with Xavière Gauthier) and *Les yeux verts*; part comes from the fact that Duras's novels, plays, and films fairly consistently focus on female protagonists. Spark, on the other hand, linked as she is with lyric poetry and religious conversion, has not, with the exception of *The Prime of Miss Jean Brodie*, captured the imagination of feminist literary critics. This is, I suspect, as much due to her novels' intriguing mixtures of realism, allegory, absurdism, and theatricality as to her 'literary-theological imagination' which seems superficially to subordinate gender issues to more abstract questions about responsibility, meaning, destiny, and morality. Where Duras is enigmatic and seductive, Spark is both harsh and playful. 'Crystalline,' Richard Todd calls her work, while Spark herself claims that 'it is a pack of lies.'[10] Both Duras's and Spark's novels, however, exhibit a consciousness of the act of telling as an act bound up with repetition, distance, false mastery and the ultimate uselessness of knowing the end.

Notes

1. This and other texts by Marguerite Duras will be cited from the following editions: *The Ravishing of Lol V. Stein*, trans. Richard Searer (New York: Pantheon Books, 1966); *Les Yeux verts* (Paris: Cahiers du Cinéma, 1987); with Xlavière Gauthier, *Les Parleuses* (Paris: Les Editions de Minuit, 1974).
2. Gérard Genette discusses prolepsis at length in *Narrative Discourse: An Essay in Method*, trans. Jane Lewin (Ithaca, NY: Cornell University Press, 1980) noting that prolepsis or 'anticipation,' 'is clearly much less frequent than the inverse figure,' an observation that he links to the predominance in 19th century literature of narrators 'who must appear more or less to discover the story at the same time' as they tell it (p. 67).
3. Laurie Edson in '"Knowing Lol" in Duras, Epistemology and Gendered Mediation', *SubStance* 68, 1992, pp. 17–31, argues that *Lol V. Stein* exposes a 'gendered mediation' where Jack's epistemophilia is a large part of the text.
4. The concept of 'Oedipus with a vengeance' comes from *Alice Doesn't: Feminism, Semiotics, Cinema* (Bloomington: Indiana University Press, 1984) p. 157.
5. McCallum's close readings of Freud's work in *Object Lessons: How To Do Things With Fetishism* (New York: Sony Press, 1998) persuasively suggest that the fetish is less a figure of disavowal and more a way of negotiating differences. It is thus an important tool for managing ambivalence.
6. See Peter Brooks, 'Freud's Masterplot', in Literature and Psychoanalysis: the Question of Reading Otherwise, ed. Shosana Felman (Baltimore: Johns Hopkins University Press, 1982, pp. 280–300) and Sigmund Freud, 'Beyond

the Pleasure Principle', trans. and ed. James Strachey (New York: Norton, 1961).

7. In 'Three Essays on the Theory of Sexuality', *Standard Edition* 7 (1905) pp. 125–246, Freud locates perversity in the middle between beginning and the 'proper' end of heterosexual intercourse.

8. In 'The Forgetfulness of Memory: Jacques Lacan, Marguerite Duras, and the Text,' *Contemporary Literature* XXIX, no. 3 (1988), pp. 351–68, Mary Lydon traces the connections and affinities between Lacan and Duras, through Lacan's phrase, quoted above as the section title. Lacan's sentence comes from his 'Hommage fait à Marguerite Duras du ravissement de Lol V. Stein', *Marguerite Duras* (Paris: Editions Albatros, 1975), pp. 93–9.

9. Joseph Hynes, 'Muriel Spark and the Oxymoronic Vision', *Contemporary British Writers: Narrative Strategies* (New York: St. Martin's, 1993) p. 164.

10. Quoted in Faith Pullin, 'Autonomy and Fabulation in the Fiction of Muriel Spark,' *Muriel Spark: An Odd Capacity for Vision*, ed. Alan Bold (London: Vision, 1984: Richard Todd, 'The Crystalline Novels of Muriel Spark', *Essays on the Contemporary British Novel*, ed. Hedwig Bock and Albert Wertheim (Munich: Max Hueber Verlag, 1986), pp. 175–92, p. 71.

3

The Suggestive Spectacle: Queer Passions in Brontë's *Villette* and *The Prime of Miss Jean Brodie*

Patricia Duncker

The spectacle was somehow suggestive.

Villette

The spectacle that Lucy Snowe, the schoolmistress in *Villette* (1853), Charlotte Brontë's haunted novel of thwarted sexual desire, is describing as suggestive is the moment in the text where Lucy , dressed as a man from the waist up, but as a woman from the waist down, takes a part in the school play (Chapter xiv, 'The Fete').[1] She sets out to win the flirtatious Ginevra Fanshawe away from the male lead role on stage and away from the man in the audience with whom Lucy is infatuated, but who is in love with Ginevra. This suggestive combination of transvestism, sexual substitution and genderbending performance is echoed in Spark' s novel, *The Prime of Miss Jean Brodie* (1961). The girls of her set become objects of sexual exchange for the ambitious, manipulative Brodie. She chooses the girl who should fill her place with the art master Teddy Lloyd, but her sexual game collapses when the girl she has not chosen betrays her. Spark, like Brontë, is interested in the ambiguous sexual electricity of single-sex classrooms.

Spark has compiled a volume of the Brontës' letters, which is still in print.[2] She first encountered Charlotte Brontë when she was under the spell of 'Miss Kay', the source of Miss Jean Brodie. 'It was when I was in Miss Kay's class that I read *Jane Eyre*, and Mrs Gaskell's *Life of Charlotte Brontë*' (CV, p. 64). In *The Prime of Miss Jean Brodie* Spark picks up the central themes of *Villette*: women's communities, spinsters, spying and female sexuality. The subject of *Villette* and of *The Prime of Miss Jean Brodie* is repression and excess, set within the claustrophobic and sexually charged environment of an all-girls' school. Neither writer is sentimental about women's solidarity or sisterhood. If anything the emphasis suggests women, beware women. The lesbian text in Brontë's novel is more subtle, but no less present than the lesbian theme in *The Prime of Miss Jean Brodie*.

Schoolgirl stories set in women-only institutions lend themselves to lesbian ambiguities and to the extension of conventional gender roles for girls. Enid Blyton's Malory Towers series of novels[3] are filled with girls whose names do not immediately signal femininity: the heroine Darrell, and even the more contentiously named Bill, short for Wilhelmina. In women-only narratives the usual men's roles of explorer, adventurer, rescuer, are shared out among the girls. Women are permitted to have adventures and ask nasty questions. They are also permitted to know things. The Brodie set in Spark's novel are 'vastly informed on a lot of subjects irrelevant to the authorised curriculum' (P, p. 5), and amongst these figure 'the love lives of Charlotte Brontë and of Miss Brodie herself' (ibid). The authors of *Villette* and of *The Prime of Miss Jean Brodie* were both intrigued by sexual knowledge of an unauthorized nature. Lucy Snowe and Miss Jean Brodie are arrogant, opinionated and passionately obsessed with power. They are both schoolteachers and they are both spinsters. They have the limited authority permitted to women as teachers and because neither of them is married or lives in her father's house they are both outside male control. Both are frequently referred to as 'Miss', underlining their unmarried state: Miss Lucy Snowe and Miss Jean Brodie. Both women are travellers, adventurers. They are women on the loose, free and independent women. And therefore dangerous.

The widow who endows the Marcia Blaine School for Girls favoured Garibaldi, the champion of liberty. Miss Brodie prefers Mussolini. She wishes to exert power over her pupils rather than empower them. Miss Brodie and Lucy Snowe are both women who take risks. As Miss Brodie persuasively argues '. . . But Safety does not come first' (P, p. 10). For the Brodie set, their years with Miss Brodie are the years of living dangerously. Lucy Snowe never lives in any other way. She leaves home, travels across the Channel, wanders the city streets at night, insists on her own opinions, looks closely and critically at pictures of naked ladies, desires men, two different men, all without scruples or hesitation. In Victorian terms she is exceedingly unwomanly and a bad example.

Spark's Miss Brodie was based on the teacher into whose hands she fell at the age of eleven during the last two years at junior school in 1929 and 1930: Miss Christina Kay. Spark herself, in her autobiography, *Curriculum Vitae*, describes Kay as 'that character in search of an author' (CV, p. 56). Outside the gossip pages of literary biography it is now peculiarly unfashionable to identify literary characters in fiction with their sources in the writer's lives. This strikes me as odd. Spark at once puts her finger on the ambiguity of this relationship between fiction and its sources. Who is the fiction and who is the character? Miss Jean Brodie is larger than life. Her force and imagination explode beyond the boundary of her classroom, Marcia Blaine's School for Girls and even her pupil's lives. Christina Kay was already a character, waiting to be written. Writers never use random elements in their lives as sources. They pick on something – or someone – who is already becoming fiction.

Teaching has a great deal in common with theatre, as do all professions which require public performances: television journalists, politicians, high-court judges. Spark makes the link between teaching and one-woman performances: 'I had always enjoyed watching teachers. We had a large class of about forty girls. A full classroom that size, with a sole performer on stage before an audience sitting in rows and listening is essentially theatre' (CV, p. 57). Miss Kay was already performing a role. To perform Miss Jean Brodie all she has to do is take on an adopted character. It is Spark who unleashes Miss Brodie. As she says, 'children are quick to perceive possibilities, potentialities in a remark, perhaps in some remote context; in a glance, a smile. No. Miss Kay was not literally Miss Brodie, but I think Miss Kay had it in her, unrealized, to be the character I invented' (CV, p. 57). It is not only children but writers who are quick to seize upon possibilities and potentialities. Making fiction is a process of building on the suggestively possible. Miss Kay has the potential to become Miss Brodie. She is already partly fiction. Her making is a process of enlargement. She grows into Miss Brodie. Only those readers of Spark's novel who already knew Miss Kay personally recognized her 'with joy and great nostalgia, in the shape of Miss Jean Brodie in her prime' (CV, p. 57). The relationship of a successful fictional character to her source in flesh and blood is parasitic. If the fiction thrives and grows strong the host is consumed and ceases to exist. Spark knew this and in *Curriculum Vitae* (1992), she devotes at least a dozen pages to Miss Kay, pointing out her teacher's influence on her own life, as if by way of apologia for her own power over her teacher. 'Miss Kay predicted my future as a writer in the most emphatic terms. I felt I had hardly much choice in the matter' (CV, p. 66). Miss Kay encouraged her own re-creator. The character who has achieved an after-life is not Miss Kay, but Miss Jean Brodie.

A teacher is always searching for the pupil who will surpass her, the pupil whose intelligence will subsume and challenge hers, the pupil who will grow beyond her. The good teacher should be looking for the intellect that will bring about the dissolution of her own power and influence. This is, of course, a tall order. M. Paul Emmanuel believes he has seen that mind in Lucy Snowe and consequently, he is furious. Miss Jean Brodie doesn't even atttempt to do it. She never lets her pupils go. And takes the consequences.The only way that Sandy can escape her is by destroying her.

Classrooms are incipient sites of revolution, the stage where power struggles are the name of the daily game. Power is a volatile element. It can pass from teacher to pupil in an instant. The potential dramatic situation in the classroom is that of the dictator, confronting the mob. Lucy Snowe's trial by fire comes when she is asked to give a dictation to the second class. 'They always throw over timid teachers '(*Villette*, p. 76) , as Madame Beck points out. The girls of Labassecour are in a state of perpetual rebellion, ready to rise up and persecute a teacher who is too weak to control them. Teaching is an exercise in authority, domination and command. Lucy Snowe triumphs by establishing her superior power and sharper wits. She jeers at one rebel's ignorance and locks another in the closet. This entire scene is of course enacted between women. But the conflict is given the status of men's conflicts. When Madame Beck challenges Lucy to take the class 'At that instant she did not wear a woman's aspect, but rather, a man's' (p. 76) Lucy takes up the gage, fights, wins. Teaching is still, largely a women's profession. Classrooms in girls' schools are the fields of conflict and battle which turn women into heroes.

And into spies. Madame Beck spies on her staff and her pupils as a matter of course. Miss Mackay never gives up pumping the Brodie set, hoping to be able to pin some colourful iniquity upon Miss Brodie. Brontë and Spark represent the mechanisms of power and rebellion inside closed systems. Both girls' schools operate with elaborate systems of surveillance and control. Information is attained by the most underhand methods. Lucy catches Madame Beck going through her private drawers. And, significantly, decides to say nothing. The schools are institutions regulated to work in the interests of those who run them. They are designed to keep order and control among young women. The watchwords are 'discipline' and 'punish'. Women are not represented in either novel as innocent, obedient and docile. The girls of Labassecour are sexual predators, knowing, callous, lazy, hardened, unscrupulous and dishonest. Brodie's girls know far too much and have all the arrogance of the chosen 'crème de la crème'. They are made in their teacher's image.

In Brontë's *Villette* her heroine follows the author's own biographical trajectory: the *pensionnat* in Brussels/Villette to the encounter with her teacher, Monsieur Paul/Constantin Héger. The final outcome of this voyage of sexual discovery was no different either in life or in fiction. Love ends in loss, absence, grief. There was only one critical difference. M. Paul sought and returned Lucy Snowe's love, unambiguously, in a way that Constantin Héger never answered Charlotte Brontë's. Silence was his stern reply to her passionate letters. And her fictional hero, while in many ways otherwise engaged, is not married.

Both novels are about sex and the single girl. The triangle patterning is the same. Lucy Snowe has two men to choose between: Dr John, a.k.a. Graham Bretton and M. Paul. Miss Brodie is courted by Gordon Lowther and Teddy Lloyd. Two other elements are crucial to the themes and patterning of both books: the paintings, which form a crucial part of the iconography of both texts, and play a critical role in the discussion and delineation of female sexuality. The second figure in the common textual carpet is the Nun.

Sandy Stranger, Miss Brodie's unrecognized antagonist, eventually becomes Sister Helena of the Transfiguration, living out her days behind the bars of another women's community. Her famous psychology book is entitled *The Transfiguration of the Commonplace*, a title which reflects exactly what Miss Brodie did for her set. She made the ordinary extraordinary and turned dailiness into fairy tales. Sandy never escapes Miss Brodie, neither her memory nor her influence. She continues to live at second hand. The Nun in *Villette* has a Gothic pedigree which goes back to Ann Radcliffe's novels of the 1790s.[4] The Nun has a remarkable consistency of cultural meaning in fiction which uses the machinery of the Gothic. The Nun is both eroticized and taboo. She signifies death, repression, madness and either warped excessive desire or the fatal denial of sexual knowledge. Lucy's Nun serves two purposes. She is a warning against the repression of desire. She is also Ginevra's cross-dressed lover, stalking round the school, male sexual desire achieving its own ends by any means available. Neither nun in either novel is quite what she seems.

Sister Helena, a.k.a. Sandy Stranger, has always been a writer, an inventor of fictions. Spark interweaves Sandy's fantastic imaginative texts – *The Mountain Eyrie* by Sandy Stranger and Jenny Gray – which contains all their secret sexual speculation on the love life of Miss Jean Brodie. Sandy's own bisexual fantasies include Mr Rochester, John

Buchan's heroes, episodes from *Kidnapped* and an upmarket police-woman whom she christens Anne Gray. The imagined narratives are not textually distinguished from Spark's main narrative. What is the effect of this? Both narratives become unstable and insecure. Neither narrative, one dominated by Miss Jean Brodie's meanings and the other by Sandy's revisions, has complete authority. Both narratives are therefore unreliable. Miss Jean Brodie's sexual clues to forbidden knowledge are planted in the texts she reads or recites to the girls of her set. Tennyson's *The Lady of Shalott* tells the tale of the prisoner of art, condemned to watch the world through the mirror and never to seize experience directly. The Lady's moment of sexual daring is also the moment of her downfall. Charlotte Brontë's love life, also a subject of Miss Brodie's lessons, can only have been her illicit passion for a married man, her master and her teacher, Constantin Héger. Miss Brodie has been seen kissing another married teacher, Mr Teddy Lloyd. Miss Brodie's narratives generate other narratives in Sandy's imagination, each one more explicit and more daring than any offered by Miss Brodie. Sandy therefore perpetually displaces Miss Jean Brodie's version with her own. Her rebellion and betrayal is silent, but constant throughout the novel until the moment when she finally betrays Miss Brodie to Miss Mackay.

Lucy Snowe and Sandy Stranger are observers, dissenters and rebels. Both of them have names that signify their outsider status. Brontë hesitated between the names Frost and Snowe for Lucy insisting to her publishers that she must have a 'cold name'. Lucy was to be the chilly observer of life, the woman who gives nothing away. Brontë's Lucy Snowe is a classic unreliable narrator, not because she is obtuse, but because she is secretive and has no confidence in the reader. Lucy's high-handedness in witholding information creates a radical insecurity in the reader. What else does she know, but is not telling? There are two other women within the structure of Brontë's fiction whose fates offer alternative narratives. Paulina de Bassompierre and Ginevra Fanshawe.

Paulina is the tiny, doll-like happy-ending heroine, the Victorian woman whose sole desire is to service men. She transfers her affection from father to lover to husband without ever interrogating her need to adore rather than criticize. This is the selfless devotion that is always rewarded with happiness in fairy tales, as it is in *Villette*. It is however, ironized. Lucy Snowe is destined for a more interesting fate and higher things. The other woman, Ginevra Fanshawe, is a flirt, fickle, light and egotistical. 'Ginevra lived her full life in a ballroom, elsewhere she drooped, dispirited' (*Villette*, p. 143). But Ginevra has the intelligence to notice Lucy Snowe, to court her attention and approval and to realize that Lucy is not all she seems. 'Who are you, Miss Snowe ?' (p. 315). Lucy's answer is intriguing. She calls attention to her own role in her own story. 'I am a rising character' (p. 317). All Brontë's heroines , Jane Eyre, Caroline Helstone, Lucy Snowe, are ambitious, rising characters. They want money and power. They want to marry above themselves. Their uncompromising desire is for sexual satisfaction and financial independence. Lucy is never humble. She trusts her own judgement and keeps her own counsel, even from her readers, which is very disconcerting. We may well demand, alongside Ginevra Fanshawe, 'Who are you, Miss Snowe?'

The presentation of ambitious, powerful women in the work of women writers is always problematic. A fixed plot already exists. Nemesis follows hubris and often takes the form of sexual punishment. It would take an uncompromisingly daring writer to overturn this particular coercive structure. Often the women who get away with it are relegated to the sub-plot. Spark and Brontë both settle for ironic compromise. We know what happens to the heroines and it is a mixture of mastery and defeat. In both texts the writers play narrative games with present and past tenses so that the future fates of the characters are present before us throughout the main action. This is a clever device, because it enables the writer to overstep the limits, to go futher in her presentation of both her heroine, the opposition and her own speculations. Brodie gets her come-uppance; we always know she will. Part of the interest of the fiction is finding out why Sandy betrays her. But Miss Brodie retains her power. None of Brodie's girls escape her influence, and their subsequent fates can all be traced back to her dominance in their early lives. Brontë never allows Lucy Snowe to experience heterosexual union, but the young women who seek her, Paulina and Ginevra, pass on into what is presented as the less charged and less interesting state: marriage. Lucy is still there at the end of the book, white-haired, independent, alone, passing judgement on other people.

Lucy waits three years for the return of Monsieur Paul. She says 'Reader, they were the three happiest years of my life' (pp. 504–5). They are the years of sexual anticipation, but also years of economic independence and the freedom to make her own decisions.

Lucy Snowe was a radically unconventional heroine for a Victorian novel. Brontë's contemporaries were perfectly aware of the writer's deliberate gender transgressions and criticized her for her boldness. Thackeray wrote in a letter to Mrs Carmichael Smyth (28 March 1853),

'I don't make my *good* women ready to fall in love with two men at once', and continued to Mrs Procter (4 April 1853), 'That's a plaguey book that *Villette* ... How clever it is ! And how I don't like the heroine.'[5] Lucy Snowe is clearly not a good woman. Anne Mozley in the *Christian Remembrancer* went further still. She was writing anonymously, but as a man:

> We want a woman at our hearth; and [Currer Bell's] impersonations are without the feminine element, infringers of all modest restraints, despisers of bashful fears, self-reliant, contemptuous of prescriptive decorum; their own unaided reason, their individual opinion of right and wrong, discreet or imprudent, sole guides of conduct and rules of manners – the whole hedge of immemorial scruple and habit broken down and trampled upon.[6]

This all sounds uncannily like Miss Mackay's views on Miss Jean Brodie. Both *Villette* and *The Prime of Miss Jean Brodie* are texts about women breaking the rules, knowingly, deliberately and without fear. Remember that 'Safety does not come first' (P, p. 10). Anne Mozley does not consider her own impersonation as a male reviewer, but accuses Currer Bell of presenting 'impersonations' of women. The fight for femininity, what it is, what it should consist of, and how it should be represented, is thus being carried on between two women in literary drag. This is what gives the debate authority in the nineteenth century and, for us, over a century later, a peculiarly piquant humour.

The key scene in *Villette*, the school play, to which I have referred as 'the suggestive spectacle', foreshadows the events of the book. Ginevra, the heroine of the piece, acts nothing but herself when she flirts with Lucy. She does just that all the way through the novel. Ginevra will reject Dr John and marry the fop, De Hamal, played by Lucy, cross-dressed as a man in the farce. Neither Ginevra nor Lucy choose Dr John, the conventional hero. Lucy falls in love with the despotic Monsieur Paul and Ginevra elopes with the cross-dressed visiting Nun. De Hamal is extravagantly feminine in appearance. 'His lineaments were small, and so were his hands and feet; and he was pretty and smooth, and as trim as a doll; so nicely dressed, so nicely curled ... he was charming indeed' (*Villette*, p. 148). Women, it seems, fancy men who resemble women and who dress up as women. In the disruption of gender roles with which the novel plays, Lucy lays claim to a man's intellect and a man's authority, but keeps her woman's sex. In the play she substitutes herself for de Hamal, and wins the girl.

Spark takes up the theme of sexual substitution in *The Prime of Miss Jean Brodie* and plays with its implications. The Brodie set become substitutes for their teacher in the paintings of Teddy Lloyd. He cannot paint her. So he paints them. All the images of the girls look like Miss Brodie. What the text does not make clear is whether this is simply a function of Teddy Lloyd's obsession with the teacher or whether it is the girls themselves who have begun to take on the likeness of Miss Brodie.

The scene in the gallery in Brontë's *Villette* (Chapter xix 'The Cleopatra') involves Lucy's judgement of womanhood and femininity. She rejects the naked Cleopatra, the conventional pornographic object of male desire, but she also rejects 'La Vie d'une Femme', the roles of maiden, wife, mother widow represented in the genre pictures. The role of spinster is not represented. The paintings present conventional versions of women. Lucy chooses none of them. For the Brodie set there is no other convincing, dynamic, desirable image of what a woman is other than their vivid mistress – therefore all Teddy Lloyd's images of the girls look like Miss Jean Brodie.

In all her imagined narratives Sandy Stranger perpetually displaces Miss Jean Brodie as the heroine and takes her place. Finally she displaces Miss Jean Brodie's chosen substitute as a lover for Teddy Lloyd and becomes the art master's mistress. The sexual substitution works both ways of course. It is unthinkable for Miss Jean Brodie to sleep with the art master, so she sends her girls. It is also unthinkable that she should sleep with her girls. So she hands them over to the art master. Then asks them to tell her all about it in detail. But somewhere or other she does think the unthinkable. 'Sandy thought, too, the woman is an unconscious Lesbian' (p. 120). Sandy thought so, and Sandy is one of Miss Jean Brodie's creations. Sandy Stranger is a familiar figure in Spark's fictions. She is the calculating observer. She wears the mask of Lucy Snowe, the 'looker-on at life' (*Villette*, p. 142). Lucy and Sandy both have the Brodie virtues, instinct and insight. Both women finally withdraw from the world. Sandy is a far less sympathetic figure than Lucy because she is always framed by Spark's ironic third person narrative. And because, in the economy of Spark's method , she is characterized as the spy. Sandy, with her tiny piggy eyes, is the woman who refuses to comply with what she recognizes as Brodie's unconscious lesbianism. What she refuses to recognize is her own lesbianism. She wanted to be chosen by Miss Jean Brodie as her sexual substitute, and therefore, by proxy, as her lover. So she steals the place that is not chosen for her and betrays Miss Brodie.

The discourse which signals the heroine's intellectual rebellion and absolute difference in *Villette* is her Protestantism; the violent anti-Catholic propaganda expressed in the novel equates Rome with a philosophy of discipline and control that is little short of Fascist. Englishness is associated with Protestantism. Yet Lucy is saved from terminal hysteria by telling all in the Catholic confessional. Miss Brodie's dedication to Fascism is at the heart of her educational philosophy, where she plays the role of Führerin. Spark finally links Catholicism and Fascism when she comments on Sandy's decision to become a Catholic nun. 'By now she had entered the Catholic Church, in whose ranks she had found quite a number of Fascists much less agreeable than Miss Brodie' (p. 125). The sharpness of this comment cuts both ways. Miss Brodie is an elitist to her fingertips, a woman who sees Hitler as a 'prophet-figure like Thomas Carlyle, and more reliable than Mussolini (p. 97). But Sandy is mean, egotistical, manipulative, with none of the colour and panache of Miss Jean Brodie in her prime. No one comes out of this conflict with the reader's sympathy for their fates still intact. And so indeed the moral seems to be: women beware women.

Passions between women, when they are unacknowledged and yet acted out, through substitution and impersonation, become twisted, dangerous things. Like Lucy Snowe, Jean Brodie is a gender transgressor, in love with power, sexual and otherwise. Spark's ironic register and the careful distance she keeps between her characters and her readers ensures that we never care too deeply about any of her characters. They are fictions. Persuasive, charismatic, vivid, but still fictions. She is a writer who gives everyone their just desserts. The narrative voices of both texts reflect the spirit of their respective heroines, Miss Lucy Snowe and Miss Jean Brodie: acid, dogmatic, eccentric, independent. The versions of womanhood on offer deliberately transgress the limits of convention. Men have key sexual roles to play, but these are essentially walk-on and lie-back parts. They are all shamelessly manipulated. The main tension, conflict, the suggestive spectale itself, is acted out between the women.

Notes

1. *Villette* (Hammondsworth: Penguin, 1994). All references are to this edition.
2. Muriel Spark, *The Essence of the Brontës: A Compilation with Essays* (London : Peter Owen, 1952) (new edition, 1993). The first essay in the book is entitled 'The Brontës as Teachers'. Spark suggests that the pupils and colleagues of Charlotte Brontë deserved some sympathy for their fate in having to work with a woman consumed by frustration and rage.

3. Enid Blyton produced 3 major series of school stories: *The Naughtiest Girl in the School* series, 1940, 1942, 1945, 6 books set at St Clare's between 1941–1945, and the famous *Malory Towers* series 1946–1951. The gorgeous Darrell Rivers is named after Blyton's second husband Kenneth Darrell Waters. The supporting tomboy heroines never stop being tomboys. Blyton's books were written especially for girls. See Sheila Ray, *The Blyton Phenomenon: The Controversy Surrounding the World's Most Successful Children's Writer* (London: André Deutsch, 1982). See also Mary Cadogan and Patricia Craig, *'You're a Brick, Angela!' The Girls' Story 1839–1985* (2nd edition) (London: Victor Gollancz, 1986).

4. Ann Radcliffe's *The Mysteries of Udolpho* (1794) is the novel which Henry Tilney praises in Chapter 14 of Jane Austen's *Northanger Abbey* (1818), 'The Mysteries of Udolpho*, when I had once begun it, I could not lay down again;-I remember finishing it in two days – my hair standing on end the whole time.' The deranged Sister Agnes, the Nun in *Udolpho*, is in fact the Lady Laurentini – nuns are never what they seem – and she serves as a warning to the heroine Emily, just as the Nun in *Villette* is a warning to Lucy Snowe. Sister Agnes suggests that unchecked irrational passion leads to madness: 'Sister! Beware of the first indulgence of the passions ... their force if not checked then is uncontrollable – they lead us we know not whither.'

5. Cited in Lyndall Gordon, *Charlotte Brontë: A Passionate Life* (London: Vintage, 1994), p. 283.

6. Ibid., p. 285.

4
In Bed with Muriel Spark: Mourning, Metonymy and Autobiography

Martin McQuillan

> In a minimal autobiographical trait can be gathered the greatest potentiality of historical, theoretical, linguistic, philosophical culture – that's really what interests me.
>
> Derrida

It is a matter of biographical fact – as far as this can be verified – to relate that one night during the summer of 1944, while unable to return to her lodgings in the countryside due to the cancellation of a train, as a result of an air raid, Muriel Spark spent the night in the house of the poet Louis MacNeice. She worked outside London for the secret services producing propaganda broadcasts for transmission to Germany. Spark had been offered a night's accommodation by a fellow traveller, who was the nanny to MacNeice's children, while the owners of the house were away for the weekend. At the time of the invitation to this house Spark was unaware of either the name or profession of the house owner. It was only during her stay there that she realized (from letters, book inscriptions, photographs) who owned the house. In subsequent writing Spark says that this singular experience in the house of Louis MacNeice encouraged her to start her career as a professional writer. She has treated this experience in writing on four separate occasions.[1]

The first instance was in a short story, 'The House of the Famous Poet', written in 1952 but not published until 1959 in *The New Yorker*. In this story a female narrator who cannot return to her lodgings in the countryside due to troop movements and air raids, takes up the invitation of a night's accommodation with one of her two travelling companions (a mother's help in a house in St. John's Wood, which is empty for the weekend). The other traveller is an itinerant soldier. The narrator subsequently discovers that this is the house of an un-named famous poet and she becomes fascinated by the space he occupies as a writer and by the serendipity of her being there. In the morning when she leaves the house, the soldier she met on the train appears on the door-step of the house and attempts to sell her 'an abstract funeral', contained in an army kit-bag, in exchange for his train fare. The story then takes off in the direction of magical-realism with the soldier constantly reappearing to discuss the 'abstract funeral' with the narrator. Ultimately, the narrator decides against keeping her purchase in favour of having her own personalized funeral and opens the kit-bag to release a large cloud of purple gas from the window of her homeward bound train. The soldier then disappears for good. Later the narrator hears that the poet's house was destroyed in an air raid, killing both the poet and the nanny.

Spark returned to this experience in 1960 (three years before the death of Louis MacNeice) when she presented a radio broadcast for the BBC entitled 'The Poet's House', a commissioned piece in which she was asked to explain how she became a novelist. In this broadcast (which did not appear in print until it was published in *The Critic* in Chicago in 1961 and in *Encounter* magazine, London, in May 1968) she outlines a similar set of events, excluding the magical soldier, with the conclusion that this experience encouraged her to start writing professionally. A year prior to this publication in *Encounter* the short story had appeared in the first volume of Spark's *Collected Short Stories*.[2] Louis MacNeice was not named in the radio broadcast, but in the subsequent publication of the transcript in *Encounter* his name appeared in the introductory blurb. In 1985 Spark placed the article 'A Footnote to a Poet's House' in the design magazine *Architectural Digest*. For the first time in any of these writings on this event, Louis MacNeice is openly discussed and quoted. In 1992 Spark once again returned to this incident in her autobiography *Curriculum Vitae*. While the article in *Architectural Digest* is a reflection on the events it describes, and the experience of writing the other two narratives, the extract in the autobiography is a 'straight' factual account of the event. Using these four pieces of writing by Spark on the same event I hope to examine a particular case of a gendered subject coming to writing.

Spark's four fragments are reassuringly similar in their self-contained accuracy of material documentation. Each of the accounts follows an identical path: the 'I' of the narrative alights from her taxi with her travelling companion at a house in St. John's Wood, she comments upon the state of the garden, then enters the house and describes

MacNeice's work table and metallic bed. Both the short story and the radio talk share near identical lines:

> I remember there was a steel Morrison shelter in one corner and some photographs on the mantelpiece, one of a schoolboy wearing glasses.
>
> (PH, p. 49)

and again:

> There was a steel-canopied bed, known as a Morrison shelter, in one corner and some photographs on the mantelpiece, one of a schoolboy wearing glasses.
>
> (CS, p. 211)

There is little question, without alternative documentary evidence, of contradicting Spark's physical description of the house. However, the interest in Spark's quadruple negotiation of this primal scene of writing is not in the empirical composition of the house, or necessarily in the chronological order of the event. It is in the relationship this event has to the author at the time of composition. In this way, the work of mourning undertaken in each fragment – and why there should be so many of them is one of the questions under scrutiny here – is constitutive, in a different way from each of its predecessors, of the subjectivity engaged in writing.

It is now difficult to read the short story in isolation from the other related fragments. However, reading 'The House of the Famous Poet' in an 'artificial vacuum' may help to begin to unravel what is going on in this narrative event. An event which offers the reader a complex knot of memory, biography and textuality. In the short story, the incident of the house is not connected with the narrative I's decision to write; rather, it is used as a station in which to locate a story which presents an allegory of the process of artistic creation. This 'allegory' allows Spark to rest her fictional narrative in a biographical ontology and to play within, and move beyond, the bounds of the intimately experienced, to expand the scope of the remembered into that of the imaginary. The domestic realism of the poet's steel-canopied bed in the first half of the story gives way to the fantastical account of the magically re-appearing soldier's abstract funeral. The story turns biography into art through the textual production of a literary fiction. In this respect it is an example of what Gaston Bachelard has described when he says, 'imagination augments the values of reality.'[3] The unnamed narrator of this short story is not the named individual Muriel Spark but rather a prosopopoeic construction (both a mask and a voice beyond the grave) of the 'semi', or, 'quasi' self. As I shall attempt to demonstrate, the named person Muriel Spark cannot be identified with any of the narrating voices in any of the fragments.

By necessity there must always be a gap between the narrating voice and the writing subject and this renders the idea of autobiography as a transparent account of the self strictly impossible. Furthermore, 'The House of the Famous Poet' represents a standard Sparkian concern, turning writing and genre inside out to exhibit the structures, conventions, and ideologies at stake within texts as part of the plot of those texts. Think of the type-writer voices which afflict Caroline Rose in *The Comforters* and which turn her thoughts and experiences into a novel, the very novel that is presented to the reader, or the theorization of autobiography and writing in *Loitering with Intent*, or the thematization of the referential illusion of drama in the play *The Doctors of Philosophy*. Examples of Spark's self-referentiality could be multiplied:

> 'And after the war,' I continued, 'When I am no longer a civil servant, I hope in a few deftly turned phrases, to write of my experiences at the house of the famous poet.'
>
> (CS, p. 216)

However, the short story does not make the same confession as the radio talk. There is no causal link (except possibly a retrospectively inferred one, and not one we might have made without reference to the other three fragments) between the narrative 'I''s presence in the house and her career as a writer. That is unless one counts this later constitutive paradox of the allegory of the author-narrator-character writing from a fictional autobiographical source.

Spark's concern in the short story is to reflect upon the processes and function of writing itself. By engaging with the autobiographical double bind she allows her text to speak in the gap between the incongruous questions of the ethical unreliability of memory and the artistic necessity of imagination:

> The blue cracked bathroom, the bed on the floor, the caked ink bottle, the neglected garden, the neat rows of books – I try to gather them together in my mind whenever I am enraged by the thought that Elise and the poet were killed outright. The angels of the

> Resurrection will invoke the dead man and the dead woman, but who will care to restore the fallen house of the famous poet if not myself? Who else will tell its story?
>
> (CS, p. 218)

On the one hand, the story can be read as a political statement about the state-sponsored terrorism of war and the ideological uses of language employed to 'sell' the idea of a war to an electorate: fine in *abstract*ion, quite different when materially encountered. The unique and unrepeatable deaths of the irreplaceable individual persons of Elise and the poet should be contrasted to the culturally received images of sacrifice and glory during wartime. This story then is not only a 'mourning' for the 'autos' of the author-narrator (the what was but is no more and is hence interiorized) but also an act of mourning for those who died during the war.

Read in this way the story demonstrates the exemplary economy of iterability identified by Jacques Derrida when he says of an autobiographical trace in a fiction by Joyce:

> This economy of exemplary iterability is of itself formalizing. It also formalizes or condenses history. A text by Joyce is simultaneously the condensation of a scarcely delimitable history. But this condensation of history, of language, of the encyclopedia, remains here indissociable from an *absolutely* singular event, an *absolutely* singular signature, and therefore also of a date, of a language, of an autobiographical inscription. In a minimal autobiographical trait can be gathered the greatest potentiality of historical, theoretical, linguistic, philosophical culture – that's really what interests me.[4]

While the autobiographical trace within a fictional narrative is what makes that narrative unique, it is also iterable. In other words, it is both inside of and outside of the delimited narrative text. At the time of the 'original' event Spark was working for British Intelligence in a 'black propaganda' unit broadcasting to Germany. This experience of creating 'fiction' from a 'true' or empirical source is perhaps a more likely root for Spark's primal scene of writing and training in her craft, than these alleged events in the house of Louis MacNeice. Thus, this primal scene of writing obeys the delayed logic of *Nachträglichkeit*, as a non-originary origin. Perhaps this is what Spark is trying to tell the alert reader. On the other hand, the above quotation from 'The House of the Famous Poet' may indicate the position this story holds within

Spark's personal understanding of the process of her own writing. As an analysis of the radio talk will show, the house is what captures Spark's febrile energy, the house is the star of the show.

On several occasions Spark has said, 'I think that the set-up of my writing is probably just a justification of the time I wasted doing something else. And it is an attempt to redeem the time.'[5] This, amongst other things, assuredly Proustian approach to memory and writing comes to the fore in the continued preoccupation with Louis MacNeice's House. Far from being through-the-key-hole-with-Muriel-Spark the role of the house in these fragments, and Spark's relationship to it, is that of a determining constituent of the narrative 'I''s subjectivity. Bachelard calls the image of the house, 'one of the greatest powers of integration for the thoughts, memories and dreams of mankind' (p. 6). He writes:

> There exists for each one of us an oneiric house, a house of dream-memory, that is lost in the shadow of a beyond of the real past ... In point of fact we are in the unity of image and memory, in the functional composite of imagination and memory.
>
> (p. 16)

Spark's narrative matrix seems to demonstrate this very point. Her short story mixes memory and imagination to lend her signature to a fictional biographical inscription. Similarly, the house which she describes (and which appears in each of her narratives) becomes a symbolically significant house which, 'is lost in the shadow of a beyond of the real past.' Whether Spark's empirical description of the house is accurate or not is immaterial because this is not what is at stake here. What is at issue is the way in which Louis MacNeice's house works, as a narrative event or event of narrative, as it appears iterably in each narrative formation. A gap exists between the house as a prosopopoeic figure to explain Spark's coming to writing and the experience which brings her to the house (secretarial training, colonialism, maternity, reading contemporary fiction and poetry, civil service). The poet's house takes on these values through the transference and translation of the narrative apparatus to occupy a pertinent position within Spark's creative imagination.

Certainly at this stage of her life, Spark's career was taking a deliberate and clear path – having escaped from an abusive marriage in Rhodesia to find employment as a single mother in wartime London. Louis MacNeice's house seems to symbolize this radical departure: it provides a material connection with the world of writing and text, it is a metonym for the metaphorical-metonymic structure of writing. That is not to suggest that the experience of spending the night in the house was as epiphanic as these texts would seem to imply. Rather, that the narrative reconstruction of these textually inscribed memories allows Spark to translate the construction of her subjectivity into the habitation of this image. This happens not necessarily because Spark believes these circumstances to be true. In the much later autobiography, she provides a good deal of evidence, from school prizes to juvenilia, to suggest that through education and socio-economic position Spark had been coming to writing for some time (she won national poetry prizes in Rhodesia). Rather, this comes about as a way of translating these experiences through narrative into a textual unit (the writer of which is aware of the dissonance between empirical event and narrative figuration). Furthermore, it is also a way of constructing a 'subjectivity' for her readership. I mean this in the sense of the construction of a prosopopoeic subjectivity (a mask of subjectivity) that Spark designs for her readers' reception.

It is not until Spark writes her first companion piece to this short story (the radio talk) that she indicates how important a place the house occupies in her imagination and in the history of her own writing:

> I don't want to exaggerate the importance in itself of this incident … but on me at that particular point in my life it had an intense imaginative effect. I had no wish to meet or see the poet … now it was the house itself which fascinated me.
>
> I went around touching everything … I think I must have felt that by some sympathetic magic I could draw from the poet's possessions some essence which would enable me to get down to my writing. Perhaps I ought to say here that I haven't been particularly influenced in my work by this poet. It was merely the will to write that I wanted to acquire.
>
> (PH, p. 49)

However, there are more ways than one in which we can be influenced. This is certainly a different narrative perspective Spark lends to the same *histoire*, to use Genette's term, of 'The House of the Famous Poet'. By this revisitation of the scene of writing the whole experience has taken on an entirely different relationship to its author, who endows it with a substantially different meaning. If it is correct to suggest that there is no singular memory, then this next article could be said to remember the house differently. This second text is the literal answer to a commissioned work which was asked to describe how she became a writer. It is again interesting to note the relation of narrative production on this event to the formalizing context of the economic circumstances which inscribe the subjectivity of the author.

It is also an attempt to theorize her own writing. She writes in introduction to the article:

> I've always been interested in what makes the adult writer start to write. Is it something compulsive within the person? Or is it, perhaps, some outward combination of circumstances? Because it's one thing to feel quite certain within oneself that one has the ability to write and to be full of ideas and visions, but it's quite another thing actually to get down to it.
>
> (PH, p. 48)

Spark is prepared to toy with the masquerades of subjectivity in order to produce four separate accounts of a single event. In so doing she redistributes the signifying effects of the history of her subjectivity over each of the texts. It is not so much a case of providing closure to an anxiety of self-inspection but rather each return to the house is part of the continual process of a developing subjectivity. On each occasion the house has a different relationship to that subjectivity and each past piece of writing is constitutive of the latest piece, because it is part of the baggage of subjectivity that Spark brings to the current piece of writing. On the one hand, each fragment is concerned with, and is a comment upon, the experience of writing the previous fragment(s). On the other hand, the fragments, with their various retellings of the same events, act as signposts for the author's continuing construction as a subject. This construction is both part of the individual writer's development and the presentation of a fiction for readerly reception. She writes:

> And so this Poet's House in which I found myself by chance became for me a symbol of what I was to attempt to make of my life.
>
> (PH, p. 50)

The ambiguity of 'I found myself' is obvious, the connotations of construction in 'make of my life' are under-stated.

Spark does not mention MacNeice by name in either the short story or the radio talk. In the introductory 'blurb' to the 1968 publication of the talk, she admits: 'I left some things out partly to save myself embarrassment' (PH, p. 48). This indicates the intrinsically incomplete nature of the necessarily selective process of narrativization. However, it also highlights the structure of transference within the practice of narrative production and within Spark's (auto)biographical writing. It might be suggested that one of the aporias of writing which these constant renarrativizations demonstrate, is the split between the writing Subject and the subject of writing. The narrative 'I' of the fragments and the author Muriel Spark can never be the same person. This is a consequence of the explicit division between author and fictional character in the short story but also of the temporo–spatial distance between the writing self and a narrativized representation of that self. Spark compounds this problem by offering four separate narrative versions of a self written from four quite different subject positions. Each fragment highlights the inescapable displacement between the 'she' that writes and the 'she' that is written about. When each fragment offers up this non-consubstantiality in time and space between the subjects of writing, they are enacting the narrative text's inability to achieve a totalization of its object of description. They also reaffirm the unsatisfactory reliance of momentary-writing upon memory as the means of access to knowledge of the subject (the exploration around which Spark places these four very deliberate documents).

Spark writes an explicitly self-referential short story which acts as an allegory for her own writing process. This is followed by a radio talk that chooses to reveal the autobiographical content upon which this story is based (which the reader would never have been able to surmise without Spark's confession/suggestion). This radio talk acts as a reflection upon both writing fiction with a biographical ontology and writing autobiography. Twenty-five years later in the most marginal and particular of places Spark chooses to return both to the singular event of the material experience of her personal history in 1944 and to the experience of writing her fragments about writing. Perhaps the importance to Spark of the materiality of the space of the house informs her decision to publish in *Architectural Digest*. The positioning of the 1985 article foregrounds the relevance of space to Spark's primal scene of writing. However, it also makes an important return to an aspect of the narrative which, although obvious in the previous two articles, was silhouetted against the pre-eminence of the writer's house. In this article the political pertinence of Spark's war-time expe-

rience moves from the background setting to a foregrounded formative causality. She writes:

> I have always known that this occasion vitally strengthened my
> resolve to become a writer. In the short-story I wrote eight years
> later, and in my radio broadcast sixteen years later, I reproduced
> some of the actual scenes of that event. It has taken me over forty
> years to realise that the quality of the experience was intensified by
> my fear of those flying bombs and the knowledge that destruction
> might fall at any moment, even on the house of the famous poet.
>
> (FN, p. 48)

From the autumnal perspective of 1985, Spark's relationship to this
most important of personal narratives has shifted focus once more. In
the twilight of nostalgia, the house returns to Spark in an exemplary
economy of iterability as a monument to her own past history, the
history of Europe, the history of the dead poets of the thirties (for the
first time in all these fragments Spark openly discusses MacNeice), and
her own past writing.

Drusilla Modjeska asks in her novel *Poppy*, 'Do we give material
shapes to our fears and remember not the fear but the landscapes we
dress them in?'[6] The whispers of mortality in all the fragments (but
which Spark chooses to foreground on this occasion) place the house
in an allegorical position. This further iteration of the narrative event
of the poet's house may suggest a particular relation that Spark's
ongoing process of subjectivity might have to the house. Bachelard
writes:

> Great images have both a history and a prehistory; they are always
> a blend of memory and legend, with the result that we never expe-
> rience an image directly. Indeed, every great image has an
> unfathomable oneiric depth to which the personal past adds special
> colour. Consequently it is not until late in life that we really revere
> an image, when we discover that its roots plunge well beyond the
> history that is fixed in our memories.
>
> (p. 33)

In this sense, the disjuncture which arises between the actual house
which Spark visited in 1944 and the role of the house as image leads
Spark to a fuller appreciation of the historico-socio-poltico-autobio-
graphical significance of the house within this narrative economy. In

as much as this significance extends beyond memory, it is difficult for Spark to assign limits to it. For the reader, it is a matter of conjecture based upon the differential evidence of Spark's set of narratives. It is a house that can be filled with, or emptied of, symbolic significance. The first three fragments account for Spark's path towards writing. However, *Curriculum Vitae*, published in 1992, is not a text which is interested in this incident's relation to Spark's writing process. Indeed, it is a text not necessarily interested in autobiography. Out of almost three hundred pages, Spark dwells for only a page and a half on the event which has so preoccupied her throughout her writing career. Perhaps she feels she has said enough about it, the careful selection of journalism offering an adequate articulation of her thought. However, the opacity of this final fragment (its lack of analytical engagement with its material, its refusal of the reflexive) is in keeping with the project of *Curriculum Vitae*. This text sets out to lay down the material facts of Spark's personal history (devoid of the deliberations of self-exploration) as a way of providing a document which steps outside of criticism by proclaiming itself as a defence of Spark's political right to be a subject:

> So many strange and erroneous accounts of parts of my life have been written since I became well known, that I felt it time to put the record straight.
>
> I determined to write nothing that cannot be supported by documentary evidence or by eye-witnesses; I have not relied on my memory alone, vivid though it is. The disturbing thing about false and erroneous statements is that well-meaning scholars tend to repeat each other. Lies are like fleas hopping from here to there, sucking the blood of the intellect. In my case, the truth is often less flattering, less romantic, but often more interesting than the false story. Truth by itself is neutral and has its own dear beauty; especially in a work of non-fiction it is to be cherished. Besides, false data leads to false premises and those to false conclusions. Is it fair to scholars and students of literature to let them be misled even on the most insignificant matters?
>
> (CV, p. 11)

Written to 'put the record straight' for future generations of Spark 'scholars and students' the text covers its trail of self-effacement in a profusion of trivial materiality. Spark still has time to mention that she slept in a Morrison shelter but allows the lists of the material to hide the aporia of disjunction between writing subjects in order to present this written account of a life as an immediate and unquestionable reality.

I do not think that Spark is unaware of the narrative (and hence both selective and 'unreliable') nature of either 'documentary evidence or eye-witnesses.' I would also suggest that Spark's litigious exercise in self-justification does not in fact trust itself to the 'neutrality' of truth. Or, at least if truth is 'neutral' then the author of *The Abbess of Crewe* and *Not to Disturb* is aware that the undecidability of a text means that the representation of truth will always be ideologically inscribed. After all if truth were neutral there would be no need to challenge alternative narrative accounts of a biography, truth would speak for itself. However, this final text does not qualify as the last word on the matter, even though as a fragment it seeks to establish a frame (by offering an imprimatur to the description of the event) for a future discussion of these narratives. Rather, by returning to the scene the text continues the ongoing process it attempts to limit. This is regardless of any ethical justification that may be required by the gesture of projected control by an author attempting to erase 'erroneous statements' by 'well-meaning scholars'. Again Spark's (the writing Subject's) relation to her material has changed. Each fragment is informed by the function Spark has required her output, on this most select of incidents, to perform at the time of production. *Curriculum Vitae* is the least 'autobiographical' of the fragments, and the fictional story is the most successful exploration of the self. For the self-reflexive and thoroughly postmodern Muriel, such an irony would not be an uncharacteristic position to occupy. 'Unreliability' always already inhabits autobiography as a necessary condition of production. Certainly it would be a mistake to confuse the ongoing process of these four separate pieces of writing as representing an advance. Nothing in the historical chronology of the texts indicates anything like a path towards greater self-illumination. On the contrary, the texts form an economy of difference in which each fragment refers back and forward to the other three (borrowing, quoting, explaining, prefiguring).

The 1981 'semi-autobiographical' novel *Loitering With Intent* (which also reads as the autobiography of its heroine, the famous writer Fleur Talbot) contains a guest (one might say ghost) appearance by Louis MacNeice. Perhaps this is a veiled reference to Spark's other autobiographical writing, perhaps it is 'surplus-value' within an exemplary economy of iterability. Taking a break from writing her first novel, Fleur goes for a drink with a young poet:

There were one or two well-known poets at the bar at whom we glanced from our respectful distance, for they were far beyond our sphere. I think the poets at the bar on that occasion were Dylan Thomas and Roy Campbell, or it could have been Louis MacNeice and someone else; it made no difference for the point was we felt that the atmosphere was as good as the Cornish pasties and beer.

(L, p. 73)

There is no difference because once again this 'spectre of MacNeice' acts as a symbol for Spark's (or Fleur's) finding of a position within social, political and cultural discourses which enables her to come to writing. As a living person MacNeice never appears in any of the fragments; rather, it is only his name which interests Spark. In 'The Poet's House' she tells of how she telephoned an editor from MacNeice's house to say where she was staying and asked whether the editor would like to read two of her, as yet unwritten, poems. Just through association with MacNeice's name the editor agreed; Spark never wrote the poems. Like the image of the house, the name of Louis MacNeice in these fragments is the rehearsal and a condensation of a complex social and cultural process which brings Spark to writing. As Spark's writing career unfolds each fragment mourns the lost subjectivity which is the theme of the preceding texts. Such a work of mourning through the metonymic condensation of figures is the work of writing itself. The scramble for memory in these oneric fragments is an attempt to conjour a past which cannot possibly be recalled. Like MacNeice's study of ancient Rome while at Oxford, it is a past which exists only in writing:

> And how one can imagine oneself among them
> I do not know;
> It was all so unimaginably different
> And all so long ago.[7]

Notes

1. Muriel Spark, 'The House of the Famous Poet', in *The Collected Short Stories of Muriel Spark* (London: Macmillan, 1995), hereafter abbreviated as CS; 'The Poet's House', *Encounter* 30(5), May 1968, hereafter abbreviated as PH (first published in *The Critic* 19(4), Feb–March 1961); 'Footnote to a Poet's House', *Architectural Digest* 42(11), 1985, hereafter abbreviated as FN; *Curriculum Vitae*.

2. Muriel Spark, *Collected Short Stories 1* (London: Macmillan, 1967; New York: Alfred Knopf, 1968).

3. Gaston Bachelard, *The Poetics of Space*, trans. Maria Jolas (Boston: Beacon Press, 1969), p. 3. All page references are hereafter contained within the text of this essay.

4. Jacques Derrida, 'This Strange Institution Called Literature', in *Acts of Literature*, ed. Derek Attridge (Routledge: London, 1992), p. 43.

5. Muriel Spark, 'The House of Fiction', interview with Frank Kermode, in *Partisan Review* Spring, 1963, pp. 79–80.

6. Drusilla Modjeska, *Poppy* (London: Serpent's Tail, 1990), p. 233.

7. Louis MacNeice, 'Autumn Journal', ix, *The Collected Poems of Louis MacNeice* (London: Faber & Faber, 1966), p. 118.

Part II
Race

'GreekJew is JewGreek'

Joyce

5
Writing against Conversion: Muriel Spark the Gentile Jewess

Bryan Cheyette

For much of the first half of 1998, Muriel Spark was the object of an unusual media controversy. Her son, Robin, claimed to have a marriage certificate which proved that his grandparents had wedded in a Synagogue and that he was, therefore, 'fully Jewish'. Spark, on the other hand, has always described herself as a 'Gentile Jew' or 'half Jew' and resented what she regarded as the rewriting of her early history.[1] This family quarrel, which continues to surface intermittently, is of little interest in itself. But what it does indicate is the extent to which Jewishness can be said to have a troubling relationship to Spark's fiction. While Spark has been marginalized as a 'Catholic Writer', it is clear that the intelligence and subversiveness of her fiction is driven not by an unchanging morality but by a radical singularity which is signified in part by her gentile Jewishness. My argument is that far from transfiguring her sense of difference, Spark's conversion to Roman Catholicism in 1954 places her many contradictions in a sustained and creative dialogue.

Destination unknown

In her short story, 'The Fortune-Teller' (1985), Spark distinguishes crucially between having a 'destiny' and a 'destination' (CS, p. 335). Once her life story is thought of as a foregone conclusion, determined by a single destiny, then other potential destinations are of necessity excluded and diminished. This determinism, which Michael André Bernstein has called 'foreshadowing', is precisely what Spark's fictional practice works against.[2] From *The Comforters* (1957) onwards, there-fore, she has insisted that her heroines, such as the Gentile Jewish Caroline Rose, challenge the Calvinistic belief in predestination by having any number of conceivable destinations. This can be seen especially at the point when Caroline is about to become a novelist. When she goes away to write her version of *The Comforters* she deliberately leaves her notes behind her which she was making throughout the book. As Bernard Harrison has argued, this paradoxical act is presumably because Caroline's fiction, if it is to be an authentic engagement with the world, will be limited and impaired by her previous thoughts and preconceptions.[3] Such open and plural figures contrast especially with Spark's more one-eyed writer's manqués, such as Lise in *The Driver's Seat* (1970) or Lister in *Not to Disturb* (1971), who mistakenly think that their myth-fictions can determine reality. Such end-directed characters clearly demean the variety and openness of life. Spark has therefore created an astonishing range of destinations for herself and her fictions. For this reason, she has routinely exposed those dangerously attractive mythomaniacs, most notably Miss Jean Brodie, who think of their lives, and those under their sway, as having a single destiny.

Spark has long since been preoccupied with her upbringing in Morningside, Edinburgh, to parents of mixed national, ethnic and religious backgrounds. Her Calvinist-inspired education in the Presbyterian James Gillespie's Girls' School has, in particular, 'bred within me the conditions of exiledom' which 'has ceased to be a fate, it has become a calling'.[4] She is explicit in her essay, 'What Images Return' (1970), about defining herself in opposition to the 'Caledonian Society aspect of Edinburgh which cannot accommodate me': 'The only sons and daughters of Edinburgh with whom I can find common understanding are exiles like myself' (WIR, p. 152). For this reason, she describes herself as 'an exile in heart and mind' and as someone who is 'moving from exile into exile' (WIR, pp. 151–2). Spark is reacting strongly against a predetermined Caledonian Scottishness, which she perceives as a determining cultural formation, and she thus places herself beyond its reach. Appropriately enough, she thinks of her Jewish father, born in Edinburgh, as being akin to the Castle Rock or the 'great primitive black crag' (WIR, p. 153) which belongs to the heart of the city and is also strangely incongruous. Like her father, Spark is both part of and out of place even in her home town.

As I show elsewhere, it is Spark's hybrid background – part English, part Scottish, part Protestant, part Jewish – which has enabled her to become an essentially diasporic writer.[5] Always shifting in time, from the 1940s to the 1990s, her fiction encompasses Zimbabwe, Edinburgh and Jerusalem and rotates, habitually, between London, New York and

Rome. No one time, place or culture has been allowed to delimit Spark's imagination. Her many and varied versions of her own biography have meant that she has refused to settle on a single account of her formative years. From this perspective, an unproblematical Jewishness (as opposed to an uncertain Gentile Jewishness) could be said to be one of many predetermined national and cultural formations which are challenged in Spark's fiction.

Hauntings

An avowed anti-determinism is especially troubling when placed next to the conversionist narrative that surrounds her as a so-called 'Catholic writer' and a convert to the Catholic faith. The convert, in this orthodox reading, is precisely meant to close off one set of possibilities, and one version of the self, and to embrace a radically new and all-encompassing *weltanschauung*. Spark's fiction has, as a consequence, been read as a 'spiritual autobiography' which distinguishes, above all, between the self before and after conversion. Each novel, according to this interpretation, becomes a kind of ongoing conversion, transforming the author anew, and distancing her from her previous self.[6] The abiding problem with thinking of Spark in this way is that it tends to set up an over-simple model of conversion which unproblematically splits the self into old and new, before and after, inner and outer. Conversion, in these terms, is turned into another form of determinism and becomes merely a self-congratulatory act of redemption. Spark's refusal in her writing to unequivocally classify and moralize herself clearly challenges the narrative of elevation implicit in this view of the convert.

The term 'convert' has an abundance of meanings and etymologies which Spark seems to be aware of. It ranges from the hardened conformities of religious conversion to a softer, more amorphous and troubling, form of exchange which includes the conversion of life into art or materiality into spirituality. Even as late as her story, 'Another Pair of Hands' (1985), she portrays a character who 'conversed' (CS, p. 338) with herself. Spark's central figures are often doubled and redoubled, such as Dougal Douglas or Douglas Dougal in *The Ballad of Peckham Rye* (1960), and thus become their own converse. The softer form of conversion as exchange enables Spark, in her writing, to connect different realms so that her fictional domain is always perceived from competing or contradictory perspectives. In many of her short stories and novels, beginning with 'The Girl I Left Behind

Me' (1957), characters are so radically divided that they literally haunt the page. The girl 'left behind' embraces her own dead body 'like a lover' (CS, p. 360) in a parody of spiritual renewal. Her fiction, in this way, questions the redemptive promise of conversion as it only momentarily is allowed to have a single transcendent vision. Far from being transformed, Spark's imagined life story always seems to return to haunt her.

Many of her stories are preoccupied with aged or dead writers who complete their novels from the grave, or have such an overwhelming ghostly presence that they inspire others to finish their life-work. At the end of 'The House of the Famous Poet' (1967), Spark's narrative voice decides that the 'angels of the Resurrection will invoke the dead man' and that her worldly role as storyteller will eventually 'restore the fallen house of the famous poet' (CS, p. 218). Here redemption takes both a Catholic and secular form and there are clearly different trajectories within these distinct kinds of exchange. Sandy Stranger, in *The Prime of Miss Jean Brodie* (1961), is inspired to write by her conversion to Catholicism and thus enables her readers, famously, to 'transfigure' Miss Brodie. The self-transfiguration of Nicholas Farringdon in *The Girls of Slender Means* (1963), on the other hand, is the endpoint of his poetic engagement with the May of Teck Club. His posthumous sceptical scrutiny, outside the sphere of words, is of a markedly different order. Conversion, as figured in Spark's fiction, is always a dual experience which not only opens up the possibilities of transforming experience through writing but also exposes the limitations of such essentially worldly transfigurations.

Models of conversion

In her well known interview with Frank Kermode, Spark described her turn to fiction from poetry, after she converted, as 'probably just a justification for the time I wasted doing something else'. She goes on to say that her novels are an attempt to 'redeem the time' so that her years before *The Comforters* 'won't be wasted – it won't be wasted until I'm dead'.[7] The introduction to her study of John Masefield confirms this unavoidable exchange between life and art: 'those parts of his life story which the poet himself has written about never fail to give the impression that life has always presented itself to him, as it were, in the narrative form'.[8] With the publication of *The Comforters*, Spark also began to use the art of fiction to turn her own life story into a 'narrative form'. In these redemptive terms, her first forty years have become the waste material for much of her subsequent fiction. As late as *Loitering with Intent* (1981) and *A Far Cry from Kensington* (1988), Spark was to imaginatively reinvent her past selves and to reclaim her wilderness years for the artistic sphere.

Those critics who have noted Spark's double conversion to both Roman Catholicism and the art of the novel have argued mistakenly that these coexisting transformations are somehow equivalent.[9] Instead of assuming that there is an organic coherence between her religion and art, Gauri Viswanathan has maintained that religious conversion, far from being a unitary form of exchange, is a model of 'dissent'. In her reading, conversion is primarily a form of doubleness which 'destabilises' modern society as it 'crosses fixed boundaries between communities and identities'.[10] According to this argument, the mixing of two different cultures inevitably creates a sense in which any one ideology can be viewed from an estranged and defamiliarized perspective. Far from merely superseding the past, conversion is seen primarily as an interpretative act which perceives one world through the eyes of another. Spark's fiction, for instance, reinterprets the secular novel as a parodic form of spiritual transfiguration, while her Catholicism is observed with an artist's sceptical eye. Rather than being an all-encompassing orthodoxy, conversion for Viswanathan becomes a form of heterodoxy which multiplies endlessly official discourse.

Although Viswanathan is correct to highlight the subversive potential within conversion, she overstates her case by focusing only on the question of dissent, as opposed to religious assent, even in relation to a figure as contradictory as John Henry Newman.[11] Spark's fiction, crucially, illustrates both the authoritarian as well as anarchic potential within the act of conversion. In fact, at the beginning of her career as a novelist, when most closely influenced by Newman, she was to reinforce the orthodox reading of conversion as a means of creating narrative and moral 'order' out of the waste and disorder of her early years. Here is Spark's much cited 1961 interview on her conversion, which she has since repudiated, where she describes Catholicism as a 'norm from which one can depart'.[12] She goes on to relate her reasons for conversion to her 'breakdown' at the time:

> The first reaction I had when I became a Catholic was that my mind was far too crowded with ideas, all teeming in disorder. This was part of my breakdown. The oddest, most peculiar variety of themes and ideas of all sorts teemed in my head. I have never known such

mental activity. It made me suffer a lot. But as I got better I was able
to take them one at a time ... It was like getting a new gift.

(MC, p. 60)

Catholicism, in these conventional terms, becomes an ordering principle as well as an act of faith: 'I used to worry until I got a sense of
order, a sense of proportion. At least I hope I've got it now. You need
it to be either a writer or a Christian' (MC, p. 63). Her conversion thus
provided her with a renewed healthy identity and the ability to write
in a controlled manner. Unlike Spark herself, critics have tended to
habitually repeat these statements, as if they were writ in stone, to
lend weight to her credentials as a wholly Catholic writer – in the great
British tradition of Ford Madox Ford, Graham Greene and Evelyn
Waugh.

Far from destabilizing different religious perspectives, Jews, at this
stage in her career, tended to be constructed as figures of confusion
and ambivalence when compared to the sanity and clarity of Christian
culture. To be sure, such authoritarian thinking at first helped fix her
identity as a Catholic writer although such distinctions were quickly
disrupted in her fiction. At the start of 'My Conversion', however,
Spark characterizes the 'very peculiar environment' (MC, p. 58) of her
childhood which she states is 'difficult to locate': 'I am partly of Jewish
origin, so my environment had a kind of Jewish tinge but without any
formal instruction' (MC, p. 58). Later on, she speaks of the 'very indef-
inite location' (MC, p 59) of her childhood as opposed to the clarity of
her Catholic identity which enabled her to find 'one's own individual
point of view' (MC, p. 61). As with T. S. Eliot's *Notes Towards the
Definition of Culture* (1948), which Spark had reviewed favourably,
Christianity is seen as a means of imposing distinct boundaries on an
excessively fluid and rootless identity. This incoherent and unstable
Jewishness, along with a sense of alienation and ill-health, thus
became a negative principle to set against a received Christian
aesthetics.[13]

It is in these authoritarian terms that Spark has been misguidedly
seen as belonging to the neo-classical 'Catholic novelists of detachment, like Joyce, whose God-like writer is indifferent to creation,
paring his fingernails'.[14] Her often cool aesthetic surface and narrative
indifference, coupled with her supposed commitment to a God-given
truth, has resulted in many of her critics viewing her mainly through
her apparently secure identity as a Catholic writer. But Spark's narrators are often aware of the dangers of coldly expunging an

uncontrollable emotional life from her fiction. In fact, as I argue in my book on Spark, her fiction was to gradually question the values of clarity and order which were so necessary to her in the 1940s and 50s.[15] As early as her story, 'Bang-Bang You're Dead' (1961), her protagonist Sybil asks 'Am I a woman ... or an intellectual monster?' (CS, p. 85) to indicate the limitations of her ordering authorial voice. The contrast in the Kermode interview between the falsity or provisionality of fiction, compared with a moral absoluteness outside of the imagination, has mistakenly acted as a manifesto for Spark's neo-classical arts. But Sybil's parodic childhood game, where she is constantly shot only to 'resurrect herself' (CS, p. 63), also demonstrates an enduring playfulness towards her most sacredly held beliefs.

Spark's critics have tended to underestimate the extent to which her conversion not only unified her but also, at the same time, enabled her to occupy more than one space in her fiction. Her faith in a universal higher authority, in other words, is thrown into disarray by a fictional practise which is plural and partial and embraces a multiple sense of self. Here the Joycean analogy is worth returning to. The Catholic authorial model, embodied in Stephen Dedalus, of the writer indifferent to creation, 'paring his fingernails', is countered in *Ulysses* (1922) by the figure of Leopold Bloom. The Greek–Jewish Bloom, in this novel, represents ambivalence *in extremis*: the impossibility of imposing meaning on the world however much his God-like author might wish too.[16] The ordering of reality in Spark's experimental fiction is similarly provisional and always open to question. That which she wishes to transfigure invariably proves to be uncontainable and returns to haunt her. This is why she continually enacts the originary histories of her 'wasted years' which includes her husband's violent nervous disorders in Africa, the uncertainty of her own part-Jewish background, and the experience of war and poverty in the 1940s and 50s and her breakdown in or around 1954. Madness, singularity and unrestrained emotion are the stuff that Spark simply cannot convert into an untroubled and impersonal narrative.

Different-from

Given the universalizing rhetoric that shapes the conventional representation of the convert, it is not surprising that Spark was to stress continually her radical singularity in relation to this generalizing and categorizing orthodoxy. This is the subject of her key story, 'Come Along, Marjorie' (1958), which is set in a Catholic retreat called Watling Abbey, a version of the Aylesford Priory which Spark had attended. All of the characters in this story are 'recovering from nerves' (CS, p. 163) although the narrator of this story, aptly nick-named Gloria Deplores-you, is alienated by the conformist demands of her fellow neurotics:

> As we walked along with our suitcases I made note that there was little in common between them and me except Catholicism, and then only in a mystical sense, for their religious apprehensions were different from mine. 'Different from' is the form my neurosis takes. I do like the differentiation of things, but it is apt to lead to nerve-racking pursuits. On the other hand, life led on the different-from level is always an adventure.
>
> (CS, pp. 161–2)

Her companion's neurosis, however, take the form of 'same as': 'We are all the same, [Jennifer] would assert, infuriating me because I knew that God had made everyone unique' (CS, p. 162). Here, in a nutshell, is the tension in the conversionist orthodoxy. The impersonal and universal higher order, which the convert is meant to assimilate into, threatens to expunge individual difference. For this reason, an unbounded individualism is at the heart of this story and much of Spark's subsequent fiction. Marjorie Pettigrew's supposedly insane refusal to conform to the norms of the retreat, and the brutal response that results from her refusal, illustrates poignantly the consequences of an authoritarian ordering principle. Instead of this conformism, Spark rewrites Gloria's Catholicism so that it can accommodate singularity and become part of the maverick arts of the novelist. In opposition to her conventional companions, Gloria responds that: '[Jennifer] believed everyone was "the same", she didn't acknowledge the difference of things, what right had she to possess curiosity? My case was different' (CS, p. 170). The curiosity of the novelist clearly cannot exist without a strong belief in 'the difference of things' however supposedly stable and unambiguous one's identity as a Catholic writer.

Gentile Jewesses and other indeterminacies

Spark's acknowledged difference as a 'Gentile Jewess' enables her to challenge, in her fiction of the 1960s, the redemptive promise of conversion. She, pointedly, does not describe her characters as 'Christian Jews' or 'Jewish Christians' which would have reinforced a traditional Catholic view of the founders of the Church. Instead, the term 'Gentile' is deliberately open and suggests both a resonant paganism in relation to Judaism as well as a rather prim and comic Edinburgh gentility. Throughout its composition, *The Mandelbaum Gate* (1965) was called 'The Gentile Jewesses' although, in the end, only a short story emerged with this title. Spark insists that 'The Gentile Jewesses' (1963) is a 'nearly factual' account of her visits to her maternal grandmother in Watford (CV, p. 81) and she has thus repeated this story in her autobiography. But whereas *Curriculum Vitae* (1992) tries to be 'factual', by assuming the air of non-figurative documentary realism, 'The Gentile Jewesses' is a story about telling stories and is playfully self-conscious about its claims to authenticity. Spark is astutely aware in her story of the extent to which identity needs to be performed and cannot be fixed by an outside or paternal authority.

In 'The Gentile Jewesses', Spark is able to embrace her identity-less Jewishness in contrast to the strictures of religious orthodoxy. After recollecting her grandmother's shop in Watford, the Sparkian story-teller comments that the 'scene is as clear as memory to me' (CS, p. 308) which gives a flavour of the inticing ambiguities in the story. The clarity of Spark's memories are, after all, precisely what is open to question. Told from the viewpoint of the granddaughter, the first person narrator stresses throughout that this is just 'one telling of the story' (CS, p. 308) and that her memories have been changed and modified with constant retellings. What is more, the granddaughter often re-enacts, in retrospect, the stories told to her by her grandmother. After recalling a visit to a group of spiritualists, she 'took my grandmother's hand to show me what spiritualists did' (CS, p. 311). Much of the story is performed in hindsight as if Spark is deliberately going through the stages necessary to construct a singular history. Her grandmother's description of herself as a 'Gentile Jewess' is, in this way, enacted by Spark's mother and, eventually, by the Sparkian narrator herself. 'The Gentile Jewesses' thus holds in tension the fixity of myth-making with the provisionality of storytelling.

Throughout the story, in fact, Spark's authorial voice stresses the extreme arbitrariness of her 'Gentile Jewish' identity. When told that she did not 'look like a Jew', she points to her small feet and claimed that 'all Jews have little feet' (CS, p. 313). At another time, referring to her father's profession, she notes mischievously that 'all Jews were engineers' (CS, p. 313). The grandmother, on the other hand, dismissed as 'Pollacks' (CS, p. 313) a group of Polish-Jewish immigrants to Watford while embracing some Londoners of German descent as honorary Jews. That Spark was to play with her part-Jewish identity in her early life can also be seen in *Curriculum Vitae*. Born Muriel Camberg, her 'foreign' name often attracted comment: 'When asked about my name I said it was a Jewish name, evidently of German origin' (CV, p. 107). On her return to an Anglican convent in Bulawayo to refuse a job, because the Mother Superior was so rabidly anti-Semitic, Spark responded by saying that, 'Of course, I'm a Jew' even though, she remembers, her 'fair skin' and 'golden locks' might indicate otherwise (CV, pp. 134–5).

Rather than perceiving a sense of confusion which needed to be resolved, her narrative voice locates her 'Gentile Jewish' identity as a creatively disruptive force. Much to the chagrin of her grandfather, her grandmother was an active Suffragette who participated in women's marches down Watford High Street. As she was to illustrate at length in *Robinson* (1958) and *The Takeover* (1976), a distinctly feminine spirituality enables her heroines to challenge patriarchal authority of all kinds. Her mother's pagan ritual of bowing to the moon three times – a ritual which Spark still continues 'for fun' (CV, p. 38) – is also, in the story, related to the Judaic lunar calendar:

> My mother never fails to bow three times to the new moon wherever she might be at the time of first catching sight of it. I have seen her standing on a busy pavement with numerous cold rational Presbyterian eyes upon her, turning over her money, bowing regardless and chanting, 'New moon, new moon, be good to me'. In my memory this image is fused with her lighting of the Sabbath candles on a Friday night, chanting a Hebrew prayer which I have since been told came out in a very strange sort of Hebrew. Still, it was her tribute and solemn observance. She said that the Israelites of the Bible and herself were one and the same because of the Jewish part of her blood, and I did not doubt this thrilling fact. I thought of her as the second Gentile Jewess after my grandmother, and myself as the third.
>
> (CS, p. 314)

By the end of the story, her mother yokes together Christianity, Buddhism and Judaism and this all-embracing pluralism becomes a version of women's otherness. At the same time, 'The Gentile Jewesses' concludes rather abruptly with Spark turning Catholic as 'with Roman Catholics too, it all boils down to the Almighty in the end' (CS, p. 315). This rather limiting point of closure contrasts starkly with her childhood home where 'all the gods are served' (CS, p. 315). The unresolved tension between the freedom inherent in a displaced multiple identity and the transfiguring power of the Catholic church was to be addressed at length in *The Mandelbaum Gate.*

Writing against conversion

Towards the beginning of *The Girls of Slender Means*, Spark imagines an 'organic' VE Day crowd made up of 'strange arms ... twined around strange bodies': 'Many liaisons, some permanent, were formed in the night, and numerous infants of experimental variety, delightful in hue of skin and racial structure, were born to the world ... nine months after' (G, p. 17). As always, Spark seems unsure of the value of these uncontrollable passions which, as Gloria Deplores-you put it, results in a 'nerve-racking' 'differentiation of things'. *The Mandelbaum Gate*, in particular, explores both the fear and desire inherent in this disruptive racial singularity which is given a historical resonance with reference to the Nazi doctrine of expunging such differences. Set in Jerusalem, this book is unique among Spark's oeuvre in relation to both its subject-matter and its literary form. It is her only novel to examine in depth her Gentile-Jewish background although this is alluded to in many of her other works. What is more, it is her longest, least serene and most ambitious novel to date. Spark clearly felt compelled to understand a key aspect of her past which had continued to haunt her long after her conversion. For this reason, Spark's eighth novel has been described as heterodox and anarchic with an 'untidy and crowded' cast of misfits.[17]

For the first time in Spark's fiction, history and her central figures all have a dangerous autonomy which escape her distinctive aesthetic command. Barbara Vaughan's Gentile Jewishness in *The Mandelbaum Gate* represents a kind of freedom which is reflected in the unusual exuberance of Spark's writing. After all, Spark spent two years composing this book as compared to, say, the eight weeks which she took over *The Prime of Miss Jean Brodie*. It became her bulkiest work, closer than any of her others to the sprawling English realist tradition of George Eliot and E. M. Forster. She acknowledged its significance at the time by describing it on publication as 'a very important book for me, much more concrete and solidly rooted in a very detailed setting' than what had gone before. But, in a later interview, she rejected the novel because it remained outside of her narrative control: 'I don't like that book awfully much ... it's out of proportion. In the beginning it's slow, and in the end it's very rapid, it races ... I got bored, because it is too long, so I decided never again to write a long book, keep them short'.[18] Given its unrestrained form and Jewish subject matter, it is fitting that this work should continue to disturb Spark long after it was written.

Appropriately enough, the second chapter of *The Mandelbaum Gate* is called 'Barbara Vaughan's Identity' and it is her self-confessed 'state of conflict' (MG, p. 23) which extends into the polarized history of the Middle East and the bisected city of Jerusalem. The eponymous Mandelbaum Gate, which separates the Israeli and Jordanian sides of Jerusalem, makes it possible for Barbara to move within and between identities. From the beginning, Barbara argues that 'the essential thing about herself remained unspoken, uncategorized, unlocated' (MG, p. 28) and later she makes explicit her conversionist credo: 'There's always more to it than Jew, Gentile, half-Jew, half-Gentile. There's the human soul, the individual. Not "Jew, Gentile" as one might say "autumn, winter". Something unique and unrepeatable' (MG, p. 37). In *The Comforters*, Jewishness is dismissed as one of Caroline Roses's 'half-worlds' (CO, p. 48) which needed to be transfigured. Barbara Vaughan, a Gentile Jewess after Caroline Rose, also stresses her transcendent uniqueness which goes beyond such racial or ethnic categories. But, unlike *The Comforters*, Barbara is aware that the too easy universalization of racial difference, especially in the Middle East, is an essentially fruitless form of transformation.

When pressed to identify herself as a Jew by her Israeli tour guide, Barbara replies in the enthused spirit of the convert. She states, 'I am who I am' (MG, p. 28) which ironically echoes God's answer to Moses from the burning bush on Mount Sinai. And yet, she soon becomes anxious at such 'mysterious truths', which 'were all right for deathbed definitions, when one's mental obligations were at an end' (MG, p. 29). Barbara's welcome intellectual scepticism can be contrasted with Father Jerome, the Catholic Priest who, with god-like authority, tells Caroline in *The Comforters* that 'she was as she was' (CO, p. 62). Unlike Caroline, who welcomes the mystification of her identity, Barbara is well aware that the effortless transformation of such ethnic, cultural and religious particularities, especially in the combustible context of the Middle East, is a too easy form of 'escape' (MG, p. 31). She questions an unthinking transcendence, as well as the Israeli tour guide's demand for definition which, she believes, resembles the false 'territorial consciousness' of other historically powerless peoples such as the Scots, Irish and the Welsh (MG, p. 29).

By refusing to either territorialize her racial difference, or to

transcend it, Barbara Vaughan stands outside of both a dominant nationalism and an orthodox conversionism. What is more, her Gentile
Jewishness becomes a model for other anarchic unplaceable individuals
throughout the novel. Barbara is attracted to her lover, Harry Clegg, for
instance, as he eludes the unspoken assumption which pigeon-holes him
as an 'Englishman of lower-class origin' or 'red-brick genius' (MG, p. 41).
The eroticizing of her Jewishness similarly qualifies her role as an
'English spinster' and she thinks of hers and Harry's refusal to be type-
cast as an 'equivalent quality' (MG, p. 41). The novel is, in fact, stuffed
full of people, such as Abdul and Suzi Ramdez, who cannot be addressed
in a conventional mode. In the end, these identity-less individuals all
seem to break down commonplace assumptions about nation, gender
and class and can be said to form an alternative community of exiles.
Spark is quite explicit about this in her account of the blue-eyed, dark-
skinned Palestinian brother and sister, Abdul and Suzi Ramdez, who
'belonged to nothing but themselves' (MG, p. 101) and yet, paradoxically, are part of a group made up of:

> lapsed Jews, lapsed Arabs, lapsed citizens, runaway Englishmen,
> dancing prostitutes, international messes, failed painters, intellec-
> tuals, homosexuals. Some were silent, some voluble. Some were
> mentally ill, or would become so.
>
> (MG, p. 101)

The warning at the end of this quotation that 'some were mentally ill,
or would become so' reminds the reader of the price that, as with
Spark's own breakdown, might be paid for such severe dislocation. At
the same time, immediately after this paragraph, the narrative voice
intervenes to repeat unequivocally that 'others were not [mad], and
never would become so; and would have been the flower of the Middle
East, given the sun and air of the mind not yet ... available' (MG, p.
101). Such is the thin line between madness and revolutionary change.
Earlier in the chapter, we are told that Abdul Ramdez categorized those
in power as 'the System' which included 'fathers, the Pope, President
Nasser, King Hussein, Mr Ben-Gurion, the Grand Mufti, the Patriarch
of Jerusalem, the English Sovereign, the civil servants and upper
militia throughout the world' (MG, p. 81). His opposition to 'the
System', essentially patriarchal power, is both a form of lunacy and a
revolutionary new way of imagining the Middle East. Spark,
throughout *The Mandelbaum Gate*, is at pains to oppose orthodoxies of
all kinds in these prophetic terms.

In fact, her preoccupation with madness as a form of creative disor-
dering refers back to 'The Gentile Jewesses' which opens with the
grandmother frightening away a 'madman' from the local asylum who
threatened to murder her in her shop. The story of this lunatic in turn
unlocks other, equally disruptive, forms of anarchy and refers implicitly to her mother's devotion to the lunar calendar in 'The Gentile
Jewesses'. Barbara, importantly, 'caught some of Freddy's madness'
when she eventually felt herself to be 'all of a piece; Gentile and
Jewess, Vaughan and Aaronson ... a private-judging Catholic, a shy
adventuress' (MG, p. 164). At this point, Freddy's madness enables her
to easily accept her manifold singularity. But all of the multiple identities in the novel, like Barbara's, are caught between being both
liberating and a form of potentially disabling madness.

The split in Barbara's double identity is writ large in the historical
backdrop of the novel when it comes to the account of the Eichmann
Trial. In stark contrast to Barbara's 'unique and unrepeatable' sense of
self, Eichmann represents the ultimate determinist and false catego-
rizer who drains people of their uniqueness. As Gabriel Josipovici has
noted, Spark characterizes Eichmann's evil as a form of 'self-love and
self-righteousness which goes with the refusal of the imagination'.[19]
To this extent, he becomes a ghastly version of a bad novelist:

> Barbara felt she was caught in a conspiracy to prevent her brain
> from functioning ... The man was plainly not testifying for himself,
> but for his pre-written destiny. He was not answering for himself or
> his own life at all, but for an imperative deity named Bureau IV-B–4,
> of whom he was the High Priest.
>
> (MG, p. 179)

The Eichmann trial exposes not only the dangers of holding an
absolute faith but also the impossible attempt to contain the particularities of history within Barbara's conflicted sense of transcendence.
During the trial, she is reminded rather solipsistically of her schooling
where she read the French *nouveau roman* or 'anti-novel' and thought
of 'repetition, boredom, despair, going nowhere for nothing, all of
which conditions are enclosed in a tight, unbreakable statement of the
times at hand' (MG, p. 177). In an anticipation of Hannah Arendt's
famous description of Eichmann's testimony as the 'banality of evil',
the judges presiding over the trial all bear the 'recognizable scars of the
western intellectual' (MG, p. 178).[20]

But Eichmann is the very real product of European history which cannot be easily transformed into Barbara's search for meaning outside of the specificities of these events. For this reason, the scenes concerning Eichmann include Spark's verbatim transcriptions of the trial, as if nothing can be added to the historical record. *The Mandelbaum Gate* attempts both to aestheticise history but, at the same time, is forced to acknowledge the impossibility of this imaginative conversion. In the end, Eichmann compels Barbara to question her belief in the value of an absolutist transfiguration. It is perhaps in horrified reaction to Eichmann as the parodic double of a true believer that Spark, after this novel, was to construct a world which was to remain radically unconverted.

International messes

Immediately after *The Mandelbaum Gate* Spark simply gave up on material – either historical or personal – which could not be completely ordered and contained by her detached and impersonal narrator. As a consequence, she chose to concentrate on artifice rather than actuality. In the novels that followed – from *The Public Image* (1968) to *The Abbess of Crewe* (1974) – there is an often pitiless tone which has been rightly described, in relation to her earlier output, as 'machine made'.[21] Angus Wilson, who used this prescient phrase, was commentating on the difference between *The Mandelbaum Gate* and what had gone before. But it is not a coincidence that many of Spark's novels of this time are dominated by machines of all kinds such as aeroplanes, automobiles, cameras, tape-recorders, telephones, food-processors, air-conditioners and sophisticated surveillance and propaganda equipment.[22] Spark, at her best, has shown that the themes of her novels dictate their form and there is a crucial link here between her heartless 'machine made' tone and her highly mechanized creations.

By the 1970s her works are full of characters who treat people, as did Adolf Eichmann, as if they were objects drained of their humanity (such as Richard in *The Driver's Seat*, or Lister in *Not to Disturb*). As we have seen, Spark in *The Mandelbaum Gate* thought that Eichmann, not unlike the authors of the anti-novel, had produced a 'tight, unbreakable statement of the times at hand' (MG, p. 177). In this light, she utilizes the 'anti-novel' or *nouveau roman* as a means of substituting conventional concerns with the inner self for a more chilling and dehumanized account of the 'times at hand'. Up until *The Takeover* (1976), her work has a cool and uncluttered surface which is the least messy, the least emotionally invested, of Spark's writings. As with the deranged subject of her story, 'You Should Have Seen the Mess' (1958), all of Spark's protagonists act as if they can turn reality into a neatly ordered narrative. In the orthodox language of the convert, they behave as if dislocation and displacement can be easily tidied away. But, in all of these books, Spark's narrators are at pains to expose the simple-mindedness of such ordering principles.

In *The Mandelbaum Gate*, Spark's community of exiles – the potentially insane or sexual and politically perverse – include a characteristically arch category known as 'international messes'. All of Spark's fiction after *The Takeover* can be described as 'international messes' modelled on the anarchic and heterodox form of *The Mandelbaum Gate*. No longer the classically concise narrator, intent on aestheticising her life story, Spark has gradually begun to relish her past lives and conflicts in such novels as *Loitering with Intent* and *A Far Cry from Kensington*. Elsewhere, she has focused on Italy, not as the place of Papal authority, but, as an essentially disruptive locale where art and life are chaotically indistinguishable. By the time of *Territorial Rights* (1979), in fact, Spark was to implicitly show that conversion is no longer an adequate response to her Jewishness. In this work, she satirizes the outrageously anti-Semitic Lina Pancev who unwittingly sleeps with a Jewish man and, once she learns of this, jumps into a nearby Venetian canal in a bid to rid herself of any potential racial contamination. Instead of purifying herself, however, the canal waters turn out to contain a high risk of infection and Lina has to take to her bed with antibiotics. As Spark's fiction has so felicitously testified, no amount of baptism can expunge the infectious and impure presence of her unconverted self from either her life or her art.

In his *The Book of God* (1988), Gabriel Josipovici has usefully placed the Pauline and Augustinian tradition of conversion at the beginning of the rise of the modern novel. According to this argument, the autobiographical narratives of both St Paul and St Augustine demonstrate the need to 'talk in order to fix the flux of inner turmoil and objectify the crucial act of conversion'. They were the first, in other words, to stress the internal life of the spirit and the consequent meaninglessness of the external world:

> With this step Paul opens up a whole new world of inwardness, a world he himself explores and describes with passionate detail, and which will always have room for fresh explorers, such as Augustine, Pascal and Rousseau. Yet the cost of this is high. Giving up this world of confusion, uncertainty and limited horizons for the apparent surer

world of the spirit, he condemns himself to the sustaining of his vision by nothing other than the sheer power of his imagination and the constant reiteration of the drama of his conversion.[23]

Although Josipovici reads Spark's fiction as opposing the Pauline and Augustinian confessional tradition, I cannot think of a more apt description of Spark's fiction than as a 'constant reiteration of the drama of ... conversion' which is sustained by the uncertain 'power of imagination'.

Notes

1. For a summary of this controversy see Martin Stannard, 'The Letter Killeth', *The Spectator* (6 June, 1998), pp. 36–7. For an implicit response by Spark's son see Samuel Robin Spark, 'Life with the Cambergs', *The Edinburgh Star* (February 1999), pp. 13–17.
2. Michael André Bernstein, *Foregone Conclusions: Against Apocalyptic History* (Berkeley: University of California Press, 1994). This book does not refer directly to Muriel Spark but it makes out such a strong anti-determinist argument, in relation to modern fiction, that it could easily have included her.
3. Bernard Harrison, *Inconvenient Fictions: Literature and the Limits of Theory* (New Haven: Yale University Press, 1991), Chapter 5.
4. 'What Images Return', Karl Miller (ed.), *Memoirs of a Modern Scotland* (London: Faber & Faber, 1970), p. 151. Hereafter abbreviated as WIR.
5. Bryan Cheyette, *Muriel Spark: Writers and their Work* (Devon: Northcote House Publishers, 2000).
6. Jennifer Lynn Randisi, *On Her Way Rejoicing: The Fiction of Muriel Spark* (Washington, DC: The Catholic University of America Press, 1991), Chapter 4, and Ruth Whittaker, *The Faith and Fiction of Muriel Spark* (London: Macmillan Press, 1982) for Spark as a Catholic writer in more general terms.
7. Frank Kermode, 'The House of Fiction: Interviews with Seven Novelists', in Malcolm Bradbury (ed.), *The Novel Today: Contemporary Writers on Modern Fiction* (London: Fontana Paperbacks, 1977), p. 132.
8. Muriel Spark, *John Masefield* (London: Peter Nevill, 1953), p. x.
9. Malcolm Bradbury, 'Muriel Spark's Fingernails', in *No, Not Bloomsbury* (London: Arena, 1987), pp. 268–78 and Peter Kemp, *Muriel Spark: Novelists and Their World* (London: Paul Elek, 1974), p. 158 for this widespread assumption.
10. Gauri Viswanathan, *Outside the Fold: Conversion, Modernity, and Belief* (New Jersey: Princeton University Press, 1998), pp. xvii and Chapter 1.
11. Viswanathan, *Outside the Fold*, Chapter 2.
12. Muriel Spark, 'My Conversion', *The Twentieth Century* (Autumn, 1961), p.60. Hereafter abbreviated as MC. While Spark's 'My Conversion' is referred to extensively in many previous critical studies of her fiction, it has recently been repudiated by Spark herself. For an annotated version of the essay, in a bid to expose its inaccuracies, see the Muriel Spark Manuscript

collection in the University of Tulsa, McFarlin Library, item 53:3.
13. Muriel Spark, 'The Poet in Mr. Eliot's Ideal State', *Outposts* Volume 14 (Summer, 1949), pp. 26–8 and Bryan Cheyette, *Constructions of 'the Jew' in English Literature and Society: Racial Representations, 1875–1945* (Cambridge: Cambridge University Press, 1993), pp. 264–7, for a discussion of *Notes Towards the Definition of Culture* in these terms.
14. Bradbury, 'Muriel Spark's Fingernails', p. 271.
15. Cheyette, *Muriel Spark*, Chapters 1 and 7.
16. Cheyette, *Constructions of 'the Jew' in English Literature and Society*, Chapter 6 for this argument.
17. Whittaker, *The Faith and Fiction of Muriel Spark*, p. 78. For a recent reading of the novel in these terms see Jacqueline Rose, *States of Fantasy (Clarendon Lectures in English Literature)* (Oxford: Oxford University Press, 1996), Chapter 3.
18. Both interviews are cited in Whittaker, *The Faith and Fiction of Muriel Spark*, p. 79.
19. Gabriel Josipovici, 'An Evil Eye Overlooking the Jet Set', *The Independent* (22 September 1990), p. 29.
20. Hannah Arendt, *Eichmann in Jerusalem: A Report on the Banality of Evil* (Harmondsworth: Penguin Books, 1977).
21. Angus Wilson, 'Journey to Jerusalem', *The Observer* 17 October 1965, p. 28.
22. Peter Kemp, *Muriel Spark: Novelists and Their World*, Chapter 5, for this argument.
23. Gabriel Josipovici, *The Book of God* (New Haven and London: Yale University Press, 1988), p. 252 and pp. 251–53. For a recent account of these issues from an uncritical perspective see Joseph Pearce, *Literary Converts: Spiritual Inspiration in an Age of Unbelief* (London: Fount, 1999), Chapter 23.

6
Muriel Spark Shot in Africa

Eleanor Byrne

According to her autobiography *Curriculum Vitae*, on August 13th 1937 Spark, then Muriel Camberg, set sail for Africa to become a married woman and take up the surname that would accompany her writing career. She would not return to Britain until March 1944. Her account of this protracted stay in Southern Rhodesia constitutes only a single yet stormy chapter in the autobiography. The status of this chapter in the autobiographical text and its relation to a number of Spark's short stories set in Africa provides the basis for my discussion.

Arguably the emigration of white British women to the colonies has most frequently been framed in terms of a 'civilizing mission'. Furthermore the 'civilizing mission' of the British, or more commonly English woman in colonial discourse has always been understood in racial terms. This is particularly clear in Britain's dealings with South Africa from the turn of the century, following the Boer War, as Jane Mackay and Pat Thane discuss.[1] It is perhaps unsurprising then that Spark's writing set in Southern Africa is preoccupied with the status of white women in the colonies. Mackay and Thane relate how Englishwomen (sic) were encouraged to emigrate, carrying 'English ideals' abroad and protecting male pioneers from the loss of their national heritage in an alien environment. For the British authorities, anxiety about the physical state of the British troops translated into fears over deterioration of the colonial British male's health, (both physical and 'moral'). This in turn was focused on the need for female emigration to establish a strong 'racial' Englishness, unpolluted by intermingling of English men with either the Boer women or (implicitly) black African women. (The routine elision of Britishness with Englishness appears as part of the deliberate absorption of internal differences neccessitated by the illusions of homogenous self and other upon which colonial power relations depended, as well as representing the material inequalities of nation within Great Britain.)

Emigration propaganda was also often explicitly anti-feminist, attempting to ensure single women in Britain were encouraged to marry and put their energy in the colonial mission and not into the women's liberation movement. Adherence to strict gender roles in the discourse of Empire – male adventure and risk, female civilizing and home-making – point to the strong challenges that gender divisions were undergoing in the early twentieth century. They also reveal an anxiety about 'racial supremacy', miscegenation and a vulnerability of white English male power, despite its supposed hegemonic status.

Spark's account of her emigration to Southern Rhodesia in 1937 appears to confront directly these perceived gender roles. The straightforward attractions of the privileges that white female status in the colonies entailed, accompanied by the 'call of adventure' rather than any devotion to a 'civilizing mission', are found in Spark's account of her emigration from Edinburgh to Southern Rhodesia in her autobiography. 'I liked the proposition that I wouldn't have any housework to do out there in Africa, that I would be free to pursue my writing. And of course, the call of adventure in a strange continent was very strong' (CV, p. 116). As a Scottish adventurer then, she was already somewhat at odds with the gendered logic of colonialism, but perhaps more implicated within colonial power than she wished to admit, the 'proposition' of not doing housework rests on the premise of a silenced and invisible black presence in the colonies who does these things for her.

Spark's account of arriving in Southern Rhodesia is marked by her sense of the impermanence of the colonial status quo in the self-governing colony, and at least in retrospect, her own sense of herself as 'passing through':

> I don't know how anyone could have thought of this situation as anything but temporary. To me at the time there was no feeling of permanence, and I marvelled at people newly arrived from England, who had every intention of remaining forever. They thought the country was an extension of South Africa ... I didn't I couldn't pretend to belong. I intended to stay for the prearranged three years and gain as much human experience as I could.
>
> (CV, p. 123)

This rather blunt characterization of her motives for marrying, and her self-conscious distancing from the white Southern Rhodesian community produces a familiar voice which resonates in many of these short stories, where her heroines might be considered to coldly inhabit a community and landscape both alien and repulsive to them. She comments further that she 'felt too young for all that formal married woman business' and was ' looking forward to getting home again' (CV, p. 125). Nonetheless, however little identification she has with this culture, she finds she quickly has to renegotiate her position as a white woman, complicating and compromising her suggestion of her role as detached anthropological investigator. This transformation operates both in terms of inhabiting a racially organized colony, where whites are a tiny minority, and further by joining a small community where white men outnumbered white women by a ratio of three to one.

This personal transformation is twofold: firstly, Spark's journey to Africa was also a journey out of childhood and straight into marriage (she notes that as she was still technically a minor her marriage in Africa was delayed whilst her father's written permission was sought). Secondly, she found herself ushered into a group of white women regarded as a rationed commodity, in a white community hugely outnumbered by the black native population. Spark's short stories set in Africa, are pervaded by the sexual tension that surrounded such a situation. In *Curriculum Vitae*, Spark relates how moving from the relative freedoms of life in Britain, she finds herself quickly interpellated by a powerful colonial discourse, where the ex-pat white woman occupies a critical position in enforcing and embodying the ambivalent logic of colonial rule. Her antipathy for the other white women suggests not only a personal dislike or snobbery, but rather like Adela Quested in India, a revulsion for what she too must become:[2]

> The white women mainly went around clutching a hundred-cigarette box of Gold Leaf cigarettes [the Rhodesian brand] in their hands, with a lighted cigarette perpetually drooping out of the side of their mouths. I didn't like these women. When we next moved, to Salisbury, they proliferated. They were very sure of themselves as women.
>
> (CV, p. 125)

This confidence which Spark finds uncomfortable, suggests a disturbing certainty about gender roles being produced in the colonies and their centrality to colonial discourses. Spark also finds with dismay that her liberal British attitudes, which drive her to befriend native Africans are simply intolerable in the colony. She only mentions two black people by name, Moses her cook and Esther her son's nanny; both relationships appear significant to her despite their curtailment by the limits of master–servant relations. She finds that her social circle is strictly policed and the fantasies of freedom are replaced by much more severe restrictions upon her behaviour and movements.

In this African chapter of her autobiography, Spark insists on a number of seemingly straightforward relationships between her experiences and artistic intentions in her short stories. She relates specific incidents, which she cites as the bases for particular stories, notably, 'The Curtain Blown by the Breeze', 'The Seraph and the Zambesi', 'The Go-Away Bird' and 'The Pawn-Broker's Wife' and her radio play, *The Dry River Bed*. However, the insistence upon direct relationships between event and fiction prove misleading; some of the 'events' do not literally happen to her and actually constitute a series of stories, told to Spark by others. These stories are embedded in the discourses of colonial Africa, and demand a different critical response to that of pursuing autobiography for explanations of fiction. Furthermore not all Spark's colonial short stories are cited in the autobiography, the notable exception being 'Bang-Bang You're Dead', a story (as I will discuss later on) which ironically might be particularly well suited to just such an autobiographical analysis.

However, by reading Spark's autobiographical account of her African experiences alongside the short stories, I am not seeking to unearth sources that can be traced back to their origins or to produce an archaeological exploration in which biography is the instigator of fiction. Rather, by placing these texts side by side I wish to emphasize, in the words of Hélène Cixous, that 'all biographies, like all autobiographies, like all narratives tell one story instead of another'. The added burden for any critic of women's writing, especially of journals, diaries, travel writing and autobiography, is the way in which such texts are poised on the threshold of the private and the public, and have been read as 'confessional' writing. The problematic status of the confessional, even for a 'Catholic' writer like Spark, is evident in Spark's negotiation of the protocols of revelation in her autobiographical style, which accompanies every personal revelation with a further erection of a stoical mask. Her tone creates the peculiar sensation that her private life has been revealed whilst simultaneously reclaimed as intensely private. It is perhaps more profitable therefore to view this chapter of Spark's autobiography as companion text to some of the short stories, interrupting any intentionalist assumptions and reading for the intertexual relationships that mark Spark's post-colonial writing.

A story which occurs in three different places in Spark's writing appears in the autobiography as a story, related to her whilst in Southern Rhodesia by a white South African woman:

> Sometimes I was horrified by the stories I was told, mainly by Africaners, or people of South African Dutch origin – who would proudly narrate this or that story of how an impertinent black had been 'fixed'. My story, 'The Curtain Blown by the Breeze' contains such an incident: a farmer, I was told, on returning home found a piccanin (as we called a small black boy) standing outside the windows of his wife's room, peeping at her through the curtains while she breast-fed the baby. For this crime, he shot the piccanin dead. This story was told me by a smug, self-satisfied South African Dutch woman of about forty-five, whom I met in one of the many boarding houses I lived in during my married life.
>
> (CV, pp. 126–7)

Completing this triangular relation between the story told to Spark by the woman and her own short story based on it, is a second story 'Bang, Bang You're Dead', which also refers to the same story in passing:

> Much had blared forth about the effect, on the minds of young settlers, of the climate, the hard drinking, the shortage of white women. The Colony was a place where lovers shot husbands or shot themselves, *where husbands shot natives who spied through bedroom windows.*
>
> (CS, p. 64, emphasis added)

'Bang-Bang You're Dead', as I have previously mentioned, is not referred to in Spark's autobiographical writing, yet it contains elements that resemble her own account of her time in Africa much more closely than any of her other African stories. The central character Sybil, a writer, finds white colonial society stifling and is unable to find an intellectual or emotional equal within its confines. When Sybil is asked, many years after her return from Africa, 'Were any of these people intellectuals?' 'No, but lots of poets', is her wry reply. Sybil narrowly misses being shot and killed by her distraught lover through a trick of the light, in which a friend of hers is mistaken for her by the killer and shot in her place. In her autobiography she also relates her own fears of possible murder:

> When Nita McEwan, a friend from school, was killed that night by her husband in the hotel where I was staying, I got seriously frightened. My husband had a small revolver, a 'baby Browning', which he liked to fire off in corridors and courtyards. I hid it, and refused to hand it over when he demanded it.
>
> (CV, p. 130)

These different fictional and autobiographical passages are tantalizing in the way that they weave in and around each other.

Spark's writing on Africa, unlike the rest of her fiction, is marked by the number of murders that take place in the stories, notably of white women.[3] The violence done against them by white men brings questions of the role of white women in the colonies sharply into focus. Many of the women that inhabit Spark's short stories set in Africa, demonstrate a distaste for any ideological commitment to colonial culture. They are women who return continually to the question of their own conflictual negotiations with, and attempts to transgress, the confines of strongly defined, indeed often menacingly policed, roles available to white women in the colonies. In both 'The Curtain Blown by the Breeze', and 'Bang-Bang You're Dead', questions about the ideological role of white women in colonial Africa preoccupy Spark. Here, questions of whiteness and gender, of racial difference, desire and miscegenation predominate.

For Sybil in 'Bang-Bang You're Dead', this ideological discomfort with the colonial production of white women goes substantially further. Asked if she had any trouble with the black population, she replies, 'No, only with the whites'. The narrative moves between the present where Sybil and friends are watching films of her time in Africa eighteen years ago, and the past, both to the days of her childhood and to the days depicted in the rolls of film they watch. 'A hundred feet of one's past life,' comments a viewer 'If they were mine I'm sure I would be shattered – I should be calling, 'Lights! Lights! Like Hamlet's uncle' (CS, p. 85). The reference to a guilty murderer watching the rehearsal of events is apt. Sybil watches the film reels apparently dispassionately; she confesses calmly that she no longer keeps in touch with any of the people featured in the films, as they were all killed in shooting affairs. The retrospective narrative however, focalised through Sybil's private thoughts, does indeed perform a kind of confessional, one which differs substantially from the highly circumspect explanation of the films that Sybil offers to the audience. The narrative reveals that these films were made on the very day in which Sybil's rejected lover shot her friend who he had mistaken for her and then turned the gun on himself. 'Was this a typical afternoon on the Colony?' Sybil is asked, 'It was and it wasn't,' she replies.

Her response is appropriate, the prevalence of shooting affairs, which appear as something of a joke in Britain before she leaves for the Colony, are far more serious and pervasive once Sybil arrives. Indeed it quickly becomes apparent that the shooting affair encapsulates a particular aspect of colonial logic in relations between white men and white women, where passions are menaced by violence and the risk of death. When Sybil's ex-lover appears on screen she explains he was the manager of an estate growing passion-fruit; 'Passion-fruit – how killing' her questioner replies. Sybil's narrow escape from being killed by the passion-fruit grower is caused by her physical similarity to another woman in the party, whose name Desirée, resonates in the text. The passions and desires that operate in the Colony are particularly marked on the white female body.

The white woman's body has a forceful ideological role to play in colonial discourse, as one of the key indices where the narrative of colonial authority is acted out. The framework of desire and disavowal which insists on the desirability of white women over black and the insatiable appetite of black men for white women produces a logic of desire and control that Sybil experiences as an injunction to desire, which if not felt must be simulated in order to conform to a monstrous norm. She 'worked herself as in a frenzy of self-discipline, into a state of carnal excitement over the men' at parties where men outnumbered women considerably, and entered into numerous affairs which she viewed as a form of heroism; 'They were an attempt', thought Sybil 'to do the normal thing'. Her affairs end when she succumbs to an attack of tropical flu, and lies in 'a twilight of the senses', on a bed with a mosquito net, 'like something bridal'. The mosquito net which suggests a wedding outfit, but also differs quite radically, produces an image of a white female sacrifice to patriarchal norms, which produces a kind of insensibility, an alienation from the body and its needs. These torments that she undergoes in order to perform the necessary function of white women in the colonies, produce in her an apprehension of her own monstrosity as she is faced with the overbearing sexual logic of the colony. 'I'm rather a frigid freak I suppose' she tells herself.

At the end of the narrative, the text returns to the present where Sybil is once again part of the audience watching the film reels. The audience begs to see the final reel again; Sybil agrees, whilst inwardly asking herself, 'Am I a woman or an intellectual monster?' Her response to her own inquiry is ambivalent: 'she was so accustomed to this question within herself that it needed no answer'. It suggests the mutual exclusivity of woman and intellectual in the colonial context where the production of physical desire is imperative to colonial narratives.

'The Curtain Blown by the Breeze', also dramatizes this policing of white women which is specifically experienced through the production of the women as sexual objects. It opens with the suggestion of the sexually predatory environment in the colony, experienced as part of the viciousness of the landscape. However, the threat to white women comes from their fellow white men rather than, as colonial discourse would have it, the insatiable desire of the natives for white females.[4] The harshness and dangers of the natural landscape appear to be complemented not by the behaviour of the indigenous people but of the pioneering white settlers:

> This was a territory where you could not bathe in the gentlest stream but a germ from the water entered your kidneys and blighted your body for life ... A young spinster could not keep a cat for a pet but it would one day be captured and pitifully shaved by the local white bachelors for fun.
>
> (CS, p. 23)

The sexual vulnerability of white women appears to be rehearsed in both the natural and social landscape that single white women find themselves in. The construction of these white women as hyperbolically desirable appears to function as a powerful social constraint upon those single white women, such as the narrator, an English nurse, who finds that the landscape appears as an alibi for a predatory sexual intimidation and policing of women who are not yet married:

> The white people seized on the slightest word. Nature took the lightest footfall, with fanatical seriousness. The English nurses discovered that they could not sit next to a man at dinner and be agreeable ... without his taking it for a great flirtation and turning up next day after breakfast for the love affair.
>
> (CS, p. 24)

The contradictory impulses in the overbearing narrative of protection (which effectively polices and produces white femininity) that operates in the colony are the main preoccupation of the story. The young black boy, shot on being discovered looking in a window at Sonji Van der Merwe feeding her baby, is the catalyst for Sonji's transformation into an 'anglicised' Sonia. She re-invents herself whilst her husband serves his (short) jail sentence for the murder. The contradictions of the colonial white woman's position then are her experience of her own disempowerment staged through her production as a potential object of attack by predatory natives. Male responses to assaults, or even the slightest threat or trace of assault, are to translate this position into a male code of honour and chivalry, where masculine white power is affirmed and rehearsed by excessive retributive revenge.

Sonji's transformation, whilst enabled by her newly discovered inheritance, is chiefly moulded by the influence of the British nurses and by her careful attention to discourses of femininity that circulate in the colony, which they introduce her to:

> She did not yet know how to travel by train and would have been afraid to make any excursion by herself far from the area, but from one nurse or another she obtained furnishings from the Union, catalogues, books about interior decoration and fashion magazines.
>
> (CS, p. 28)

The transformation from poor white housewife on a farm, Sonji, to lady of leisure in a fabulously flamboyant house, Sonia, is critical as it marks her retreat from an Afrikaner women's identity (as the name change suggests). The importance of the Afrikaner Volksmoeder (mother of the nation) for the construction and affirmation of Afrikaner identity has been well documented by Anne McClintock.[5] Her iconography is one of paradoxical containment in the political sphere and power, albeit restricted in the domestic sphere. Sonji's transformation then operates not merely as a personal indulgence in luxury and eccentricity, but constitutes a betrayal of the nationalist discourse of Africaner identity, which, McClintock argues, was increasingly turned to, following the Boer War and the First World War. McClintock comments that 'The family household was seen as the last bastion beyond British control and the cultural power of Afrikaner motherhood was mobilized in the service of white nation building' (p. 379). Taking note of McClintock's very pertinent comments about the critical ideological importance of the domestic realm in the assertion of Afrikaner nationalist narratives, Sonia's transformation of herself and her house, her sending the children to boarding school, her abandonment of all farming on her land, constitute an act of considerable rebellion.

Spark arrived in Southern Rhodesia in 1937, only a year before the centenary anniversary of the Great Trek, celebrated in 1938, by the Tweede Trek (second trek) in South Africa.[6] Whilst the celebrations and the spectacle were in the adjacent colony, their impact cannot have been negligible on a colony that Spark herself notes, 'considered itself an extension of South Africa' (CV, p. 123). The ideologies of white womanhood circulating at this time then were, as McClintock notes, 'the controlling of women's sexuality, exalting maternity and breeding a virile race of empire builders'.[7]

The British nurses are very much implicated in the transformation; the narrator is one of these nurses whose fiancé is eventually stolen by Sonia as her power and ostentation increase. Sonia is encouraged by them into outlandish purchases, in their own seemingly unspoken collusion to create a fantastical, ridiculous new identity for Sonia, what the narrator terms, their 'bizarre cultivation' of her:

> She was our creature, our folly, our lark. We had lavished our atten-
> tion upon her eager mind and had ourselves designed the long voile
> 'afternoon' dresses, and had put it to her that she must have a path
> leading down to the river and a punt on the little river and a pink
> parasol to go with the punt.
>
> (CS, p. 30)

The nurses themselves seem confused about their interest in her, uncertain of their motives for becoming involved in the creation of a mocking pastiche of femininity. The narrator appears to view the process from a distance, Sonia's gullibility is ruthlessly exploited both for its comic potential – 'I think it was I who suggested the black-and-white bedroom being a bit drunk at the time' – and for any material advantages the nurses might gain – 'We taught her how not to be mean with her drinks':

> (CS, p. 28)

However, whilst the English women have contributed to the creation of Sonia's bizarre interiors, dressed and coached her as if for the most frivolous of entertainment, contrary to their estimations, her status as a mocking fantasy, burlesque femininity, is barely recognized by the men of the colony. Sonia dazzles the white English community and quickly rises through the social strata of its small hierarchy, gaining access to the most elite and powerful circles: 'government officials took it for granted she had ruled the district for years, and, being above the common run, pleased herself how she dressed and what she did' (CS, p. 28).

Equally, though, the nurses' ironic distance from the trappings of a fantasized and patently parodic version of white colonial womanhood is overturned within their community, such that the women no longer appear to recognize her as a 'monstrous creation' but also become seduced by her. Whereas the men accept and desire her, the women who have been instrumental in creating her are increasingly attracted to her and collude with her dominance in their small social circle. Hence, whilst the nurses initially believe her to be a joke, Sonia becomes unusually liberated from the usual constraints upon women's behaviour, and becomes influential enough in local hospital politics to decide which of two men (the narrator's fiancé and her brother) receive a promotion they badly want.

Sonia then becomes a contradictory symbol, both of the oppression of white women in the colonies and of their liberation; also of their racism and stupidity; of their undeserved privilege in the stark inequalities of the colony. The desire that the nurses invest in creating her appears as, simultaneously, attraction and repulsion. She exposes the constructed nature of white femininity – which doesn't detract from its desirability or efficiency. The nurses themselves have much more invested in Sonia than frivolous enjoyment at her expense. They quickly come to realize that Sonia is not a joke but a kind of imaginary intervention in the colonial status quo. The horror of their own position as colonizers, and of the origins of her newly found status (the killing of a young black child), are also sources of fascination. By contrast, Sonia herself appears not in the least horrified by her husband's actions, complicit with a virulently racist discourse, and yet is equally repulsive and attractive to the nurses.

In Spark's narrative those who appear at the margins of the text, the two black characters, two boys, return to the centre of the narrative, outlining the fundamental injustice of white oppression in Africa and the ambiguous complicity of white women in the history of this dispossession. The first boy is already dead when the narrative begins, his death having been the impetus for her story. But the marginality of his story to that of Sonia's is starkly changed at the climax of the narrative when Sonia too is shot by her husband on his release from jail. Jannie Van der Merwe, shoots Sonia and her lover Frank as they alight from a trip down the river on the aforementioned punt. He has previously walked round the newly refurbished house and tested all the appliances. This inspection of the transformed domestic scene followed by his discovery of his wife in the company of another man culminates in the double murder.

But rather than representing the oppressions of race and gender as types of equatable suffering, the narrative suggests that constructions of race and gender are intimately linked and operate in complex relations with one another. The narrative itself exposes the colonial white woman's contradictory position, her implication in colonial violence, her interpellation as a sexualized object, and also the signs of what McClintock calls 'racial stigmata' which are attributed to Sonia. The focus of sexual energies around her from the other women extends to the point that she takes on the narrator's fiancé as her new lover, which the narrator appears resigned to and complaisant of. But also her flamboyance appears paradoxically raced: her sexualized image which is so readily consumed by the white men has a racial aspect; her black and white bedroom appears pointedly mischievous; black and white stripes in the bedroom are not merely avant-garde, they are suggestive of the most forbidden of sexual liaisons in the colonies. The narrator also comments that Sonia is reputed to have 'some coloured blood', which the narrator 'reads' from her behaviour when she crouches on her living room floor, 'like a native in his hut' whilst a storm passes overhead.

At the heart of such a throwaway comment is the intimation of a profound instability in the construction of white colonial identities. Whilst whiteness is appealed to as an indisputable essence, a clear division between colonized and colonizer, this story suggests it is little more than an ideological necessity, for the continuation of dominance. Its production in colonial discourse is reliant on its inscription on women's bodies. Sonia's white identity is an impossible contradiction, a performance that is accepted as the 'real thing', revealing the discursive construction of white femininity. Physically, her body, clothes and house offers a space upon which the redundancy of the colonial project is rehearsed in collusion with the English nurses. Here the 'civilizing mission' of the white woman appears as a gross parody, flamboyantly exaggerated until its ideological status is revealed.

Sonia's murder underlines the contradictions of her transformation, recalling as it must the initial murdered black child who had looked in at her through her bedroom window. The child's murder is punishable by a six-year sentence but Sonia's murder is a hanging offence. Yet this apparent valuing of a white life above a black one appears as no more than the ambivalence of colonial discourse, in that the 'protection' of women which extenuates the first murder, is belied by the violent retribution of the second. Rather, by connecting both deaths, the ambivalent logic of white colonial femininity and that of the civilizing and taming of colonial discourse is revealed, where 'protection' is merely an alibi for white male intimidation of the black native population and for policing of white women. The equation of the murder of a black child for the indiscretion of glimpsing a white women suckling her baby with Sonia's double infidelity (sexual and cultural) returns as the outrage haunting the narrative. This is the horrible paradox of Sonia's brief transformation.

Ultimately refusing the possible roles in colonial Rhodesia, the English nurse narrating decides to leave Southern Rhodesia and return to England. This conclusion appears not escapist or an act of avoidance of the hard political facts of white oppression in Africa, but as a conscious personal decolonization, necessitated by a recognition of complicity with rather than detachment from the operations of colonial power. This is suggestive of Spivak's injunction to the critic to interrogate that position or identity which one cannot avoid inhabiting. In this case though, self-reflexiveness results in the rejection of an untenable position, the only moral choice possible in the narrative.

This choice is however marked by the privileges of class and nationality. The narrator saves herself, just as Sybil escapes from the madness of the passion-fruit farmers. Both texts might seem anxious to draw a line between the racially organized colonial context and the relative safety of England, but as Spark demonstrates in 'Bang-Bang, You're Dead', the images of long-dead lovers and friends return through the spectral medium of the home movie, and play themselves over repeatedly in the English living room. The images of colonial 'splendour' already fetishized and misread by the watching audience, appear as ghosts from the future (as yet unrecognized), pregnant with the imminence of political change.

Notes

1. Jane Mackay and Pat Thane, 'The Englishwoman', in *Englishness, Politics and Culture 1880–1920*, pp. 199–229. Conflations of the terms English and British appear to be very common in colonial discourse in the late nineteenth and early twentieth century. Mackay and Thane suggest that despite a desire to differentiate between the different ethnic or national groups in

Britain the exegiencies of the British Empire demanded a claim to a 'British race'.

2. E. M. Forster *A Passage to India* (Penguin: London, 1936).

3. See 'The Portobello Road', 'The Curtain Blown by the Breeze', 'Bang-Bang You're Dead', 'The Go-Away Bird', all in *The Collected Stories*.

4. For detailed discussions of the construction of colonial white women in India see Jenny Sharpe, *Allegories of Empire: The Figure of the Woman in the Colonial Text* (Minneapolis: University of Minneapolis Press, 1993); for discussion of colonial desire and miscegenation see Robert Young, *Colonial Desire: Hybridity in Theory, Culture and Race* (London and New York: Routledge, 1995), Chapters 6 and 7.

5. Anne McClintock, *Imperial Leather: Race, Gender and Sexuality in the Colonial Contest* (New York and London: Routledge, 1995), p. 378.

6. For an in-depth analysis of the role of white women in the 'Tweede Trek', see Anne McKlintock, *Imperial Leather*, Chapter 10.

7. Ann McClintock, *Imperial Leather*, p. 47.

7
A Bit of the Other: *Symposium*, Futility and Scotland

Alan Freeman

In preparing the dinner party that the action of *Symposium* revolves around, Hurley Reed visits two of his invited guests, William Damien and his mysterious new wife, Margaret. Referring to her new, rich and influential mother-in-law, Margaret describes Hilda Damien as being immersed in the philosophy of *Les Autres*:

> 'The philosophy', said Margaret, 'of *Les Autres* is a revival of something old. Very new and very old. It means we have to centre our thoughts and actions away from ourselves and entirely on to other people.'
> 'Oh, meaning the others. Why is it expressed in French?'
> 'It's a French movement,' said Margaret. 'Well, Hilda, as I say, exemplifies *La Philosophie des Autres*. She really does.'
> 'Good, well, we'll see you on the 18th. Ten of us, informal.' Hurley left half of his drink, and William saw him to the door.'
> 'Isn't she wonderful?' said William. 'An amazing sweet character. Do you know where we met?'
> 'Where?'
> 'Marks and Spencer's. I was buying fruit. Do you know what she said? – She said, "Be careful, those grapefruits look bruised." And so they were.'
> 'Good luck,' said Hurley Reed.
>
> (S, p. 35)

This passage illustrates central elements of the novel, which depicts the organization and execution of the dinner party. Scenes interchange between the dinner itself, usually reported in the present tense, and the events surrounding it, in the weeks beforehand, delivered in past tense. We learn much about the characters before they get together around the dinner table and, in characteristic Spark style, dialogue implies as much as it says; undercurrents abound.

As this scene suggests, the characters are educated, sophisticated inhabitants of metropolitan life, for whom evening drinks and chat about philosophy are commonplace. They are also, largely, liberal-arts orientated, creative rather than commercial, concerned with the common weal along with their private wealth. They share with Margaret a concern for others and admiration for Hilda Damien, the media magnate. Hilda, here, is discovered via other characters' opinion of her; and so indeed is everyone concerned. Further, William appears somewhat naive about his whirlwind romance, eager to find merits in minor details of his wife's manner; the wily Hurley is less convinced. In their exchange, Margaret's rather arch altruism is sidestepped by both men. Such minor disjunctions will gather momentum among the guests-to-be, as their discomfort with Margaret crystallizes into specific suspicions about her motivations and past. Her philosophy will have its most dramatic effect in unintended ways for all concerned, as their surface impressions give way to deeper narratives, which in turn are underpinned by assumptions from which none of the cast would imagine they suffer. Contemporary perspectives on cultural formations generally and on Scotland's in particular are placed within Spark's artistic vision. Margaret herself will be treated according to her reputation, constructed as other to the others, as local presumption infests a metropolitan elite, in a tale of aspiration and futility.

I

Spark's novels often address the relation of realism and the surreal, of body and spirit, the patterns by which *we* order our experience. Plato's *Symposium* concludes with Socrates hectoring Aristophanes and Agathon into accepting that the traditional separation of comedy and tragedy is artificial, and that they are in fact aspects of a larger whole, and Spark's *Symposium* shares with Socrates the rejection of tidy demarcation of our experience within an order amenable to our mortal knowledge.[1] Beneath the surface of her wit, humanity is portrayed in its stark limitation, higher harmony by implication unknowable to us.[2] 'With its array of Catholics, butlers, bachelors, nuns, charlatans, malign plotters and the super-rich, its self-reflexive asides and prolepses, and its passing biblical quotes and mentions of Venice', as Ian Rankin observes, '*Symposium* comprises a veritable compendium of its author's concerns'.[3] The novel goes on to locate these in the generalities of the New Europe emerging from an expanding European Community (as it was then called), and the declining Soviet empire at the start of the present decade: the new freedom benefits the mobile few, a bourgeois elite which crosses state frontiers to arrange the cultures its exponents readily traverse. And the novel also comes back to Scotland, to play with literary and cultural expressions of its peripheral status within these secular structures.

In both respects, as we would expect from Spark, it is not quite historical reality or social realism that she addresses, but the historical relativism of their perception: the *invention* of meaning that is a community, whether confined to a few individuals or encompassing a nation. Her fiction accords with contemporary identification of the local and historically specific basis of cultural value. If God is inaccessible under the sun, the transcendental ideal remains out of reach and the 'universal' value is no more than the dominant mortal one. The plots of many of Spark's novels turn on the attempts by her characters to create meaning for their lives, often by open deceit, though also at times through self-delusion. Her acerbic comedy confirms the absurdity and the profanity of assuming divine knowledge, and narrative detachment from such efforts provides discreet commentary on the accuracy of characters' claims. One effect of Spark's portrayals is a rootless quality which can be as disturbing as the strange events she depicts. The characters who wander through London or Venice or Tuscany are oddly unspecific, unconnected to each other, or to place; the London whose portrayal in Spark's early novels led to her celebration as a realist writer, for example, is peopled by two-dimensional individuals who belie the usual concerns of realism. And of course they frequently reveal quite bizarre traits such as hearing themselves being written as characters in a novel, or believing their friends to be Satan. Their quest for transcendental meaning may involve religious interest, usually of the quack variety; more often it features paid inventors of fictions, or those paid to discover truths: the writers, actors and producers of film and literature, and the detectives and spies who labour to create or uncover reality.

But the ambitions and actions of central figures always end in failure, as what is serious on their social level is found to be futile, and incidentals overlooked by everyone affect plot outcomes. In *The Public Image* (1968), actress Annabel Christopher manipulates the image which is making her famous, in competition with her husband Frederick who sets out to sell another version for profit. That Annabel's public image in Spark's novel obscures quite different depths beneath her surface is an age-old, indeed classical, trope; and that in the world of modern media the condition of celebrity should most pointedly exemplify this disjunction is enjoyable if not startling. But Sparks's acute insight identifies her characters accepting their reputations as real and reality as false; and most importantly, she shows the relation of the two: as far as can be understood on our mortal plane, human reality may to all intents become what its manipulators make it. But this invention will never constitute a higher truth, and Annabel will share with many a Spark protagonist an outcome quite different from that desired or expected. That she takes on the fuller import of her Madonna-like posturing implies without explanation a larger, Catholic frame of reference beyond mortal machinations in the novel. Contemporary relativism is itself relativized within the unstated absolute to which the narrative alludes.

Likewise, the writing of reality is contested by Sandy Stranger and Jean Brodie in Spark's *The Prime of Miss Jean Brodie* (1961), as the pupil resists her teacher's schemes. Just as Sandy listens to Miss Brodie with 'double ears', so must the reader: the narrative largely comprises their competing accounts of both what takes place, and what it means. Having designated herself as some kind of deity, and her girls as the Elect, Miss Brodie's efforts all come to nothing, her plans failing at every turn. She is quite devoid of God-like powers after all. Sandy similarly steps outside moral convention to betray her erstwhile mentor. She too seeks a higher truth, but is also doomed to frustration. Having disavowed this world, a world of transient, ersatz values, she cannot discover another. God's realm is inaccessible to our personal stories, and for Sandy, truth remains stranger than fiction. She ends the novel enigmatically, clutching the grille through which the public may speak with her. Placed outside of this life, but also cut off from the other she seeks, Sandy is caught between them, a prisoner on either side of the grille. In these novels, the pursuit of causal effect of a higher nature flounders on the futility of human agency, as dreams turn to dust, and actions lead mostly nowhere. Spark presents a twentieth-century version of *The Vanity of Human Wishes*, though mercifully with more laughs. *Symposium* provides us with a world being written from the centre by the voices of evolving modernity, alongside a fictional reality that refuses to succumb to that merely human imposition.

II

'This is rape!', expostulates Brian Suzy, the wheedling Lord, 'This is violation!', to be followed by the narrator's blank contradiction: 'This was not rape, it was a robbery.' (S, p. 7) From the first, *Symposium* switches between third person, first person and free indirect narrative styles. Within a credible realist report of the aftermath of the Suzys' robbery, we see the dissonance between people familiar with each other, their social relations arbitrary, an awkward fit owing more to expediency than to depth of inter-personal communication. Peace is disturbed by unpredictability, and we are warned that truth, whether closely resembling or far removed from our subjective interpretation, should not be taken as identical with it. In the midst of plotting, mad Uncle Magnus 'poured himself a drink of the liquid, good malt whisky as it was, and continued his discourse' (S, p. 153). Discreetly confirming the relativism of outlook, the word 'discourse' acts like an editorial disclaimer, alerting us that the opinions expressed herein should not be identified with those of the author – whether Spark, or the one upstairs. Devoid of social as well as higher grace, Lord Suzy will continue his self-pitying whine throughout the dinner-party, imposing on the other guests his account of what the robbery means to him. Transforming a robbery into a rape is the conversion of fact into metaphor; and this process of interpretation becomes central to the stories the characters tell themselves and each other about their lives. Spark brilliantly captures the artistic practise at the heart of ordinary experience, in which inner subjectivity mediates external fact. The range of characters also share with Suzy a degree of self-absorption beyond their own insight. Each is the centre of his or her solipsistic universe. And where their views appear to coincide, we discover the local cultural presumptions underpinning them. The range of discourses passed around the table cohere around three recognizable, influential narratives.

Firstly, there is the broad practice of self-composition. The dinner party itself, the symposium, is emphatically the composition of the creative Chris Donovan and Hurley Reed, as they fuss to achieve the right balance of people, lighting, food, wine and liqueurs. Their guests share with them a stake in constructing reality. The waiter, Luke, is a history student who advises his friends the Untzingers to move to Bloomsbury, with all its literary associations. Roland Sykes is an investigator. Though an honest one, as the narrator points out, his name and job are reminiscent of Dickens's low-life Bill, and of that great star of the dumbing of contemporary television's ideals, Roland Rat. Annabel Treece is an assistant TV producer; Margaret Damien *née* Murchie herself works temporarily in televisual research, while her new husband William specializes in artificial intelligence. Hilda Damien is a media magnate, Australian by origin but easy in her internationalism, a burgeoning female Rupert Murdoch. Ernst Untzinger, a European Community financier who commutes between Brussels and London, comments on the inability of TV to be accurate: 'Can't the television make it more convincing?' (S, p. 25) Is being convincing or convinced the same as being true? Hurley Reed is to be the subject of a TV documentary, and gives advice regarding representational authenticity in the making of a programme about an artist. Assuming his own form of omnipotence, he maintains his mastery of all he surveys. Of any activity he undertook, he asserts, 'I would know how to do it' (S, p. 57). Whether economically powerful or specialists in language, history or the visual arts, the inhabitants of this milieu enjoy social status, their beliefs standing for the higher value. They shape the way that reality is viewed in a containing, or framing process, which features throughout Spark's novels.

From the start, preferred compositions cannot be held in place, and limitations are not hard to find. The clatter of a serving fork as Ernst Untzinger attempts to touch the waiter, Luke, breaks the aesthetic order of the dinner table, while Suzy's recurring invocations of rape tarnish the hosts' canvas like a misplaced daub. Hurley tells Suzy's second wife, Helen, about St. Uncumber, to whom women might pray for assistance in relieving them of their spouses. The young woman's murmured reply, 'Then I might try the Uncumber method', (S, p. 13) confirms the insecurity of the Suzys' marriage, but also the unreliability of such societal institutions. We hear of the translator in Brussels who interprets everything wrongly during an international meeting before running around threatening everyone with a knife: 'The world is going mad', Ernst bewails (S, p. 174), his words spoken before the party, though recorded late in the novel, making the parallel between two symposia whose assumed cosmopolitan accomplishment, uniformity of language, purpose and belief, are suddenly rent asunder. 'Simultaneous interpreters have nervous problems', Ella replies to her husband, her observation applying beyond that specialist career. For the interpreter in Brussels, and the interpreters at the dinner party, words appear to exist as objects as much as they represent other things: 'Ernst often said one thing with reference to another' (S, p. 174). The apprehension of reality flounders on its collapse into metaphor, language refusing to yield stability. An absolute order may inhere in reality but is not available to even the smartest set. The deepest human insights join the most banal in this narrative characterization as simultaneously local and alien, subjective and absurd.

Where Jean Brodie leads her pupils through the Grassmarket in Edinburgh, providing them with a glimpse of another reality beyond their ken, like a window on another world, in *Symposium* we are introduced to alternative belief systems adhered to by the characters. Most striking is the curious innovation of the nuns who displace their Christian grand narrative with that of Marxism. As Sister Lorne is reported by Margaret to remark, 'there is no power in Church or State that can stop the inexorable march of Marxism into the future' (S, p. 105). The nuns' historical materialism flies in the face of traditional Christian spirituality, as well as its moral injunctions against violence, adultery, and theft; theirs is a polarizing pattern, supplanting a truth of the spirit with one of the flesh, the inevitable triumph of the proletariat. When the Bishop sends a dictionary to Sister Marrow to discourage her swearing, to be rebuffed as 'a fart and a shit' (S, p. 105), we are reminded that the higher status of language, 'the accurate epithet', is moot. But it is moot for the claims of the Nuns as well as their hapless leader. History is the nuns' sacred text; and like all texts, it offers more than the conclusion they seek. Likewise, Sister Marrow's mural depicting Lenin and Marx suggests saints or a dragon to the visiting TV crew, and is described in the finished documentary as a scene from Tolstoy. The presence of the TV crew introduces another, contemporary process of framing, and Marrow's art cannot claim a final meaning. As with the mural of Alasdair Gray's infuriating Duncan Thaw (*Lanark*, 1981), interpretation will continue to elude the closure sought by its creator.

Sister Lorne's ideology is also 'the result of thinking of *les autres*' (S, p. 104), but this version of the others more markedly betrays secular patterns imposed on experience when giving it names and meaning. This is the attribution of otherness, another other, constituting difference as identity.[4] Such signification is premised on an implicit teleology, a prior causality, in the nuns' case that of history itself; and it requires the projection of alterity onto an identified other. For the nuns this other is the property owning classes but, as the frail Mother Superior implies in her ribald symbolist speech, not only will they fail to contribute to the onward march of history, the nuns' ideals will resolve into base motives and petty ambitions. What they believe is not actually seen; what can be seen is not believed. Acceptance of the

Mother Superior's confession to murdering Sister Rose contradicts the agreed facts, for instance, and Lorne's large-handed husband goes unquestioned. Though intended to honour Truth, the nun's actions serve merely their ambitious sister: their holy aspirations are ultimately forlorn. As well as the coincidence of Margaret's presence among them, the nuns are linked to the party guests by this projection of construed identity. The episode at the convent ends with Margaret's indignation at Magnus's hints of her culpability: 'Do you know he [Magnus] even quoted Schopenhauer at me against my alibi – 'Chronology is not causality.' Poor old fellow. I could sue him for that.' (S, p. 122) Suspicion seems to follow Margaret Murchie around, and typifies the response of the party guests to her arrival in their lives.

The second discourse proffered in the novel is the tale of Margaret's evil. This echoes the dismissal by Chris and Hurley of their Mauritian chef Corby in terms of his racial otherness: 'Of course Mauritius still has a very primitive element, you know. Their witchcraft. They sense things.' (S, p. 179) Following a similar pattern, the hosts and their guests construe Margaret according to her Scottishness, in all its traditional alterity to their centre. Magnus's nurse assents to his claim that nobody does sunsets better than Walter Scott – 'that's a fact' (S, p. 161) – and in this respect, Scotland is the outcome of another imaginative framing process. Margaret certainly presents as a Scot of gothic splendour, attractive, striking, odd and discomfiting, a Scot of the Scott kind. Faced with Hurley's initial scepticism Chris continues to elaborate Hilda's anxieties: 'She [Hilda] told me that it was very spooky there in Fife at the wedding. Nothing you could put your finger on':

> 'Oh, that's Scotland. All the families are odd, very odd.'
> 'Hilda said', Chris went on, 'that they weren't so odd. In fact they were too much all right.'
>
> (S, p. 87)

So in classic binary caricature Margaret is cleaved into excessive strangeness *and* excess ordinariness, a status at once above and beyond the level of her metropolitan observers, and beneath them. Scottishness becomes the source and explanation of her other-worldliness and her apparent potential mendacity. Projected outwith the rational realm the guests imagine they inhabit, Margaret constitutes an active threat to the material trappings on which their social status is founded. She embodies for them the return of that which their culture represses. A pallid Pict and dark-skinned primitives alike can be conflated into one cartoon of special senses, arcane knowledge, under-developed ethics. Vague unease experienced by those who meet the strange bride cohere into specific fears about her motives for marrying William Damien, namely, that she must be after his mother's money: since she appears to have engineered the meeting with William, she must be devious and scheming. And that she could cause William to fall in love with her equates with aptitude beyond the ordinary. Margaret must has special agency, and she clearly intends some evil. You'd think there must be an EU directive against such scapegoating but, no, Margaret is convicted as a sister weird.

Margaret's ability to enter into bourgeois London life and still retain a difference coloured by Scotland's distinctive cultural traditions reflects the curious ambivalence of Scotland within the British imperium. Jocks on the make have always enjoyed mobility across the expanding empire, contributing to the subjugation of many non-white peoples in its name; and yet they have also always remained partly distinguished by their otherness within Britain. The relation between Scottish markers of identity and those of the metropolitan centre are inextricably linked, each dependent on the other for its formation, other to each other, in an awkward little reel. Scots have traditionally been defined in opposition to the civilized and moderate centre, but so too have they enjoyed the terms of opposition to the putative material comfort and narrow consciousness of that centre, and Spark's characters play out this interdependence. Just as Jean Brodie scorns Scottish vowels, many a Scot has adopted a bourgeois English accent to get on in Britain. Accommodating to the bourgeois pronunciation of her name, Margaret shifts from Murchie to 'murky'. 'Here in Scotland', opines Magnus, champion of Scottish folklore, 'people are more capable of perpetrating good or evil than anywhere else' (S, p. 159). The mad uncle frequently affirms the witchiness of his niece via the ballad tradition so often invoked by Spark:

> O was it a wer-wolf in the wood,
>   Or was it a mermaid into the sea,
> Or was it a man or a vile woman,
>   My true love that mis-shapit thee?

> (S, p. 141)

Symposium plays with the cultural artefacts by which collective iden-tity in the land of her birth is forged, manipulated, trivialized, shaped and misshaped.

Of course, matters aren't helped by the evidence which does then come to hand. Following another key trope in Spark's fiction, strange events accumulate, defying the cast and the reader to resist assuming underlying connections. In this case our awareness of the already recounted murders of Margaret's grandmother and Sister Rose is supplemented by revelation of the mysterious drowning of a school friend and disappearance of a teacher, each while in Margaret's company during her childhood. Such evidence inevitably points to the common participant; it is difficult not to ascribe causal agency to the strange Scot. We are restricted to circumstantiality and our own scale of probabilities, which suggest the sequence extends beyond coincidence. Directly or indirectly, Margaret must be implicated. And so Margaret herself accedes to the otherness attributed to her over the years, and the scheme to lure a rich husband and secure his fortune gets underway. That the projected plan and the chain of events which take place so resemble each other leads Magnus to assert success, but the facts are not that reliable. Warren McDiarmid, the first target selected by sticking a pin in a list, shows no interest in the beautiful redhead; when the pin sticks between two names, Magnus recommends Werther Stanhope rather than William Damien; Magnus claims accuracy in predicting the suicide of Stanhope when it is McDiarmid who does the deed. No more than similar to their scheme, coincidence does not confirm causal effect. In keeping with the wealth of sinister events to which Margaret has found herself adjacent in her life, the climactic murder of her new mother-in-law evades her active agency too. As the narrator notes, Margaret's parents might have been consoled if they could have seen that, 'there was absolutely no link of any rational, physical or psychological nature between Margaret's personal activities and what went on around her' (S, p. 142). Trust Schopenhauer: chronology is not causality, proximity is not participation.

As incriminating as the facts appear, as much as the guests suspect her of unnatural influence, and no matter how hard she herself believes in her capacity to do evil, Margaret cannot alter her destiny. She is condemned to coincidence, the world in which she finds herself unamenable to her will. Enacting the designated other to Spark's effete elite fails; there is no wicked witch of the East Neuk, and another narrative of self-creation founders on human futility. Scots may believe themselves doomed, as Private Fraser used to proclaim in *Dad's Army*, but with Spark they're doomed to be unsure if they're doomed. Inconclusiveness underlies the extremes imagined: perhaps this is more typically Scottish, a metaphysical nil–nil draw. Far from possessing a special propensity for evil, Spark's Scots join the rest in displaying gullibility, complacency and superstition over and above the intelligence on which their social status is putatively based. Under their very noses, meanwhile, the facts of the story unfold.

The third discourse in the novel is that which underlies the other two. Postmodern art has broken the demarcation between high and low; Spark has always enjoyed pricking the presumption of higher art, and her worlds can lapse into the crassest of cliché, stock responses and plot outcomes. As characters attempt to make reality accord with their own accounts of it, events, as described by the narrator, share more with genre fiction rather than aspirational art. *Symposium* is a whodunnit, in which the random element – to human eyes – is responsible for the multiple mortalities, including Hilda's murder; and the detection of the criminals by the prosaic-minded constabulary is swift and simple: all the clues are in the opening chapter and, far from malign arcana, the plot ends in 'a fair cop, guv'nor'. Innocent of all charges, Margaret's assumed guilt is the kind of framing process found in crime fiction.

Oblivious to the connections which intertwine them, characters ignore literal facts in favour of social symbols. Suzy's conversion of robbery into rape starts proceedings; the end is upon them when he remarks that robbers want dinner guests to discuss their treasures in front of inside-informants, blind to the fact that he is doing exactly this throughout the dinner. For poor Hilda too, the frame in which she places reality fails the test of truth. Like the artwork whose intended theft leads to her death, Hilda's reality is just an impression; supreme materialist that she is, it's a case of her Monet or her life. Wry laughter greets the name of Charterhouse the butler, but association with the prestigious school in his employers' minds outweighs the suspicions of a dark-skinned chef. And in the case of handsome Luke, the guests miss the hint in his name. The Untzingers even concoct exotic tales of sexual adventure to explain his inappropriate affluence, preferring to invent when they only had to look. Which is why they fail to recognize an outcome determined by the oldest cliché of the crime genre: in the end, it was the butler wot did it. Ridiculing the vanity, presumption and power of the metropolitan sub-culture, the novel satirizes colonial dreams of final control. It's not concerned with the specifics of Scottishness, or even the failure written into influential scripts of Scottishness by the metropolitan centre; rather, it points to the futility of any attempt to impose such a script in absolute terms on reality at all. The relation of metropolitan centrality and Scottish marginality appears powerful but mutable, and destiny remains a whodunnit beyond human detection.

Among the meanings mobilized by the events of the novel, a curious one emerges from the coincidences and collisions to tease a progressive reader. Should an alternative causality be inferred from the chronology of the action, we might consider the changing of the grandmother's will by the Murchie family. If the error of the cast in the novel is to presume higher agency, then here is a major example. The alteration replaces equal inheritance among the family with primogeniture. Grandmother's money was her own, we are told, not her husband's: a democratic order is superseded by a patriarchal one, fairness by arbitrariness. Perhaps there is a causal sequence at work in what follows, the consequences of another human transgression? After all, the women in the story appear more worthy than the presumptuous men; Hurley acts as a deity, but Chris funds his life and is more capable; even her name is closer to Christ. Ah well, that's another story. Like the businessman whose brief appearance ends the novel in recognition that he has an extraordinary tale to tell, the connections continue, the final pattern still unseen. Spark's characters seek to write their lives, all the while enacting a life sentence of a higher author's devising. In pursuit of wholeness, of body and spirit, of here and the beyond, they set about dividing, hierarchizing and projecting otherness onto individuals and cultures in all too traditional human terms, aspiring, conniving and expiring. New Europe, old error: *Symposium* is a caustic little novel which restates Socrates's refusal of simple demarcations while revisiting the cliches of Spark's native culture; its cast members aspire to deification while indulging in a bit of the other, convinced of their superiority, condemned to futility.

Notes

1. See Lorna Sage, 'Seeing Things as They are', *Critical Essays on Muriel Spark*, ed. Joseph Hynes (New York: G.K. Hall & Co., 1992), pp. 275–8.
2. See Ruth Whittaker, *The Faith and Fiction of Muriel Spark* (London: Macmillan Press Ltd, 1982).
3. Ian Rankin, 'The Deliberate Cunning of Muriel Spark', *The Scottish Novel since the Seventies*, eds Gavin Wallace and Randall Stevenson (Edinburgh: Edinburgh University Press, 1993), pp. 41–53, p. 50.
4. Edward W. Said, *Culture and Imperialism* (London: Vintage Books, 1993), p. 201.

Part III
Deconstruction

'... postmodernist, mostly, whatever that means.'

Muriel Spark, 'The Same Informed Air'

8
Muriel Spark's Uselessness

Jeremy Idle

I

In *Prague to Paris*, J. G. Merquior's polemic against avant-garde Parisian and para-Parisian thought, Georges Bataille has a cameo role as a bookish, impotently evil Walter Mitty, in a world not too distant from those of *The Comforters* or *Loitering with Intent*:

> A quiet librarian dreaming of violence and of violation, [Georges Bataille] was a prize instance of a typical figure among the French intelligentsia: the pyromaniac in slippers, the wild barbarian who does not hurt a fly. But this Sunday immoralist was to haunt the post-existentialist mind.[1]

Merquior's Bataille would fascinate Muriel Spark: this study will indicate possibilities of a Sparkian reading of Bataille while attempting to justify a Bataillean reading of Spark. Merquior's rapid dismissal of Bataille makes one wonder if he would have liked Bataille better if the Bibiliothéque Nationale were a more dangerous place to work in, and if the work of a thinker is invalid if its practicalities are questionable. The creativity of Bataille's imagination is ignored in *Prague to Paris*. Trusting Bataille outside the library would be like trusting Freud inside the consulting room, but this is no reason to ignore his provocative ideas on waste, excess and evil.

The vehemence of Merquior's condemnation is matched by the breathless approval of some of Bataille's interpreters. Denis Hollier celebrates Bataille as a proto-deconstructionist in *Against Architecture*, showing how his work embodies the endlessly splitting nature of meaning in an ambitious, playful piece which attempts to '*write* on Bataille' rather than simply 'writing *on* Bataille'.[2] Nick Land is also *write* on, his Bataillean meditation in *The Thirst for Annihilation* recording the impulse to vomit at mere writers *on*, accusing deconstruction of 'playing with its willy', and, most daringly, claiming that he stayed up terribly late to write the book, sometimes after three o'clock in the morning.[3] In a paper by John Lechte in *Textual Practice*, reading Bataille seems to involve a continual confusion of painful shuddering and great joy, especially at the sexy bits.[4] There are, though, cooler evaluations: Michael Richardson attempts an empirical evaluation of Bataille as anthropologist, and a corrective Geoff Bennington subjects Bataille's notions of general and restricted economies to deconstructive assault.[5] This paper, inspired by the concerns of *The Accursed Share*, will avoid the overheated language of Land and Lechte while asserting Bataille's usefulness for literary criticism.

The first volume of Bataille's *The Accursed Share* details the lavish, non-recoverable expenditures of different pre-modern societies on human sacrifice (among the Aztecs), potlatch (destruction of one's own goods among Native Americans), holy war (in Early Islamic tradition) and monasticism (in Tibet).[6] Western capitalism, so intent on accumulation, rationality and planning, is odd one out. A broad logic of comparison works here, even if the verdict on capitalism is incomplete, the interpretation of Aztec culture is flawed, and the use of Mauss on gift-giving is characterized by strong misreading. Bataille then describes his theoretical object in later volumes as 'a general critique of the ideas that subordinate man's activity to ends other than the useless consumption of their resources' as 'it is a matter of discrediting those ways of looking at the world that are the basis of servile forms'[7] and of identifying our 'sovereign moments' when 'nothing matters except what is there' in antithesis to the attention and demands of the future.[8] Crudely put, every useful act is useless because in the long run we are all dead, and every useless act is useful in that it challenges our slavery to mere necessity. Key ideas of *The Accursed Share,* such as excess, expenditure and loss, find varying expression in such work as *Theory of Religion, Eroticism, Inner Experience* and *Literature and Evil*.[9] Bataille's categories are generally useful for literary interpretation; they are particularly useful for Spark.

Muriel Spark's fiction contains an abundance of actions which lead to nothing, of cancelling movements, of excessive expenditures. Her characters buy or steal unnecessary clothes, die pointlessly, conceive useless poems and frivolous fictions, waste time, take days off work, teach useless subjects and pointlessly thrust letters into others' pockets. Others pathetically attempt to save things up, like money, cakes and matches; others still – seen much more positively – dwell on the importance of the gift. Spark's interest in extravagance and the useless relates in part to the rational, calculating accumulation problematized some time ago by Jesus Christ – 'You fool! This very night your life will be demanded from you' says God to the farmer who complacently accumulates in the parable of Luke 12: 16–21 – and more recently by Max Weber, who makes his scorn obvious for Benjamin Franklin's mania not to waste a second of time.[10] There is also Norman Brown, who thinks that Protestantism is anal.[11] But though her fiction would not wholeheartedly endorse the prodigal expenditure of time, money, energy and bodily fluids advocated in George Bataille's writing – 'pisseur de copie' (K, p. 49) is hardly a compliment to Hector in *A Far Cry from Kensington* – Spark's expenditures go beyond any formulaic 'Catholic' disagreement with the accumulation ethic into her own idiosyncratic territory.

Some critics, Catholic or just over-friendly, represent Spark as some kind of model Catholic who would never dream of forcing religious principles beyond due bounds. The issue is, however, an open one. Bataille's work on art, evil, money and death enables a rereading of Muriel Spark's work. The two writers share similar concerns, though they are, admittedly, hardly natural allies. Spark is so often withering about the sort of barminess that excited Bataille:

> 'He ought to pay you for all that work,' Alice had said. But to Elsie it was a labour of love typing out all [Father Socket's] papers on the subjects of the Cabbala, Theosophy, Witchcraft, Spiritualism, and Bacon wrote Shakespeare, beside many other topics.
> 'It's a labour of love,' Elsie said to Alice.
>
> (BA, p. 118)

II

However vainly, Bataille wants art to be useless. The arts in general are included in his list of 'unproductive expenditures' (why war?) in the early essay which laid the foundations for *The Accursed Share*:

> The second part [of consumption] is represented by so-called unproductive expenditures: luxury, mourning, war, cults, the construction of sumptuary monuments, games, spectacles, arts,

perverse sexual activity ... all these represent activities which, at least in primitive circumstances, have no end beyond themselves.[12]

Another essay from the 1930s, 'The Psychological Structure of Fascism', develops the concept of 'the heterogeneous', the 'trash' on the margins of society which cannot be reconciled to it, which includes 'vermin ... dreams ... mobs ... the warrior, the aristocratic and impoverished classes ... those who refuse the rule (madmen, leaders, poets, etc.)'[13] While these idealizations of artistic activity clash – the first list concerning an older state-organized activity and the second an activity opposed to the state – the idea of unproductive expenditure still links them. But Bataille also describes types of art which make their peace with orthodoxy and are complicit with a kind of unwelcome production. In *Literature and Evil* he breezily dismisses Romanticism's challenge to utilitarian society: 'There is obviously nothing less dangerous, less subversive, or even less wild than the wildness of rocks.'[14]

Romanticism is, then, mere compensation (unless we're talking about Blake or Emily Brontë). Mere beauty is another pitfall for art. In the notes to the bizarre 'L'impossible', he denounces bland art: 'If there is no subversion, poetry stays trapped in the realm of everyday activity, which reduces it to the status of merely "beautiful poetry", that is, pure rhetoric, or poetic verbiage.'[15]

In Spark's *Mandelbaum Gate* Abdul, a Jordanian, reads a private letter sent home by Freddy Hamilton, a British diplomat and friend. The letter speaks of trying to find a rhyme for 'Capricorn' to put in a poem – the technical exercises of Fleur in *Loitering with Intent* are similar. Abdul's response:

> He was fascinated by the entire vision of that state of heart in which one wrote to a Fellow of All Souls about a rhyme for Capricorn. It could not result in any large benefit to Hamilton or his friends, nor could this piece of information damage Hamilton's enemies. It was disinterested and therefore beautiful, even if it was useless to the immediate world. And this was something Abdul could never make his middle-class Arab acquaintance understand – how it was possible to do things for their own sake, not only possible but sometimes necessary for the affirmation of one's own personal identity.
>
> (MG, p. 88)

For Bataille, this sort of unsubversive poetry, this poetry which does not grasp after infinity and the unknowable, would be irredeemable. The poetry does, though, function as a fairly disinterested gift, in a novel centering on disinterested gifts, such as the seeds of flowers scattered by the British in Israel, and the main character's pilgrimage, characterized as a gift to God.

Freddy might seem elsewhere to devote himself to the sacralizing of written material, the purposeless splendour of the moment and the acceptance of the impossibility of permanence, when he flushes burnt letters down the toilet (MG, p. 138) or burns what he claims is a poem in front of Suzy, Abdul's sister, 'as a symbol of consummation' (MG, p. 239). In the latter case, though, he is destroying intelligence information in order to stop it falling into the hands of a possible enemy. Spark enjoys destructive fires, given that gerontological research burns in *Memento Mori*, Mary McGregor burns in *The Prime of Miss Jean Brodie* and The May of Teck Club burns in *The Girls of Slender Means*; but while these are random and capricious, Freddy's burning is the reverse. If Suzy had Bataille's passion for sacrificial destruction, though, she might have taken Freddy at his word.

The division between art and utility, so apparently clear-cut in *The Mandelbaum Gate*, was more problematic for Mill and Arnold. Mill, preaching to the cultured in *Utilitarianism*, claimed that 'every writer, from Epicurus to Bentham, who maintained the theory of utility', included 'the agreeable or the ornamental' among useful things.[16] Conversely, Arnold, preaching to the Philistines in *Culture and Anarchy*, proposed that 'culture' included 'all the love of our neighbour, the impulses towards action, help and beneficence, the desire for removing human error, clearing human confusion, and diminishing human misery'.[17] Does utility subsume culture, or vice versa? Spark's *Ballad of Peckham Rye* dramatizes some extreme consequences of the former assumption. Druce, a factory general manager at Meadows, Meade and Grindlay, tells Dougal Douglas, an incoming personnel consultant and arts graduate from Edinburgh University, that 'industry and the arts must walk hand in hand' (BP, p. 15). If Druce's phrasing suggests an equal partnership, his aim is to harness, to make whatever Dougal has learnt at Edinburgh University about the ordinary human emotions to serve the needs of production targets. Druce has previously taken on 'a Cambridge man' to perfect factory routines with a time-and-motion study, obtaining 'the least loss of energy and time' (BP, p. 16). Looked at this way, there is a reciprocal logic in Dougal's aim to use whatever human material exists in the factory to serve the Bacchanalian revelry, the encouragement of absenteeism, the double-crossing of different firms and the abuse of personal confidences, which leads to a ruined wedding, frequent fighting and a murder. Dougal is provoked to cultivate waste and destruction by Druce's utilitarianism, by the obsessive, frequently-alluded to money-saving habit of his friend Humphrey's fiancé, which as Humphrey indicates 'takes the sex out of a girl' (BP, p. 57), and by the habit at the local shops of making sure Dougal, among others, wastes no money on unnecessary ounces of cheese (BP, p. 19). Horned Dougal makes industrial production deteriorate but excels in the production of stories. Dougal must be a near-relation of the Father of Lies, creatively fictionalizing his police connections, his emotional state, his availability for work, and his ghost-written old lady's life. For Alan Bold:

> There is, [Spark's] novels show, a world of difference between false faiths and spiritual aspirations, between criminal plots and fictive ploys. Art is, by its aesthetic energy, affirmative.[18]

Dougal sabotages Bold's formulation, given his false, criminal, fictive and artistic nature. Marginal and threatening ('heterogeneous' in Bataille's terms) he is a 'succubus' in the narrator's words, and in the words of other characters 'a pansy', 'probably versatile', 'handicapped', deformed', 'a cripple', 'different' and 'a diabolical agent'. He continually encourages turbulence and rule breaking around him, changing the otherwise dull rule quoting, Trade Union stalwart Humphrey such that the latter muses on his bride's germs hopping over to him as they approach the altar, and (after jilting her) pays double for his half-empty bed at his honeymoon hotel.

It is *The Prime of Miss Jean Brodie*, though, that deals most obviously with art as supplementary to life and yet essential to it. Brodie makes sure her pupils are informed on 'subjects useless to the school as a school' (P, p. 5), concentrating on art and poetry to the exclusion of the practical and scientific: 'Art is greater than science' she tells her girls (P, p. 25). Above and beyond this, though, she makes the arts the essential and everything else secondary:

> It is witty to say that a straight line is the shortest distance between two points ... it is plain witty. Everyone knows what a straight line and a circle are. (P, p. 82)

Going further than Dickens' *Hard Times* (see Valentine Cunningham's

In The Reading Gaol) which identifies fact-obsessives like Bounderby as the most indulgent rhetoricians and fictionists, Brodie identifies mathematics itself as an absurd fiction.[19] Brodie's girls thus realize that 'the solution to [mathematical] problems would be quite useless to Sybil Thorndike, Anna Pavlova and the late Helen of Troy.' (P, p. 82) Anna Pavlova, incidentally, can scream at others as she is a great actress, but Brodie does believe in restraint: she opposes Baldwin's slogan 'Safety First' not by saying that recklessness must come first but 'Goodness, Truth, and Beauty'. (P, p. 10) She is against 'a frivolous nature' like Sandy's, as the latter is too adept at parodying the Sybil Thorndike walk (P, p. 23). She claims that opening a window more than six inches is 'vulgar' (P, p. 46), makes them march in a line round Edinburgh, and preaches the gospel according to Mussolini. Thus she opposes the school's stultifying bourgeois order with her own quasi-Fascist one, as Sandy recognizes. Jean Brodie ought to have found more critical favour, given the passion of Eagleton and Kristeva for right-wingers of unsound mind like T. S. Eliot and Céline when they write anything that might upset the bourgeois liberal subject.[20]

While Brodie is a radical within the overall context of the school, and while she points in the direction of excess, exuberance and passion in actresses, literary characters and herself, she still de-radicalizes an art and literature which is perilously close to becoming, for the girls, merely a field of knowledge relevant to academic success. Few better treatments of this perpetual problem exist than Alan Chedzoy's essay 'Arnold in Coketown' which conflates the opening scene in *Hard Times* with an Arnoldian model of the 'Facts' pupils in English are expected to grasp.[21] What culture means in *Prime* is some way off from what it means in Bataille:

> In their major form, literature and theater, which constitute [the category of symbolic rather than real expenditure], provoke dread and horror through symbolic representations of tragic loss (degradation or death); in their minor form, they provoke laughter through representations which, though analogously structured, exclude certain seductive elements.[22]

For Bataille, then, literature is not merely a matter of the expenditure of ink and paper but of tears and breath. Certainly the whimsical Freddy in *Mandelbaum Gate* seems to miss out on this; art as a theme in Spark connotes the elevated and the pleasant, even if her art itself at least gestures at provocation to dread and horror, as one sees in the closing lines of *The Driver's Seat*. The police, the narrator tells us, wish to insulate themselves with their holsters and epaulets and other trappings from 'fear and pity, pity and fear' (DS, p. 107), leaving us with the possibilities of these Aristotelean modes of prescribed feeling, although the deadpan narration discourages them. Spark frequently does provide 'representations of (potentially) tragic loss', even if farce persistently haunts these tragedies.

III

Constantly hovering in *The Ballad of Peckham Rye*, death is more interesting still in *Memento Mori* and *The Driver's Seat* – not so much from the religious point of view, but from the point of view that the thought of death is terrifying and exhilarating. It is difficult, even for Christians, convincingly, to imagine anything much after death's annihilating finality. Few good novelists, however Christian they are supposed to be, have tried this century to imagine the afterlife in any sustained way. Spark's fiction, we are often told by both critics and herself, scrutinizes a world *sub specie aeternitatis*. Such a Christian *aeternitas* is flimsy, even if Spark speculates at moments.

In *The Bachelors* the speaking dead are only frauds. The 'other world' referred to at the very end of *The Ballad of Peckham Rye* is a parallel universe, not a subsequent one. 'The Portobello Road' and 'The Executor' involve a dead character making a living one feel guilty, but in each case the ghost is wandering the earth rather than anywhere else.[23] *Memento Mori* is morbidly playful: 'Lisa Brooke be damned' says a friend (MM, p. 21), not knowing she has, after taking nine months to die, died that day. A poet imagines her body burning as he attends her cremation, and suggests that Lisa has gone to hell for 'aiding and abetting' Dylan Thomas 'in his poetry so-called' (MM, p. 28). One character's spirit goes to 'God, who gave it' (MM, p. 52) and another to the 'sweet Lord' (MM, p. 115) but no further details emerge. Death is the end for Spark characters as far as the reader can see. Were it not the end, it would not be so compelling.

Memento Mori's main business is to follow the later lives of a number of old men and women and chronicles their passing. On a number of occasions a character is mysteriously told over the phone 'Remember you must die', and this offender is identified as 'Death himself' (MM, p. 142) by Mortimer, a former policeman. Most of them should be aware of death as they are so old. There are, though, those like Godfrey

Colston who worries about his wife discovering infidelities decades ago, clings on to the last vestiges of a sexuality by paying women to show him their thighs, and bizarrely saves up cakes and matches despite his comfortable wealth. The book ends with a catalogue of deaths, by accident or illness, of Godfrey, his wife and a number of others. Here death is out of everyone's control, and confirms the misery that was life, whether it comes suddenly by murder or slowly by illness and deterioration.

The crucial advice on death given by Inspector Mortimer is not taken up by others. Indeed, at the very point that it is given it is misunderstood by a minor character. For Mortimer:

> I would practise, as it were, the remembrance of death. There is no other practise which so intensifies life ... Without an ever-present sense of death life is insipid. You might as well live on the whites of eggs.
>
> (MM, p. 150)

A listener interprets witlessly: '[w]hat Mr Mortimer was saying just now about resigning ourselves to death is most uplifting and consoling. The religious point of view is too easily forgotten these days.' Mortimer's response is polite in the circumstances: 'Why, thank you, Janet. Perhaps "resigning ourselves to death" doesn't quite convey what I mean.' Resigning oneself to death is Christian; Mortimer is not recommending this. He is surely close to the stance of Bataille in 'The Practice of Joy Before Death' – a stance which is, however, perhaps satirized in the treatment of *Memento*'s perverse poet Percy at a cremation: 'each new death gave him something fresh to feel [...] he grinned like an elated wolf' (MM, p. 22). Here is Bataille's 'The Practice of Joy before Death' from *Visions of Excess*:

> Before the terrestrial world whose summer and winter order the agony of all living things, before the universe composed of innumerable turning stars, limitlessly using and consuming themselves, I can only perceive a succession of cruel splendors whose very movement requires that I die: this death is only an exploding consumption of all that was, the joy of existence of all that comes into the world.[24]

Here, on the other hand, is Spark critic Ruth Whitaker's reading of Mortimer's role. Given her guileless enthusiasm for the banal, her stance might be defined as belonging to the Meringue School of literary criticism:

> In contrast to the world of petty jealousies and ancient feuds indulged in by most of the other characters, his retirement with his wife is placid and happy. He enjoys gardening, fishing and sailing, and the visits of his grandchildren. Mrs Spark builds up a picture of the Mortimers as an ordinary, suburban couple, who, being neither self-important, nor melodramatic, accept their evident mortality with ease.[25]

Lise in *The Driver's Seat* has a solution to the problem of the control of death implied in *Memento Mori*, selecting not only the time and manner of her death but her killer also, recognizing someone who killed a few years ago but is supposed to be reformed, and ordering him to put a knife into her. He kills her as instructed, and she accurately predicts that her killer will get caught. All goes to plan, then, except that she tells him she does not want sex and he 'plunges into her' regardless before stabbing her and 'as the knife descends to her throat she screams, evidently perceiving how final is finality' (DS, p. 107). No afterlife is hinted at here. The problem of choosing death, then, is that beyond a certain moment all possibility of choice is lost forever. She has, however, selected the clothes, country and manner to die in, has worked relentlessly towards it as if it is the meaningful culmination of her life in the manner of Bataille's 'Joy Before Death'; we also see in Lise a success in final self-definition, to borrow from Bataille's 'Sacrifices', in which the moment of death finally defines a 'me' which has remained otherwise unrealized and elusive (compare the graveyard in *Memento* (p. 70) proving for Jean Taylor that 'people exist'). Thus Bataille, 'the *me* accedes to its specificity and to its integral transcendence only in the form of the *me* that dies'.[26] In 'Hegel, Death and Sacrifice' the point is elaborated:

> In order for man to reveal himself ultimately to himself, he would have to die, but he would have to do it while living – watching himself ceasing to be. In other words, death itself would have to become (self-) consciousness at the very moment that it annihilates the conscious being.[27]

Lise does her best, although at the moment of death she realizes that it is not as desirable as she thought. Her story is that of a quest for self-definition, involving aggressive and inappropriate self-assertions, the wearing of tasteless clothing combinations and the laying of a murder trail for the police following in her wake. All these trail-laying acts, such as the leaving of a passport in a taxi, are only given meaning by her death. If after death her body will mean different things to different people (she says she doesn't mind the murderer using her body sexually once she's dead), her story, her identity, will signify something to the extent of getting on European television news, even if in a Baudrillardian reading (as also with *The Public Image* or *Not to Disturb*) she will become mere simulacrum and mean not very much.

IV

Lise's end blurs sex and death in a Bataillean manner, although ideally sex for him means what *The Driver's Seat* misses, 'the negation of the isolation of the ego which only experiences ecstasy by exceeding itself, by surpassing itself in the embrace in which the being loses its solitude.'[28] Spark's sex isn't like this: egos remain isolated, as individuals refuse the risk of opening themselves up to others. Jean Brodie only 'gave' herself to a lover in the pastiche of Brontë written by an adolescent Sandy; Elsie in *The Bachelors* may have 'given and not received' but the phrase remains only a phrase, of a rather melodramatic kind. But another kind of excess related to sex in *The Bachelors* does bear examination.

The most morally impressive of the novel's males, Ronald Bridges, seems to have found a divine calling to bachelorhood which acts as a substitute for failing to become a priest or husband. Overall, though, bachelorhood is cause for suspicion (marriage is natural and God's will) and homosexuality cause for worse. Sex without usefulness equates with perversion. Moments after we are told in a Hampstead club by one of their own number that the 'filthy beasts' known as bachelors 'pee in sinks and basins', the revolting homosexual Father Socket appears (BA, p. 73). One fluid wrongly directed and going to waste indicates another. Socket is useless not only due to his sexuality but also because of his failures in perjury, business and pornography. While Bataille is most interested in willed, magnificent waste, here Spark associates useless activity with meanness and inadequacy. 'I hate queers. I want to conceive a child', says Elsie, a former acolyte of Socket's (BA, p. 161), as if homosexuals' personal non-reproduction means they must somehow act as a force against reproduction in general.

Elsie and her temporary lover Matthew Finch intellectually embarrass heterosexuality. Matthew overstates the case for universal marriage, with his unintentional irony:

> There's no justification for being a bachelor and that's the truth, let's face it. It's everyone's duty to be fruitful and multiply according to his calling either spiritual or temporal, as the case may be.
>
> (BA, p. 69)

Finch – whose fundamental claim on the reader's attention lies in his eating onions to put Elsie off sex because it will make him feel guilty – uses God's command to Noah, whose mere eight-strong family had to replenish the earth after the flood. London, with its 'six hundred and fifty-nine thousand five hundred' 'unmarried males' (Matthew's words) and ten million population is hardly in urgent need of superfertility. 'Don't be so excessive' says Ronald a little later (BA, p. 76) and he has to deal with Elsie too, who wants to 'be in love with a man and to conceive his child'. Ronald's admonition: 'You can't go round having babies all over the place. It's impractical.' (BA, p. 164) If reproduction means being 'fruitful', too much of this good thing is made to sound wanton and spendthrift. Elsie's friend, though, is pregnant for the first time; Elsie wants *one* baby to keep up with her. Ronald seems to have an aversion to the idea of childbearing. Elsie's implicit nightmare is a world full of perverted bachelors in which natural sex and thus conception and thus humanity become extinct: Ronald's implicit nightmare is a world full of stupid women copulating without discrimination and bringing forth child after child into London. Extremes, then, are to be avoided, including the extreme of homosexuality.

Spark is not always good on desire, and where she is best at it, the desire is strongest for a dress rather than a person. In *The Girls of Slender Means*, rationing and austerity in 1945 are the crucial background to a beautifully-spoken rendition of 'The Wreck of the Deutschland' getting erased from a tape for reasons of economy, to one character trying to get money by writing to famous authors and at least getting their valuable signatures back, and to the theft of a gorgeous, rustling, multicoloured floral taffeta dress – the only thing that ever makes the narrator of a Spark novel say 'Oh!' – by one of the more glamorous and slender girls of slender means (G, p. 89). The conversational exchange on the theft is classic, minimalist Spark:

'Not very nice of her to pinch another girl's dress, especially when they've all lost their wardrobes in the fire.'
'It was a Schiaparelli dress.'

(G, p. 136)

Why choose Bataille as master-thinker for a piece on Spark and utility when Marx, Weber, Mill, Brown and others might have competing claims? Because he writes with an excitement foreign to the others on going too far and the relation of excess to art, and because he provides an extensive rationale for Spark's characters to act as they do, however stupid or evil Spark may believe they are.

Elsa Schiaparelli, the designer who worked with Dali and Cocteau among others, is the perfect choice of dressmaker in *The Girls of Slender Means*. Her autobiography *Shocking Life* froths that while she had the odd interlude of negotiating with Stalin's Russia about designing the ideal cheap, utilitarian dress, more representatively she 'went up into the rarefied skies of her most fantastic imagination and set off cascades of fireworks' and that 'fantasy and ingenuity broke forth, with complete indifference to ... what was practical'.[29]

Notes

1. J.-G. Merquior, *Prague to Paris* (London: Verso, 1986), p. 112.
2. Denis Hollier, *Against Architecture: The Writings of Georges Bataille* (Cambridge: MIT Press, 1992), p. 24.
3. Nick Land, *The Thirst For Annihilation: Georges Bataille and Virulent Nihilism* (London: Routledge, 1992) pp. 155, 26, xiii.
4. John Lechte, 'George Bataille', *Textual Practice* 7:2 (1993), pp. 173–91 (p. 173).
5. Michael Richardson, *Georges Bataille* (London: Routledge, 1994); Geoffrey Bennington, 'Introduction to Economics I: Because the World is Round' in *Writing the Sacred*, ed. by Carolyn Bailey Gill (London: Routledge, 1995), pp. 46–57.
6. Georges Bataille, *The Accursed Share*, vol. 1, trans. Robert Hurley (New York: Zone, 1991).
7. Bataille, *The Accursed Share*, vols 2 and 3, trans. Robert Hurley (New York: Zone, 1993), p. 14.
8. op. cit., p. 283.
9. Bataille, *Theory of Religion; Literature and Evil; Inner Experience; Eroticism*
10. Max Weber, *The Protestant Ethic and the Spirit of Capitalism*, trans. Talcott Parsons (London: Routledge, 1992), pp. 48–52.
11. Norman Brown, *Love Against Death: The Psychoanalytical Meaning of History* (London: Routledge & Kegan Paul), pp. 234–304.
12. Bataille, 'The Notion of Expenditure', in *Visions of Excess: Selected Writings 1927–1939* (Minneapolis: University of Minnesota Press 1985), pp. 116–29 (p. 118).

13. Bataille, 'The Psychological Structure of Fascism' in *Visions*, pp. 137–60 (p. 142).
14. Bataille, *Literature and Evil* (London: Calder & Boyars, 1973), p. 42.
15. Bataille, 'L'Impossible', qt. in Marie-Christine Lala, 'The Hatred of Poetry in George Bataille's Writing and Thought' in *Writing the Sacred*, ed. by Carolyn Bailey Gill, pp. 105–116 (p. 108).
16. John Stuart Mill, *Utilitarianism* (London: Everyman, 1995), p. 6.
17. Matthew Arnold, 'Culture and Anarchy', in *Selected Writings*, ed. by Peter Keating (Harmondsworth: Penguin, 1973), p. 205.
18. Alan Bold, *Muriel Spark* (London: Methuen, 1986), p. 119.
19. Valentine Cunningham, *The Reading Gaol* (Oxford: Blackwell, 1994), pp. 129–51.
20. Terry Eagleton, *Literary Theory: An Introduction* (Oxford: Blackwell, 1983), p. 41; Julia Kristeva, *Powers of Horror* (New York: University of Columbia Press, 1982), p. 135.
21. Alan Chedzoy, 'Arnold in Coketown', in *Matthew Arnold: Between Two Worlds*, ed. by Robert Giddings (London: Vision, 1985), pp. 47–55.
22. Bataille, 'The Notion of Expenditure', p. 120.
23. Spark, 'The Portobello Road', 'The Executor', in CS, pp. 1–22 and 316–24.
24. Bataille, 'The Practice of Joy before Death', in *Visions of Excess*, pp. 235–9 (p. 239).
25. Ruth Whitaker, *The Faith and Fiction of Muriel Spark* (London: Macmillan, 1982), p. 58.
26. Bataille, 'Sacrifices', in *Visions of Excess*, pp. 130–6 (p. 132).
27. Bataille, 'Hegel, Death and Sacrifice' in *The Bataille Reader*, ed. by Fred Botting and Scott Wilson, pp. 279–95 (pp. 286–7).
28. Bataille, *Literature and Evil*, p. 5.
29. Elsa Schiaparelli, *Shocking Life* (London: Dent, 1954), p. 73.

9
Muriel Spark's *Mary Shelley*: A Gothic and Liminal Life
Julian Wolfreys

It must all be considered as if spoken by a character in a novel.

Roland Barthes

Introduction

Muriel Spark's first publication was a biographical and critical study of Mary Shelley.[1] Published in 1951, entitled *Child of Light: A Reassessment of Mary Shelley*, it appeared at a time when many of Mary Shelley's own publications were unavailable. Spark's biography served significantly in bringing into the light an author who was known chiefly for being the wife of Percy Bysshe Shelley, and for her novel *Frankenstein*.[2] Arguably, even the novel was known only in a second-hand fashion to many, through James Whale's film adaptations in the 1930s (particularly his *Frankenstein* and *Bride of Frankenstein*). *Child of Light* included an abridged version of Shelley's *The Last Man*, as that novel was out of print at the time the biography was published, and had been out of print for some time. The significance of this biography is best attested to by the fact that, while it was published in Great Britain, it did not have an 'official' publisher in the United States. Despite this, a pirated edition found its way into print in North America, as Muriel Spark recounts in her preface to her revised edition (MS, p. x), retitled *Mary Shelley: A Biography*, which was published in 1987. Spark republished the biography, as she remarks, in large part because of the existence of the photocopied edition being sold in the USA. Taking into account much of the scholarship on Mary Shelley which had appeared in the three decades since the initial publication, Spark revised the work extensively, dropping the abridged version of *The Last Man* (MS, p. x).

Mary Shelley: A Biography is divided into two distinct sections. The first – '*Biographical*' – having ten chapters (MS, 1–146), the second – '*Critical*' – being comprised of six (MS, pp. 149–235). The biographical chapters not only follow Mary's life, but explain, in some detail, the lives of her parents, William Godwin and Mary Wollstonecraft, as a means of providing the reader with an understanding of the psychological traits of Mary's character, which Spark interprets in the biography as Mary Shelley's 'inheritance' from her somewhat famous parents. The critical chapters address the form, influences and aesthetic merits of Mary's principal publications, *Frankenstein, The Last Man, Perkin Warbeck,*[3] as well as her activities as a critic and a poet. In particular, Spark is at pains to distance Shelley's writing from Gothic fiction, especially *Frankenstein*. As she argues, calling the novel Gothic is, at best, a 'loose definition' (MS, p. 153). While it may be taken as 'both the apex and the last of Gothic fiction' (MS, p. 154), it should be read rather as 'the first of a new and hybrid fictional species' (MS, p. 153). Such a hybrid, suggests Spark, is one which combines scientific and philosophical knowledge with an eye for realist detail. This in turn, Spark argues, is quite distinct from the narrative and descriptive conventions of Gothic fiction. The question of detail in Spark's biography is itself important, and will be returned to below.

This resistance on Spark's part to the Gothic label is mentioned here because it goes against the grain of much of the detail, if not the principal narrative direction of the biographical part of the book, which, as we shall go on to explore, is marked repeatedly by instances of Gothic detail and modes of representation. What in life may seem merely tragic or terrifying moments can become transformed into Gothic events in writing, especially if the tendency is, in the writing of a life, to emphasize those events as a network of punctuating instances, or a certain rhythmic pulse. Such moments of iterative punctuation provide Spark with a skeletal structure for the life, so to speak. They may also be read as iterative instances of a certain, constantly returning trope, written by Spark as that which haunts Mary Shelley's existence, often tragically. The focus here will therefore be on the biographical, rather than the critical, part of *Mary Shelley: A Biography*.

This essay will address two aspects of Muriel Spark's biography. These are, first, the liminal, marginal, or seemingly often subservient position Shelley occupies in relation to those around her during her life and the subsequent marginality of that life as it is written by Spark. The second aspect of the biography which concerns us here is what may either be described as the Gothic element of Mary Shelley's life or, otherwise, the Gothic mode of representation within which Spark writes that life, already mentioned. The two aspects – the liminal and the Gothic – are, we will contend, mutually interdependent. Mary Shelley's apparent marginality in her own life and the role she is made to play in the subsequent retelling of it are inescapably informed by Gothic details, as the biographer emphasizes these. Reciprocally, and no less importantly, the incidents in Mary Shelley's life which are either Gothic or made to appear as Gothic in condition belong to the sense, given by Muriel Spark, that Mary Shelley led a life at the border of other more self-promoting or otherwise public lives, particularly those of her father, William Godwin, her husband, Percy Bysshe Shelley, and Lord Byron. What we can read from Muriel Spark's *Mary Shelley: A Biography* is that a liminal life is one led amongst penumbra, often cast by figures who shine brightly by comparison. Such shadows are, inescapably, the places from which the Gothic event can appear. The story Muriel Spark tells of Mary Shelley is of someone who is, while the subject of the biography, nonetheless and perhaps paradoxically, always hovering in the wings, rather than appearing centre stage.

A doubling effect then, in this biography, and an effect which tends in two directions simultaneously. This double effect, an effect of writing, *in writing*, is registered in this essay already, in the paragraph above, as I attempt to orientate my own writing in response to Muriel Spark's biography. I note, for example, that the Gothic is either that mode of representation chosen by Spark or that it is an expression of Mary Shelley's life: the Gothic doubles itself, in the text that we call a life, and in the life that is configured by the text through which we come to apprehend that life. This is not really an either/or dilemma, for it is important that we acknowledge how both aspects of the Gothic are inseparable, and that they may be said to be mutually overdetermined by one another. Similarly, – and this is, once more, a double figure – I suggest above that the biography both marks and remarks on the liminality of Shelley's existence, even as it seeks to narrate her as its principal subject. Put somewhat baldly, Mary Shelley occupies a shadowy and marginal place in relation to others throughout her life, and this particular narrative thread becomes retraced in the act of seeking to emphasize her singular significance. Thus, the text of Muriel Spark weaves the border patterns it appears to observe, reiterating through life-writing the *parergonal* as the place–between – between what is often expressed as 'life and work' of a particular biographical subject – from which Mary Shelley can be made to return, and, equally, from which she writes, writing herself the shadowy existences of Victor Frankenstein, the Last Man, and Perkin Warbeck.

Gothic liminality or, the writing-effect and the example of the first chapter

What is called a 'life' always exceeds and escapes biography, even, or perhaps especially, when the biography appears in the most conventional form. Writing a life necessarily entails processes of selection, of inclusion and exclusion simultaneously, which occur in the configuration of any narrative subject. In writing a life the biographer is constrained by writing *a* life, one possible life as a narrative thread pursued, retold or traced among a number of possible, potential lives. As such, the biography is that act of writing in which the intertext, composed as Roland Barthes suggests of *interventions, fictions*, 'splinters, fragments ... overlappings, returns, affinities',[4] stitches the corpse together into an apparently seamless subject, which then appears reanimated. Biographical inscription is therefore the double act of writing while appearing to hide that which writing effects, or, to put it another way, the writing-effect which announces this *therefore will not have been writing*. As a textual paradigm, the subject is thus gathered *and* dispersed, as Barthes makes plain.[5] This double and seemingly contradictory movement is most readable in Spark's repeated return to the intertext fashioned from the overlapping of, and affinities between, fragments of the life-narrative and the Gothic mode. Despite its original title, *Child of Light, Mary Shelley: A Biography* is a narrative clearly organized according to some of the darker effects available to literary inscription. These effects of rhetoric and fiction ineluctably take hold, dispersing the 'life' so-called they serve to assemble, across the fragments of the Gothic.

The first chapter of *Shelley* provides an exemplary moment of liminal and Gothic interanimation in a narrative fashion which it is hard to dissociate from the stage-managed effects of what we call 'fiction'. It deals almost exclusively with Mary Shelley's famous parents, their personalities and their circle. They are presented by Spark as subjects of an age of intellectual and ideological transition,[6] marked by political fervour, popular agitation, the debate over human rights, and radical rationality. We are told that Godwin's personality is marked by 'intellectual stoicism', while Wollstonecraft's is one of 'passionate pessimism' (MS, p. 7). These psychological traits discerned by Spark, or otherwise overlaid in her act of purposeful reading, are singular and strong enough to warrant a reading of the biographer's assignation of type rather identity, where bold, gendered delineation may serve as the mould from which the character of the biography's principal character may spring. Spark's identification of the cardinal qualities of Mary's parents functions economically to foreshadow the writing and mediate the reading of Mary Shelley's life throughout the rest of the biographical narrative. It is important that we keep in sight these determining and, for Muriel Spark, incisive *traits* as literary figures, as much as we should regard them as the markers of psychological verisimilitude culled simply from the study of the past. Spark may be read as in the process of determining the parameters for her biographical subject in a manner which owes as much to certain fictional conventions of the late eighteenth century, as it does to any historically verifiable record of the lives of Wollstonecraft and Godwin.[7] Indeed, in marking out the limits of Mary's identity in so forceful and simple a fashion, Muriel Spark could easily be forgiven had she titled her first chapter 'Sense and Sensibility'.

There is, then, clearly a sense on Spark's part of self-conscious determination of the outline of the subject 'Mary Shelley' in so 'literary' or figural a manner. Like a character in a novel, Mary Shelley will arrive with a ready-made moral personality, to paraphrase Mark Currie, which exhibits not the subject herself so much as what Currie describes as the 'technical control' over the narrative of a life, the narrator's point of view, and the reader's response.[8] The extent to which she may go, and no further, is acknowledged throughout this opening chapter by the fairly frequent use of conditional clauses married to collective pronouns, in phrases such as 'if we...' or 'should we...'. In no other chapter do such phrases appear so frequently, and there is readable here a teasingly tentative exploration of the speculative limits permitted the biographer. The rhythm of reading dictated by such remarks suggests a constant tension or oscillation as an effect of trying those limits or margins.

But to reiterate: we are not concerned here principally with exploring the limits to which biography as a genre or form may be taken, even though this is potentially fascinating. Rather, it is with a life lived and subsequently written, in certain margins, at the borders of others' lives and the limits of those lives, in which we are interested. To pursue the formal limits of biography might seem to be an unjustified, and unjustifiable strong reading of *Mary Shelley*, given that, on a first or even second reading Spark's study appears a wholly conventionally shaped, albeit interesting, narrative. There is little about it which is obviously 'experimental', in the sense that *Roland Barthes by Roland Barthes* or *Jacques Derrida* by Geoffrey Bennington and Jacques Derrida both play with the limits they refuse to assign to the *biographical mode*, even as they overflow them. Nor is there anything obviously playful or transgressive in the form of Spark's account as there is in Peter Ackroyd's *Dickens*, which is by turns seemingly Edwardian and then self-consciously postmodern in its dalliance with identities. However, and to return to an earlier point, in an essay concerned with liminality and, by extension, with apparently minor narrative detail, it is perhaps the little, marginal – and marginalized – details which should claim our attention, despite the ostensible conventionality of the narrative's broader gestures.

One such detail is, quite literally, marginal. It concerns also the limits, seen from either side of the edge, of a life, of two lives, the ending of one involving and intimately connected with, the beginning of another. It is precisely the type of formal device considered as a writing effect which should draw our attention for being at once so apparently 'natural' in terms both of the event being narrated and its use as a means for concluding a chapter, while presaging the start of another, while being equally the mark of a double writing. There occurs at the conclusion of the first chapter, Mary's birth. This moment, which from certain perspectives might be read as something of an afterthought, is introduced as the chapter comes to a close. The subject of biography is brought in at the very margin of the first chapter. Yet if on the one hand the birth seems inauspicious, on the other it's narrative location may also be read as portentous. With Mary's birth comes the other narrative instance of the limit – Mary Wollstonecraft's death at the instance of giving birth, which tragic moment threatens to overshadow momentarily the birth of Mary Godwin.

It was of course quite common for women to die in childbirth or as its result in the eighteenth and nineteenth centuries, as any reader of novels from the time will confirm. It was also, doubtless, reasonably common practice for children to be named after their parents. However, such commonplace occurrences when transformed into narrative can function in a wholly different fashion, especially when their placement suspends narrative so dramatically, and when that suspension is formally re-enforced through so artificial a hiatus as the close of a chapter. The effect of the scene, with all its doubling resonances is thereby heightened, made to seem an even greater tragedy in the literary sense, and given a literary and rhetorical oscillation which continues in effect into the silence of the space beyond the chapter. Mary's death and Mary's birth are at once the most natural and the most artificial events in the world. Such a resounding climax is also a *crisis*, a decision-making which determines violently and strongly the reading and writing of a life. The climax is clearly both an end *and* a beginning. Here is written the limit of one life and/as the limit of another; it's placement seduces with the promise of the Gothic portent. Spark's decision to close the chapter with a double inscription, both death and life in writing resonates beyond its merely factual and historical instances, which life-writing overflows, and to which it cannot be reduced. The death of Mary Wollstonecraft might even, in a strong reading, be comprehended as a possibly Gothic moment wherein may be anticipated a troubled and tragic life for the as yet unconscious heroine.

Whether this is too strong a reading of so liminal a moment is open to debate, although I would suggest that we subject the moment to the force of reading *because* it is figured in so marginal and 'throwaway' a fashion. Given what we call the literary context in which Mary Shelley's most famous publication, *Frankenstein*, has been placed, and, by extension, Shelley herself, it may be all too easy to read Mary Shelley's life as a Gothic life. The risk is there, doubtless, a risk which is at work in both the writing of the biography and any subsequent commentary on it, and in the reading of its details.[9] Certainly, as suggested before, Muriel Spark is scrupulous in her efforts in the second part of the biography to dissociate Shelley's publications from any simple understanding or reading of them as Gothic narratives, even though she acknowledges, in passing, the literary contexts and genres which they acknowledge to greater or lesser degrees. Yet, despite this, and despite the separation of 'life' and 'work', the text that the life becomes is significantly punctuated by events that are narrated in a decidedly 'Gothic' manner as if, as with Mr Dick's trouble over King Charles, Muriel Spark just cannot keep the Gothic out. Whether the return of the repressed or the anxiety of influence marks this biography, there are some decidedly Gothic elements in the telling of Mary's life. Perhaps 'telling' is not the most apposite word at this juncture. Given my conjecture that the biography is shaped, or at least punctuated, by discernible Gothic narrative details and conventions, it might be more appropriate to speak of the biography of Mary Shelley as a 'reading' of her life – which of course it is. In reading the life according to particular literary and rhetorical rhythms of the late eighteenth and early nineteenth centuries, Spark gives herself over to what Paul de Man has described as the 'intuitive presence of the moment', appearing passively to fuse 'past and present' in order to reach a 'more fundamental continuity, which is the continuity of the source, of the creative impulse itself'.[10]

The rhythm of Gothic detail, or appearances notwithstanding

If, as Roland Barthes, George Orwell, and Naomi Schor assert in different ways,[11] a characteristic feature of realist writing is its attention to superfluous detail, what may be said of Spark's biography, in which Gothic detail is, seemingly, superfluous *and* necessary? The details are superfluous in that they are written as textual apparitions designed to set the scene or mood, to provide a *frisson*. They are necessary in that, together, they provide a rhythm of reading, marking the text as a series of rhetorical sutures in the act of remembering the life-in-writing, the life as text. If as Schor suggests in reading Freud's reading of detail,[12] that an excess of detail guarantees truth – or, in the case of a biography, verisimilitude – we would argue, following this, that it is the very excess of Gothic detail which is itself excessive, properly speaking, as well as being fragmentary. The Gothic mode is, as we know both excessive and fragmentary in its discursive and narrative patterns; these are amongst its defining features. Yet, while Spark would draw our attention to the 'facts' of Shelley's life in order to read truthfully the life of Mary Shelley, she does so in so markedly a stylistic manner that we are made to read in two directions at once, confronted by the writerly tension between verisimilitude and stylization. What we might suggest, in keeping with the Barthesian sense of the work of detail, contrary to any manifest will, intention or articulated desire, is that Gothic detail in its double service, appearing pointedly and repeatedly at the margins of the central narrative, serves the role of the *punctum*, as defined in *Camera Lucida*. Against the conscious will of the photographer, a detail appears and draws the attention. It 'occurs', writes Barthes, 'in the field of the photographed thing like a supplement that is at once inevitable and delightful'.[13] The Gothic detail is definable in this fashion, as a detail *within* or *of* a detail, to borrow from Naomi Schor's discussion of Barthes.[14] It is that chance fragment which, despite the attention to the understated in *Mary Shelley* as a sign of its realist-biographical credentials, draws our attention as it participates in the 'economy of meaning'.[15]

The first moment of Mary's life after her birth which draws the reader's focus occurs when she is seventeen. Arguably, Spark's brief narrative of Mary's stay with friends in Scotland, in the setting of the north bank of the River Tay, adjacent to Dundee, might be considered to provide a gloomy atmosphere, but it is in itself not necessarily Gothic, while it does provide what Spark describes as the background for Mary's 'creative gestation' (MS, p. 18).[16] When she is seventeen, Mary's life takes a decidedly Gothic turn, when she begins meeting secretly and regularly with Percy Bysshe Shelley. They take to meeting, we are informed, at her mother's grave in 'St. Pancras Churchyard' (MS, p. 19). This uncanny moment is only one of a number of events and details overdetermined by the Gothic sensibility in Mary's life with Shelley, who is nearly always referred to by Spark solely by his surname, as though he were the product of fictional narrative himself, some Byronic hero–villain. The detail of the meeting, the mention of the grave and graveyard fulfil the requirements of the Barthesian *punctum* of being both 'inevitable and delightful'. Spark seeks to thrill even as she attempts to convey the thrilling, if somewhat morbid element in Mary's life, as she and Shelley hover around the limits of the living world. The graveyard scene suitably punctuates a moment of transition in Mary Shelley's life; rhetorically it serves to mark the limit between her earlier and later lives. If, up to this point, Mary's life had been unremarkable (Spark spends almost as much time on the second Mrs Godwin in the first part of Chapter Two as she does on her principal subject), she had at least been more or less central, albeit subserviently, to her own biography. When Spark introduces Shelley on the stage, like a somewhat camp vampire among the gravestones of North London, Mary is placed in a supplementary role in her own narrative, at least until the poet's death some six chapters later.[17] This is a position which she is either unable or unwilling to escape, as though, again like some Gothic heroine, she was held in thrall to the genius of her partner, and his demonic circle.[18]

It is certainly Percy Bysshe Shelley – about whom 'frightful tales' circulate, and who tells terrible stories of himself for the amusement of his company (MS, p. 89) – who brings the Gothic to the relationship, scaring Claire Clairmont for example into convulsions with his tales (MS, p. 33) and describing to his publisher the production of *Epipsychidion* as containing a 'portion of me already dead' (MS, p. 76). Furthermore, the poet, later in his marriage, becomes enamoured of Emilia Viviani, a friend of the Shelleys who is imprisoned by her mother in a convent. Spark interprets Shelley's interest in the following way: 'But the fact that her convent prison rendered her unattainable and suggested untold mysteries which in reality Emilia did not possess, sent the poet into high raptures' (MS, p. 75). Spark is as much responsible for filling in the Gothic detail as she is for reporting it, once again investing the narrative with the double writing of the necessary and the delightful. Picking up on the various details, the author weaves a skein of writing effects, such as the problems caused by vindictive and untrustworthy foreign servants (MS, p. 73), so that the biography pulses with the Gothic. At another moment, Spark cites a letter from Shelley to Leigh Hunt, in which the poet describes William Godwin's demands on his daughter: 'he heaps on her misery, still misery' (MS, p. 72). There is a play at work in Spark's writing between carefully chosen citations from the past, which come back to haunt this biography, and the rhetoric of the biography itself. Even Shelley's debts are given a somewhat Gothic, albeit parenthetical turn:

> (The theme of debt throughout the nineteenth century is a social study by itself: debt was the equivalent of fraud; debt had its own prisons, its own police. Debt was a psychosis and by its dangerous nature positively mesmerized its victims.)
>
> (MS, p. 61)

To the reader of the 1990s, there is perhaps something vaguely Foucauldian in this pathology of debt. Extending the discourse beyond the personal instance, Spark at once constructs a psycho-cultural identity for debt, capable of acts of seduction and hypnosis, reminiscent of the powers of Dracula or Svengali. At the same time however, the Gothic genealogy of the discourse of debt which Spark sketches is placed in a markedly marginal position to the narrative, secured firmly between those parentheses. It would not be going too far, we suggest, to see or certainly to read in this gesture of Spark's, whether consciously or no, a performative, liminal and Gothic detail, a manifestation of the *punctum* beyond the individual subject, which focuses the reader's attention in a highly economic fashion on one particular impulse behind the writing of the biography. At once material and spectral, the spectre of economic hardship haunts both the Shelleys and the nineteenth century.

Hard-hearted fathers, malevolent Italians, and the pressing nature of debt aside, Spark also chooses to emphasize the Gothic narrative of the lives of Mary and Shelley together in other ways. On their first journey together through Europe, described in Chapter Three, detail is provided from their jointly kept journal of a Cossack raid and the report of rats crawling over Claire's face in her sleep. In Chapter Four, relatives die violently: Fanny takes her own life in Swansea, through an overdose of laudanum (MS, pp. 52–3) while Harriet Shelley drowns herself in the Serpentine (MS, p. 54). Subsequently, there are the deaths of the Shelleys' children, Clara and William (MS, p. 68). Juxtaposed to the deaths of Fanny and Harriet in the fourth chapter is the residence in Switzerland, with Byron and Polidori, where the tale of *Frankenstein* is first conceived. Later on, Mary will write of Byron to Claire, describing him in explicitly Gothic terms (MS, p. 81), while her descriptions of her illness, in a letter to Leigh Hunt, are also suitably Gothic: 'I wish I could break my chains and leave this dungeon' (MS, p. 98). Even Byron gets in on the act, imprisoning his own daughter (by Claire) in a convent, while Claire devises a kidnapping plan (MS, p. 81). Claire's child will also die however, plunging Mary 'once more into that abysmal gloom' engendered by the death of her own children (MS, p. 94). Everywhere, the everyday is overdetermined by the haunting inscription of the Gothic, so that events are never themselves but always much more, always arriving from some other place to disturb and displace the identity of the biography.

Chapters Six and Seven give details of the Shelleys' lives in Pisa and Liguria. As Shelley's circle widens, so Mary's importance appears to dwindle further, her role being as a supporting character for the most part. At the same time, the family, we are told had become 'inured to [the] *ever-present daemons of fortune*' (MS, p. 73; emphasis added). Furthermore, Spark suggests, in describing the growth of the Shelley circle, that '[i]t was as if, in response to some dramatic law, the actors were assembling on a stage, each a unit of suspense in attendance on the tragic dénouement' (MS, p. 78). This is the most pronounced moment of deliberate artifice in reconstruction on Spark's part. Having set the scene, having recounted the arrival of Trelawny to the party, and the telling of terrible tales, the beginning of Chapter Seven provides a frame for the events which are to follow:

> Mary was always conscious of the transience of things. Experience had endorsed this awareness, and in every appearance of tranquillity she saw, and saw correctly so far as her own life was concerned, an approaching turmoil. It often seems that such people invite the Furies by their own apprehension, that misfortune gains confidence, as a fierce animal will at the sense of a stranger's fear.

It was not long before Mary's 'prognostications of evil' took shape.

(MS, p. 84)

Constructing the biography in this manner, Spark brings into play that certain sense of evil, which she is able to attribute as Mary's own words. The division in the opening paragraph of the chapter makes a strong impression, moving as it does from the representation of Mary's own feelings, drawn from her letters and journals, to the more speculative, emotionally heightened consideration of a quasi-classical tragedy waiting to occur. While this is not directly Gothic in its expression, as an opening passage, it nonetheless relies heavily for its effect on its placement and the general air of mystery and foreboding which it desires to evoke in its rhetorical slippage from the personal to the universal. It is perhaps Gothic in register rather than language.

Such 'Gothicization' continues through Chapter Seven, in the description of the residence of the Shelleys and their guests Edward and Jane Williams: 'They were isolated in a small, and at that time quite savage fishing community on the Ligurian coast. On the night of 22nd June 1822, Mary was awakened by Shelley's scream' (MS, p. 98). The isolation and savagery are purely Gothic effects, and what is all the more disturbing in this brief moment of scene setting is that double effect once more, where the narrative strains between its factual element – the precision of the report of the date – and the sudden disturbance of sleep. Shelley has screamed, we learn, because of a dream in which the bodies of Jane and Edward Williams are seen with torn and bloodstained skin (MS, p. 98). Moreover, and as if to add to the overall effect of this one incident, Spark tells us that both the Williams and the Shelleys allegedly experienced hallucinations and visions. And of course, all of this is to lead up to the sailing accident, and the deaths of Percy Bysshe Shelley and Edward Williams, the news of which is given by that teller of horrific tales, Trelawny, who brings the '*ghastly* information' to Mary and Jane (MS, p. 99; emphasis added). Thus the tragic events of the summer of 1822 become reshaped, reinvented, to become a tale of Gothic detail, where the detail halts the reader's attention. Yet even this is not quite the end of the Gothic, for there is the moment with which Spark chooses to begin Chapter Eight, at Shelley's funeral pyre when the dead poet's heart is snatched from the burning body by Trelawny (MS, p. 100).

Conclusion

Was there life after Shelley for Mary? From Chapter Two on, until his death, Percy Bysshe Shelley occupies a central role, both in the life of Mary and in her biography. Arriving like some Byronic figure his effect on writing and on those whose lives he comes into contact with is inevitable and inescapable. The necessary and unavoidable inclusion of the poet in *Mary Shelley* transforms the biography as much as he transformed his wife's life, a central significance which Mary acknowledges in her journal, and which Muriel Spark dutifully reports in her biography (MS, p. 101). If Mary had come to occupy a less than central role during her time with Shelley, the strange and the uncanny undoubtedly punctuated her life, at least in Spark's version. And even though Shelley was dead, he continued to haunt Mary's life, not merely through the 'dark mood [which] had overtaken her' (MS, p. 106), but also through the tolerance and condescension shown Mary by many of Shelley's friends, as Spark makes quite plain. Mary assumes a marginal role even after Shelley's death, seeking patronage from her father-in-law, editing her late husband's poems, and finding herself ostracized by Shelley's circle (MS, p. 131).

Appearances notwithstanding, *Mary Shelley: A Life* is imprinted throughout by the trace of the Gothic. Narrative event and historical detail are contaminated by the constant return of an other form, which is all the more haunting because it is disguised, as the ghost of the Gothic appears in the form of biography. In this fashion, Muriel Spark fuses past and present, to recall the words of Paul de Man, cited earlier. Or rather, and to recall also de Man's insistence on the writer's passive role in the act of fusion, Spark allows the Gothic past to return through, and in the guise of, the present biography. The return occurs most frequently from the margins of the text, and from the margins of a life, made more liminal in its re-creation. The narrative of Mary Shelley may not be a life she would necessarily recognize; it is, though, perhaps a narrative she may have written, we like to imagine, in other words. In overlapping the fragments and details of one genre onto the constraints of another, Muriel Spark brings to our attention Mary Shelley's Gothic affinities.

Notes

1. Muriel Spark, *Mary Shelley: A Biography*, revised edition (New York: E.P. Dutton, 1987). First published as *Child of Light: A Reassessment of Mary*

Shelley (London: Tower Bridge Publications Ltd, 1951). All references to the biography are taken from the revised edition.

2. Amongst the biographies available, two of the most interesting are Anne K. Mellor's *Mary Shelley: Her Life, Her Fiction, Her Monsters* (London: Routledge, 1990) and Emily W. Sunstein, *Mary Shelley: Romance and Reality* (Boston: Little, Brown & Company, 1989). Neither takes much interest in Spark's biography, even though both share Spark's own interest in the separation and interanimation of life and work. In a concluding chapter which assesses biographical and critical work on Shelley, Sunstein describes Spark's biography briefly as sympathetic yet misleading (p. 400), without suggesting why it is misleading, other than to intimate that this is the case because Spark did not have all Shelley's material available to her in 1951. The question here is one of aesthetic evaluation, and of treating the biography as 'straight' biography.

3. *Perkin Warbeck* is not obviously a Gothic novel. It is however an historical romance, influenced by and in the style of the Waverley Novels of Walter Scott, as Spark points out (*MS*, p. 199). The relationship of the historical romance to the Gothic is made explicit by Scott himself in his introduction to what is considered the first Gothic novel, Horace Walpole's *The Castle of Otranto*. Walter Scott, 'Introduction to *The Castle of Otranto*' (1821), rpt in Horace Walpole, *The Castle of Otranto*, intro. Marvin Mudrick (New York: Crowell-Collier, 1963), pp. 115–28.

4. Roland Barthes, *Roland Barthes*, (1975) trans. Richard Howard (Berkeley and Los Angeles: University of California Press 1977), p. 145.

5. Ibid, p. 143.

6. Which a critic with historicist tendencies may be tempted to connect to the period in which Spark first published her study of Shelley.

7. Which arguably is still a textual intervention rather than a simple representation.

8. Mark Currie, *Postmodern Narrative Theory* (Basingstoke: Macmillan, 1998), p. 17. While Spark's biography is not in any obvious sense 'postmodern' in the currently understood senses of that word, Currie's discussion of narrative convention is usefully broad enough for me to draw upon in making this point.

9. It is possible to argue, after Harold Bloom, that Muriel Spark's 'life' of Mary Shelley, is an act of misprision, a strong reading or misreading, which swerves away from the documenting of a life in seeking to create as strong an effect as the writing of its subject.

10. Paul de Man, *Blindness and Insight: Essays in the Rhetoric of Contemporary Criticism* (New York: Oxford University Press, 1971), pp. 84–5.

11. Roland Barthes, 'The Reality Effect', trans. R. Carter, in Tzvetan Todorov, ed., *French Literary Theory Today* (Cambridge: Cambridge University Press, 1982), pp. 11–7; Naomi Schor, *Reading in Detail: Aesthetics and the Feminine* (New York: Methuen, 1987), p. 85; George Orwell, 'Charles Dickens', in *Collected Essays* (London: Secker and Warburg, 1961), p. 75, cit. Schor, pp. 160–1 n.6.

12. Naomi Schor, *Reading in Detail*, p. 75.

13. Roland Barthes, *Camera Lucida: Reflections on Photography*, trans. Richard Howard (New York: Hill & Wang, 1981), p. 47, cit. Schor, *Reading in Detail*, p. 90.

14. Schor, *Reading in Detail*, p. 91.
15. Ibid.
16. Not too many overtly Gothic tales have been set in Scotland, though a notable example is, of course, Ann Radcliffe's *The Castles of Athlin and Dunbayne*.
17. Although space does not permit us to address the second part of the biography in any detail, it is important to note two instances of Spark's re-enforcement of Mary's shadowy and marginal position. The tendency to subjugate Mary Shelley's position to those around her is reiterated in the form of the biography, as Spark moves to, what is for her, the greater importance of Mary Shelley's writing, thereby displacing the writing of a life with the discussion of the text. She suggests as an imperative for the reader of Mary Shelley that, it is in 'her writings themselves, then, [that] we must seek the imaginative complement to an "imperfect picture"' of Mary's life (MS, p. 146). Of *The Last Man*, Spark writes that the novel 'most manifestly reveals her as Godwin's daughter, as Shelley's wife, and as a student of Platonic literature' (MS, pp. 183–4). Spark's somewhat Gothic rereading and reinvention in Mary Shelley is important in part, we would contend, because it provides a Bloomian act of misreading, which, from the evidence of Mary's life as presented by Spark, Shelley herself was never able to present.
18. Against such a reading there is, once more, an implicit *caveat* to be acknowledged. No biography can be written, conventionally at least, in which the principal subject of that biography can be narrated without recourse to other figures, social settings, historical events, and so on which serve in the reconstitution of that life. At the same time, however, there is of course the question of how the material is shaped by the biographer, how the subject is situated rhetorically amongst the factual, cultural, historical details. Mary's liminality in her own narrative, where she is read as simultaneously the subject of the biography and yet also a subsidiary figure to others, a reflection first of her parents and then of her husband, is noticeably pronounced. This is particularly so whenever Shelley is present. We might read here Spark's struggling with the power of the poet's character as it is consolidated in narratives about him, without ever being able to control it wholly, and her subject suffering as a result. Of course Mary may have been cast frequently into the shadows by Shelley's brilliance, especially when surrounded by his friends, but Spark's biography writes itself into this same process figuring Mary on occasions as a supplement, a marginal detail of another narrative.

10
Not to Deconstruct? Righting and Deference in *Not to Disturb*

Willy Maley

Father O'Malley gave her the benefit, after her conversion, of his Jungian therapy.[1]

The press and the police are coming, and there are only sixty-four shopping days to Christmas.[2]

Operating on the 'nevertheless principle' does not mean that anything goes, that absolute relativism is the ticket, or that one must settle for despair and/or deconstruction. On the contrary, Spark insists not that any single reading is impossible but that one's reading must accommodate numerous subreadings. Morally, such an attitude leads to charity in one's reading of and presentation of people and characters ... Spark is decidedly a 'both/and' writer, rather than an 'either/or' writer. In my opinion, the better criticism of her work is that which recognizes and tries to explain the particulars of this assertion.[3]

Swift directs servants to be arrogant, to do as they please, to be felons and vandals.[4]

In the face of a common misconception of deconstruction, a 'subreading' of it, I want to argue in this essay that Muriel Spark's writing – affirmative, open, playful and determinedly materialistic – is much more disturbing and 'deconstructive' than critics have allowed, and morality or charity have nothing to do with it. Indeed, one consequence of the comparative lack of theoretical criticism of Spark has been a neutralizing of her radicalism. Spark attracts admirers rather than critics, whose comments are not quite critique. A polite criticism, Catholic and conservative, attaches itself to her work, a criticism whose watchword is 'do not disturb', rather than 'not to disturb'. As if. Nevertheless, in principle there is no disagreement between Spark and Derrida. Both are suspicious of a literature of commitment, of committed writers, those 'interventionists' who wear their politics on their sleeve and wipe their noses with it. Both are wary of social realism, and sceptical about the idea of the 'engaged' intellectual. Both prefer politically conservative authors who are radical in their approach to form, and who tamper with language, loiter with intent, and fool around with time. Equivocation, aporia and indecision are the driving force of deconstruction and the key to Spark's ignition.

Spark is arguably one of the most disturbing writers of prose fiction in contemporary literature, yet proponents of literary theory remain largely impervious to her work. In this essay, through a deconstructive encounter with one of Spark's most disturbing novels, ironically entitled *Not To Disturb*, I shall argue that theory has in fact much to learn from Spark. *Not to Disturb* is a dark tale of class and revolution, lit up by Spark's literary pyrotechnics. An author sometimes represented as reactionary, despite her innovative approach to literary form, she is here seen to be engaging with material that can be interpreted as radical and subversive. Several key concerns of deconstruction can be witnessed in *Not To Disturb*. There is the unfolding in the margins, or the subtext of 'downstairs', as the servants plot the downfall of their masters. There is the element of repetition, of a destination that is always already reached, as the programmatic nature of the narrative emerges. There is, finally, the two stages of deconstruction, opposition and displacement, enacted in perfect harmony, as we see the risk of a revolution that merely repeats rather than uproots the worst features of the system that is to be overturned. The monstrousness of the ruling elite is mirrored in the monstrousness of its gravediggers. The servants' intention is not to redistribute, but to mimic, and to make money out of the ignominious end of their employers, an end which they manipulate and effectively 'produce', in the cinematic sense, but which they also consume, whether as passive observers or as paid extras. While this can of course be regarded as a glib and reactionary conclusion to a scenario of social upheaval, as the new masters sell the film rights of their masters' vice, it can also be read as a critique of a limited and carefully staged uprising that leaves everything intact, in its place, exactly *not to disturb*. In focusing on the unsettling effects of the novel, I shall also be drawing on the idea of a textual 'disturbance', or breach of the peace, as mapped out by Alan Sinfield in an essay on political subversion in *Macbeth*.[5] A disturbance is an undercurrent of a text that in some way upsets the equilibrium of a surface reading and creates a disturbance at the deepest levels of language.

Not to Disturb is replete with metaphors of staging, screening, casting, corpsing, directing, producing, spinning, and setting. In flagging the finale, Spark undercuts, edits out, any sense of anticipation, exposing from the outset the plotting that parodies rather than points to the denouement. *Not to Disturb* is a satire of the three estates of police, press, and informants who are both consumers and producers of scandal and gossip.

Spark is one of the most rigorously materialist writers around, yet she is erroneously described as anti-materialist. Joseph Hynes speaks of 'that materialism sharply and effectively bashed in so many Spark novels'.[6] But how does this square with Spark's own remarks concerning matter, and the fact that it is what gets left out of other religions (like the religion of criticism)? In fact, in the resistance to realism evident in 'The Desegregation of Art', reminiscent of Robert Louis Stevenson's critique of Zola, Spark is taking up a rigorously materialist stance, and a theoretically sophisticated one.[7] Spark also anticipates the postmodernist perspective on realism. The 'only definition' of realism, according to Jean-François Lyotard, 'is that it intends to avoid the question of reality implicated in that of art'. For this reason, realism 'always stands somewhere between academicism and kitsch'.[8]

Determinism and materialism are held by critics to be anathema to Spark, but in speaking of her conversion to Catholicism, Spark reveals that it was matter rather than pater that drove her: 'One of the things which interested me particularly about the Church was its acceptance of matter. So much of our world rejects it. We're not happy with things. We want machines to handle them'.[9] Spark, according to Joseph Hynes, 'rejects the world-bashing determinism of Calvin and Knox in favour of a vaster inclusiveness that she finds in orthodox Catholicism'.[10] This vaster inclusiveness includes a vaster and more inclusive materialism than was dreamt of in Marxism. Derrida's *Specters of Marx* was an effort to put the matter of religion and spirit back into Marxism, and like it is for Derrida, it is the materialism of language and of form, as well as that of spirit and religion, that engages Spark, and with which she is engaged.

The kind of commitment and engagement practised by Spark is largely invisible to her critics. Patricia Stubbs, for example, sees Spark as an escapist: 'Fiction for Miss Spark is play, escape from life; her view of the low status of fiction encourages her to fritter her talent in humour and pun, thus invalidating any true seriousness'.[11] Spark's is a serious playfulness. Like Derrida's, her attachment to style and to satire is fundamentally political. *Not to Disturb* is a contradiction in terms. The very title itself, with its odd grammar, like a phrase taken out of context, is already unsettling. It recalls the 'be not disturbed' of the Psalms, but it has the opposite of a calming effect. The repetition of the title, in various guises, throughout the novel, adds to its eerie and unorthodox accent and intonation, and extends the impression of a world that is unbalanced, unhinged and out of joint. This is a deeply disquieting novel, heavy with 'disturbulence'. The word 'disturb' derives from 'turbulence', meaning 'having irregular variations in the course of time', which in turn stems from the Latin 'turba', meaning 'crowd'. *Not to Disturb* would be a very different novel if told from the viewpoint of the doomed ménage-à-trois within the library. The parcel of rogues in the rest of the house are equally unlikely to elicit the sympathy of the reader, but by giving us a glimpse of aristocratic decadence and decay through the keyhole, as it were, Spark offers a crowd scene, a snapshot – or a crotch shot – of a lower class 'take' on high society.

Spark's identity is many-sided. She is Jewish by birth, Presbyterian by schooling, Catholic by choice, anarchist by ethos, deconstructive despite herself, and postmodernist before her time. With Spark, as with Derrida, the accent is on infiltration and overturning from within. Like Derrida, Spark is an outsider even in regard to her own country. She describes herself as a 'constitutional exile', and concedes that it was Edinburgh that instilled in her 'the conditions of exiledom'.[12] Spark is at once wandering Jew, cloistered Catholic, and posh Presbyterian. To paraphrase Joyce, she forsook an absurdity which was illogical and incoherent and embraced one which is logical and coherent.[13]

Spark and Derrida share more than their Jewishness, their exile, and their formalism. There is also a commitment, if I can call it that, to entering a system in order to upset it. Derrida's most recent work is quite explicit about this movement from the margins to the centre in order to upset its codes and norms, but to do so with the utmost respect and politesse, in a language that would not be out of place in the tea-rooms of Edinburgh or the salons of the Left Bank.[14] Derrida goes so far as to say that for him the accent is on the posh and the pure when it comes to language: 'I am not proud of it, I make no doctrine of it, but so it is: an accent – any French accent, but above all a strong southern accent – seems incompatible to me with the intellectual dignity of public speech'.[15] And he adds that 'this hyperbolic taste for the purity of language is something I also contracted at school'.[16] It is exactly this mix of the proper and the improper, of poshness and pushiness, that characterizes Spark. She is at once Scary Spark – and nowhere more so than in the dark Gothicism of *Not to Disturb* – but she is also Posh Spark, quaffing her goblet of blood with a pinkie extended. Sparklife is a blurred phenomenon. Spark's critics show their class and their politics more than she does. Norman Page depicts the flight of the royal family with parquet flooring and door knobs in hand in terms of 'violent and tragic events, revolution and exile'.[17] Revolutions can be violent and tragic events, but they can also be beautiful and necessary, not to mention artful and instructive, even or especially when they bring you back to where you started.

There is a great deal of wit and wordplay in *Not to Disturb*, as in all of Spark's work. At one point Heloise expresses concern, both belatedly and prematurely, for her master:

'The poor late Baron,' says Heloise.
'Precisely,' says Lister. 'He'll be turning up soon. In the Buick, I should imagine.'

(N, p. 7)

Note the layers and lairs here. The Baron, who is rich, is also poor, as the object of sympathy and the victim of a triple betrayal, by his wife, his secretary, and his servants. He is late in his discovery of this, and imminently late, as in soon-to-be-dead. The Baron will turn up in the 'Buick', and in the book. Of course, on one level the cast of characters in *Not to Disturb* are little more than ciphers, cardboard cut-outs drawn from a board game, refugees from Cluedo – Lister the butler, Clovis the chef, Hadrian his assistant, Sister Barton the nurse, Pablo the handyman, Heloise the maid, not to mention Theo and Clara, the odd couple – oddly normal, in this context – who live in the lodge. But if the characters are one-dimensional the narrative has four dimensions at least, and the underlying argument of the book is as serious as it is disturbing.

Page – who turns up in this Buick – characterizes *Not to Disturb* as 'a sardonic commentary on the fictive nature of "news" as reported by the popular press and other media'.[18] Page sees the novel in terms of 'its sardonic exposure of the power of the mass media in the contemporary world: the main characters are motivated by the wish to get their hands on the vast fortunes to be made by supplying sensational and scandalous material to the mass-circulation magazines and the film industry'.[19] Malcolm Bradbury shares this view of a novel intent on exposing the intimate connection between the crowd-pleasing requirements of the media circus and the events it invents to a large extent: 'It is these traditional fiction makers and reporters of the crimes of high passion, of the corpse in the drawing room and the shouts in the night, these non-participant observers, who in *Not to Disturb* have learned to ape the manners of their betters, acquiring press-agents, and aspirations to film-script writing, and also that gift of forward plotting of which Miss Spark herself is an exponent. They also serve who only stand and wait: having worked out the ending before the event, these avant garde servants have a fiction to preserve'.[20] The servants also have a social order to preserve, for despite their subversive tendencies they are determined to leave things as they are.

In her Gothic critique of gossip and scandal, Spark puts the hell into *Hello*. Spark reverses the order of things, and she does so because that's the way things are. Journalism is not yesterday's news today but today's news tomorrow. As Page puts it, 'in *Not to Disturb* media exploitation precedes instead of following a sensational event'.[21] As Page points out: 'What had been shown in *The Public Image* in relation to a particular profession, the film industry, is here shown to be true of a whole section of society'.[22] What Spark is attacking is the mediatization of the culture at large, the global village that is emerging with postmodernity. In Lister and Company's elaborate posing and exposing, making and marketing of their story, and in their determined promotion of what is to come, Spark is pointing up the prophetic nature of news, its self-fulfilling profit motive. Their action and inaction is the logical consequence of a vicarious interest in the sex lives and deaths of the rich and famous, a morbid fixation upon celebrity and publicity.

If her conversion to Catholicism gave Spark a voice and a cathartic sense of self, it also informed her work in mysterious ways. A Catholic aesthetic, critics argue, manifests itself in her fiction. For Malcolm Bradbury, Spark is a writer who pares and compares:

> Muriel Spark's aesthetics and her religion, her Catholicism, are closely involved – a point that has been tellingly made by David Lodge ... this might serve to remind us to what an extraordinary extent it is the Catholic novelists who have contributed self-

conscious aesthetics to the English literary tradition and have, in so doing, given those aesthetics a casuitical, or Jesuitical, streak. Concern with the analogue between God's making and the writer's tends wonderfully to generate a large frame of reference for art and a sense of high presumption, in more than one sense of the word, in the writer; meanwhile Protestants have realism.[23]

Spark doesn't just pare her fingernails, she uses them to claw the face off society, leaving hair and blood and skin underneath for forensics. Spark foreshadows, or rather forelightens, for her prolepses are not so subtle as to deserve the shade. Spark, like the servants whom she directs, like a ruthless tabloid editor in search of something for the front-page, sells the story in advance. She is a 'prolepsed' Catholic, to give it a Morningside inflection. Spark says 'nevertheless' was pronounced 'niverthelace' in the tea-rooms of Edinburgh. Although she says first that her teachers used the phrase, then that 'All grades of society constructed sentences bridged by 'nevertheless'', she goes on to characterize it as the kind of final flourish favoured by old ladies in the tea-rooms of Edinburgh (EB, p. 22). Nevertheless, always the more, where Spark is concerned. As Malcolm Bradbury observes, Spark's work 'is hardly designed not to disturb'.[24] According to Patrick Parrinder, she 'is a genuinely disturbing writer – one who disturbs our deepest convictions and prejudices about novel-writing, and about more fundamental matters as well'.[25]

Spark's formalism and her faith are seen to be complicit or contradictory. Parrinder says: 'She is a notoriously anti-humanist novelist, who ultimately puts down a large proportion of the manifestations of human nature that she portrays to the ragings of the devil' (p. 25). This seems contradictory. One could argue that Spark's humanism extends, like Derrida's, to animals and to those 'occulted by hegemonic canons', to cite Derrida. Parrinder sees Spark as a writer who, in opposing realist fiction, produces an equally dogmatic view of the world:

> Spark is self-consciously fictive, playful and cynical; she is wryly despairing about the social world in which we live and anything to which this world seems likely to lead ... She is resolute in destroying utopian illusions, and romantic only in the extent of her negations. Yet, like Socialist Realist novels, her plots tend to be propaganda vehicles manipulating her characters' destinies for a dogmatic purpose. She is, in fact, a reactionary allegorist.
>
> (p. 25)

Conversely, Spark could be seen to be disturbing the equilibrium between radical and reactionary, deconstructing them even, in order to show their implicatedness, their underlying complicity.

Even if we accept Parrinder's charge that Spark is a 'reactionary allegorist', there is still the question of what implications this might have for her reception as a writer. Derrida has remarked on the ways in which authors of a conservative political bent are often the most interesting in terms of formal experimentation and rhetorical richness: 'Our task is to wonder why it is that so many of this century's strong works and systems of thought have been the site of philosophical, ideological, political "messages" that are at times conservative (Joyce), at times brutally and diabolically murderous, racist, anti-semitic (Pound, Céline), at times equivocal and unstable (Artaud, Bataille)'.[26]

Parrinder maintains that Spark's 'novels express not only formalism and Catholicism but a controlling personal vision; a vision which reveals itself through the manipulation and, as it were, the anaesthetisation of strongly emotive aspects of reality'.[27] Parrinder contends that Spark's 'deepest allegiance has always been to the fictional sub-genres – and especially to the Gothic – rather than to realism and its apparent successors' (p. 27). Something is being overlooked in the claims to sub-genres and subreadings. Parrinder asks 'what are we to make of Spark's heavy use of the fantasy, the Gothic, and the thriller?' (p. 27). Light work is the answer. The real interest lies elsewhere, in the savage and subtle deconstruction of personal and political interests and in the disturbance of discourse.

Parrinder points out that Spark's settings themselves are 'closed and allegorical communities', that they lack the 'typicality and focal validity demanded by the realist tradition' (p. 28). As an example of Spark's artifice and excess Parrinder cites a troubling passage in one of her novels that he reads in a curious way. Parrinder speaks of the VJ night scene in *The Girls of Slender Means*, and of the juxtaposition of a seaman's stolen kiss and another seaman's cruel knifing of his female partner, concluding that 'it is typical of Spark's sensationalist vision that the beery kiss had to be counterbalanced by a murder' (p. 29). This seems to me to be an inattentive reading. The sexual harassment of Jane and the violent assault on the unnamed woman are part of the same congruence of misogyny and militarism, in precisely the same way that suicide and murder are the consequences of media intrusion and scandal in *Not to Disturb*. This is the moral heart of the novel, and of Spark's writing as a whole, the heart of Sparkness. What Spark exposes is the repression and violence that arise from the fear of exposure, as well as the ambition and avarice that engender it. *Not to Disturb* continually points up the connection between sex and violence, a connection that the culture at large, and the state as a whole – including the machinery of media and order, the press and police – serves to promote and uphold. There is throughout the novel an alluring mix of understatement and outrage, gossip and gospel, as we take stock of Klopstock, film stock, and small talk.

Parrinder maintains that Spark's 'blend of artistic desecration and artistic blackmail may, ultimately, induce some of her readers to share her own refuge of Catholic piety; but it is the sensationalism and inherently anti-utopian bent of her imagination that stand out'. He argues for a productive tension between Spark's fiction and her faith in that she became a novelist when she became a Catholic and the novels are an escape hatch rather than an expression of her religious beliefs (pp. 30–1). In fact, in her Catholicism, Gothicism, formalism, and dispassionate rendering of the struggle between good and evil, Spark resembles in many ways Flannery O'Connor, a Southern writer who was herself familiar with Spark's work.[28]

Spark's moral and political vision, individualist and anarchist and endlessly irascible in the face of bureaucracy and institutional tyranny, is often overlooked, and instead she is characterized as cool and dispassionate and uncaring, as if aspects of the writing were being confused with authorial attitude. Parrinder, for example, is 'troubled by her sensationalism, and her lack of compassion'.[29] Spark disturbs her critics as well as her readers. In an essay on *Macbeth*, Alan Sinfield invites us to 'draw a more careful distinction between the violence which the State considers legitimate and that which it does not'.[30] *Not to Disturb*, like *Macbeth*, is about usurpation through imitation and corruption. According to Sinfield:

> Violence is good ... when it is in the service of the prevailing dispositions of power; when it disrupts them it is evil. A claim to the monopoly of legitimate violence is fundamental in the development of the modern State; when that claim is successful, most citizens learn to regard State violence as qualitatively different from other violence and perhaps they don't think of state violences as violence at all (consider the actions of police, army and judiciary as opposed to those of pickets, protesters, criminal and terrorists).[31]

Like in the context, a disturbance is to be found *in the text*, and not just around it.

Spark's conversion, like her resistance to social realism, has about it a touch of the search for subaltern status by someone who might otherwise be deemed relatively privileged: 'I was living in very poor circumstances and I was a bit undernourished as well. I suppose it all combined to give me my breakdown. I had a feeling while I was undergoing this real emotional suffering that it was all part of the conversion. But I don't know. It may have been an erroneous feeling' (MC, p. 25). Religion was Spark's bit of rough beast, slouching towards the suburbs of Edinburgh. Catholicism provided her with her catharsis and contact with high clericalism and the underdog. A con-version needs hard currency. Lo and behold, if suffering brought her to her faith, a little money from Macmillan brought her to her fiction: 'I hadn't any money to write a novel with and so they offered to give me some. I started one when I got better' (MC, p. 25). Funny how funds can inspire fictions. As Jane Austen remarks, a very narrow income has a tendency to contract the mind. Spark needed a Rome of her own.

Spark resists the idea that her commitment to Catholicism places constraints upon her work: 'You mentioned the problem of the committed writer, but I don't feel committed in that way. It may be that I am one of those people who are in chains and don't know it. People who don't know say it's like Soviet Russia, as if we get directives from priests and from the Pope telling us how to write. What nonsense! It may be different in countries where there's a censorship run by priests, but we are on toast here in England. If you make a name for yourself, everybody is your friend' (MC, p. 26). Writers are sharing in the recent theoretical obsession with roots and identity, in the search for authenticity and for an originary position from which one can run different self-generated software. Terry Eagleton's born-again Irishness and Raymond William's emphasis on his Welshness are contemporary instances of privileged intellectuals seeking marginal status. Jacques Derrida's recent book on his Algerian origins – or 'nostalgeria' – is another instance of this desire for otherness by major metropolitan figures.[32] Catholicism gave Spark all the edge and attitude and individuation she needed.

Indeed, Spark's Catholicism can by no stretch of the imagination be called communitarian, and is in fact quite in keeping with Protestant individualism:

> I take this attitude to Catholicism because it's really a Christian thing to me conducive to individuality, to finding one's own individual personal point of view. I find I speak far more with my own voice as a

Catholic and I think I could prove it with my stuff. Nobody can deny I speak with my own voice as a writer now, whereas before my conversion I couldn't do it because I was never sure what I was, the ideas teemed but I couldn't sort them out, I was talking and writing with other people's voices all the time. But not any longer. This is the effect of becoming a Christian. People talk about Catholics as if it's the Co-op, a kind of spiritual Co-op which you join and get so many dividends. But the Catholic Faith really has enormous scope.

(MC, pp. 26–7)

Spark makes Catholicism sound very catholic, so catholic as to be Protestant, perhaps even Presbyterian. Not a Co-op, but a designer label. It was also a safety net and a called-for back-up: 'I didn't get my style until I became a Catholic because you just haven't got to care, and you need security for that' (MC, p. 27). Catholicism thus gave Spark a sense of selfhood rather than social responsibility. In search of a non-tribal, non-national identity, one that wasn't class-based, Spark found a space somewhere between ego and empire. All roads for the writer lead to Rome.

From Proust, Spark learned the value and relevance of digression, 'though of course I cut it down in the English way' (MC, p. 27). The English way? A digression on Spark's Scottishness is in order. Spark insists that 'the puritanical strain of the Edinburgh ethos is inescapable' (EB, p. 22), and speaks of imbibing 'just by breathing the informed air of the place, a haughty and remote anarchism' (EB, p. 23). That 'haughty and remote anarchism' is the key to Spark's politics. Like James Kelman, she is a champion of the individual against institutions, bureaucracies, and the state. While from one Marxist perspective such a standpoint can be seen to be petit-bourgeois and limited in terms of its social efficacy, from another it can be seen to be a valid form of anti-authoritarianism. When Spark says 'I can never now suffer from a shattered faith in politics and politicians, because I never had any' (EB, p. 23), her anti-electoral, anti-establishment, anti-institutional stance could come straight from Kelman, even from Irvine Welsh.[33] Spark is Scottish in a variety of ways, and nowhere more so than in her eschewing of class consciousness or community politics in favour of anarcho-individualism, though this may be a matter of the form of the novel as much as the history of any particular nation, whether colonized or colonizing.

Spark also shares with contemporary Scottish writers a suspicion of the aura of intellectualism with which some authors overlay their elitism. Spark's idea of the role of the writer is of a servant rather than a master: 'I think of the artist as a minor public servant. If he starts thinking of himself as a public master, he's in trouble. Your beliefs should check you there. What can upset you is the arrogance of some intellectuals – they feel themselves apart from ordinary people – and on the other side the oppression of ignorance' (MC, p. 28). Spark situates herself between arrogance and ignorance, exposing both with in a merciless and consequent fashion.

In a notorious polemical exchange, Derrida drew an analogy between the separate development of faculties within universities and the state's separate development of races in apartheid South Africa.[34] Spark too, in 'The Desegregation of Art', uses a word that is racially and politically charged – desegregation – in order to advocate an opening up of art. Concretely, she begins by praising social realism before going on to bury it:

> We have in this century a marvellous tradition of socially-conscious art. And especially now in the arts of drama and the novel we see and hear everywhere the representation of the victim against the oppressor, we have a literature and an artistic culture, one might almost say a civilization, of depicted suffering, whether in social life or in family life. We have representations of the victim-oppressor complex, for instance, in the dramatic portrayal of the gross racial injustices of our world, or in the exposure of the tyrannies of family life on the individual. As art this can be badly done, it can be brilliantly done. But I am going to suggest that it isn't achieving its end or illuminating our lives any more, and that a more effective technique can and should be cultivated.
>
> (DA, p. 34)

The irony of course is that if 'we have a literature and an artistic culture, one might almost say a civilization, of depicted suffering, whether in social life or in family life', then this is the legacy of Christianity in general and Catholicism in particular. A culture of depicted suffering might capture succinctly Spark's own predicament, as a de-picted writer, one whose Scottishness is picked out, if not written out, both depicted and de-picted.

Spark goes on to make a Derridian argument about the catastrophic model of the committed writer, and the risks of closure in a certain kind of committed writing (DA, p. 35). She describes the experience of closure drawn by a reader from such a committed art:

He has undergone the experience of pity for the underdog. Salt tears have gone bowling down his cheeks. He has had a good dinner. He is absolved, he sleeps well. He rises refreshed, more determined than ever to be the overdog. And there is always, too, the man who finds the heroic role of the victim so appealing that he'll never depart from it. I suggest that wherever there is a cult of the victim, such being human nature, there will be an obliging cult of twenty equivalent victimizers.

(DA, p. 35)

But Spark too 'has undergone the experience of pity for the underdog' through her conversion to Catholicism, and has emerged as an overdog. The art of ridicule Spark advocates is an art of looking down the nose at those beneath contempt, an attitude that is at once satirical and 'sniffy':

But the power and influence of the creative arts is not to be belittled. I only say that the art and literature of sentiment and emotion, however beautiful in itself, however striking in its depiction of actuality, has to go. It cheats us into a sense of involvement with life and society, but in reality it is a segregated activity. In its place I advocate the arts of satire and of ridicule. And I see no other living art form for the future.

Ridicule is the only honourable form we have left ... And I say we should all be conditioned and educated to regard violence in any form as something to be ruthlessly mocked.

(DA, p. 35)

In her charged advocacy of 'the art of ridicule', the stigma or stigmata of satire, which, she says, 'can leave a salutary scar', Spark both opposes and underwrites, subverts and subscribes to violence (DA, p. 36). Derrida might add that writing in general, and satire in particular, was a form of violence in itself.[35] Spark's contention is that 'the art of protest, the art which condemns violence and suffering by pathetic depiction is becoming a cult separated from the actions of our life' (DA, p. 36). This in other hands would be a critique of Christianity and of Catholicism in particular, with its cult of Christ crucified.

Derrida and Spark have both been labelled anti-humanists, but it is fairer to say that they share an affinity for animals that makes them question the limits of subjectivity as applied solely to humanity. Spark describes herself as 'a sort of writing animal' (DA, p. 36). In this she comes close once more to Derrida, who when asked where he gets his ideas, replied: 'A sort of animal movement seeks to appropriate what always comes, always, from an *external* provocation'.[36] Indeed, Derrida has gone so far as to say that 'man is not the only political animal'.[37]

If Spark's view of writers is that they are servants, then some of her critics, judging by their attitude to servants, have a low regard for writers. Lister, according to Joseph Hynes, 'is listening to the three voices quarrelling in the locked library, from which the commonsense reader would have the servants rescue them. But common sense is merely realistic, so that Lister can ignore such inquiry or expectation and can instead say, "What is to emerge must emerge"'.[38] The commonsense reader would have a better class of servant. You just can't get the servants these days. Hynes proceeds thus:

> Up to a point, no doubt, we can say that these are simply servants who, like many servants, know the upstairs residents so well that it is not at all unusual for them to call some shots (so to speak) and to see some outcomes as inevitable: married couples of certain appetites and incomes and morals may (perhaps even will) almost certainly come to ends of a sort.
>
> (p. 242)

Hynes writes: 'every reader is familiar with maidservants turning up pregnant, and everyone can admire the opportunistic use to which Lister and his crew put the pregnancy in their quick decision to attribute the deed to "him in the attic" and thereby marry Heloise and themselves into inheriting the estate' (p. 246). Does the claim that 'every reader is familiar with maidservants turning up pregnant' refer to the experience of reading a certain kind of fiction, or to a particular way of life? (I tend not to read the kind of books that have servants in them.) Heloise fears that 'him in the attic', the split heir, 'might create or take one of his turns'. And he does create, and he does take his turn. In Allan Massie's phrase, 'the natural order is disturbed'.[39] You just can't get the servants these days, or the critics worthy of them.

Peter Kemp describes *Not to Disturb* as 'a very noisy book', and chilling one too, with 'a vampire crew of servants metaphorically battening upon the blood of others', but who are the parasites here and who are the hosts?[40] Spark's contention, at least in my view, is that there is a mutually assured destruction between aristocracy and peasantry, between the arrogant and the ignorant (however knowing in the ways of the world). Kemp, however, goes on to acknowledge a kind of poetic, if not social justice: 'What happens has a retributive rightness. Those unwilling to be disturbed are caught in a deadly drama they cannot disturb. Having lived by fiction, these people are destroyed by it' (p. 136). Kemp goes further, and suggests that Spark is exposing the extent to which class is a construct dependent on image as much as economics: 'aristocracy, the book constantly implies, is itself an illusion, totally dependent on setting and indicative of no genuine *noblesse*' (p. 137).

In an interview, Spark spoke of *Not to Disturb*, admitting that: 'One of my motives is to provoke the reader; to startle as well as to please'.[41] Spark is a disturber of the peace, a disjointer of time, of narrative drive and sequence. 'Let us not', as Lister says, 'strain after vulgar chronology', and let us listen to Eleanor when she advises Heloise: 'Don't be crude or literal' (p. 66). 'Let us not split hairs', says Lister, 'between the past, present and future tenses'. Let us instead split heirs, as the servants do, and as happened in *Hamlet*, a work that has as much to do with sex and ghosts and split heirs as *Not to Disturb*, and a key text for deconstruction. Derrida has gone so far as to say that deconstruction could be summed up in a single phrase from *Hamlet*: 'The time is out of joint'. According to Derrida, deconstruction consists precisely in 'deconstructing, dislocating, displacing, disarticulating, disjoining, putting "out of joint" the authority of the "is"'.[42] Pablo the handyman's closing comment about 'Ghosts and fantasies rising from sex repression' is apposite (N, p. 92), as is Hadrian's allusion to 'The flight of the homosexuals', a flight that has dearly departed (N, p. 91). Andrea Dworkin's famous dictum that 'pornography sexualises inequality' is implicit in Spark's suggestion that scandal is an effect of class difference, as well as a consequence of media manipulation. As Peter Kemp puts it: 'Most relevant to the catastrophe ... are the sexual charades the Klopstocks have a taste for, pornographic scenarios fleshed out by an affluence-procured cast of servants, secretaries, and cousins'.[43]

Not to Disturb ends with a disquieting image, that of couple of unconscious and invisible policemen, unconscious because dozing, invisible because out of uniform:

> The plain-clothes man in the hall is dozing on a chair, waiting for the relief man to come, as is also the plain-clothes man on the upstairs landing. The household is straggling up the back stairs to their beds. By noon they will be covered in the profound sleep of

those who have kept faithful vigil all night, while outside the house the sunlight is laughing on the walls.

(N, p. 96)

Jacques Derrida would fasten onto this passage, since he is obsessed by the police, haunted by them, whether in uniform or in plain clothes:

> Let us take the example of the police, this index of a phantom-like violence because it mixes foundation with conservation and becomes all the more violent for this. Well, the police that thus capitalize on violence aren't simply the police. They do not simply consist of policemen in uniform, occasionally helmeted, armed and organized in a civil structure on a military model to whom the right to strike is refused, and so forth. By definition, the police are present, sometimes invisible but always effective, wherever there is preservation of the social order. The police aren't just the police (today more or less than ever), they are there, the faceless figure ... coextensive with the *Dasein* of the *polis* ... In so-called civilized states the specter of its ghostly apparition is all-pervasive ... It is the *modern* police, in politico-technical *modern* situations that have led to *produce* the law that they are only supposed to *enforce* ... While recognizing that the phantom body of the police, however invasive it may be, always remains equal to itself, he admits that its spirit ... the spirit of the police, does less damage in absolute monarchy than it does in modern democracies where violence degenerates ... The police become hallucinatory and spectral because they haunt everything; they are everywhere.[44]

Though he is inclined to extend the notion of policing to reading and to criticism, both in its close reading, soft-boiled detective guise, and in its hard-boiled, deep cover, 'contextual' or historicist form, elsewhere Derrida says 'there are police and police':

> There is a police that is brutally and *rather* 'physically' repressive (but the police is never purely physical;) and there are more sophisticated police that are more 'cultural' or 'spiritual', more noble. But every institution destined to enforce the law is a police. An academy is a police, whether in the sense of a university or of the *Académie Française*, whose essential task is to enforce respect for and obedience to ... the French language, to decide what ought to be

considered 'good' French, etc. But I never said that the police as such and a priori ... There is no society without police even if one can always dream of forms of police that would be more sublime, more refined or less vulgar.[45]

Spark too dreams of a more sublime police, of servants who keep their masters in line, though her dreams have a nightmarish quality. To be or not to be disturbed, that is the question. The key for me to Spark's political force as a writer lies in her mercurial manipulation of language. According to Derrida:

In many departments what is considered threatening is not a politically revolutionary position, if it is expressed in a coded and traditional way, rather, it is something which sometimes doesn't look political but disturbs the traditional ways of reading, understanding, discussing, writing, using rhetoric, etc. – because this undermines, or not necessarily undermines, but at least discovers, what was hidden in the institution.[46]

Spark is a disturbing writer, and, with one or two reservations – her individual and self-deluding pacifism spring to mind – a deconstructive one too.

Notes

1. Alan Bold, in Joseph Hynes (ed.), *Critical Essays on Muriel Spark* (New York: G. K. Hall, 1992), p. 94.
2. *Not to Disturb*, p. 30.
3. Joseph Hynes, 'Introduction', *Critical Essays on Muriel Spark*, p. 2.
4. Jean-François Lyotard, discussing Swift's *Directions to Servants*, in the 'Foreword' to Andrew Benjamin (ed.), *The Lyotard Reader* (Oxford: Blackwell, 1989), p. x.
5. Alan Sinfield, '*Macbeth*: History, Ideology and Intellectuals', in Colin MacCabe (ed.), *Futures for English* (Manchester: Manchester University Press, 1988), pp. 63–77.
6. Joseph Hynes, 'Muriel Spark and the Oxymoronic Vision', in Robert E. Hosmer, Jr. (ed.), *Contemporary British Women Writers: Texts and Strategies* (Basingstoke: Macmillan, 1993), p. 163.
7. Spark's critique of socially conscious art echoes Robert Louis Stevenson's response to Zola. See 'A Note on Realism' in *The Collected Works of Robert Louis Stevenson*, Vol. 24: *Essays Critical and Literary* (London: Waverley Press, 1925), pp. 77–83. I am grateful to Graeme Macdonald for drawing my attention to this reference.
8. Jean-François Lyotard, 'Answering the Question: What is Postmodernism?',

in Thomas Docherty (ed.), *Postmodernism: A Reader* (Sussex: Harvester Wheatsheaf, 1993), p. 41.

9. Muriel Spark, 'My Conversion', in Hynes (ed.), *Critical Essays on Muriel Spark*, p.28. Hereafter abbreviated as MC. Regarding this essay see p. 128 n. 12.

10. Hynes, 'Muriel Spark and the Oxymoronic Vision', p. 170.

11. Patricia Stubbs, 'Two Contemporary Views on Fiction: Iris Murdoch and Muriel Spark', *English* 23, 117 (1974), p. 110.

12. Spark, 'Edinburgh-born', in Hynes (ed.), *Critical Essays on Muriel Spark*, p. 21. Hereafter abbreviated as EB.

13. '– I said that I had lost faith, Stephen answered, but not that I had lost self-respect. What kind of liberation would that be to forsake an absurdity which is logical and coherent and to embrace one which is illogical and incoherent?' James Joyce, *A Portrait of the Artist as a Young Man*, p. 358.

14. Jacques Derrida, *Monolingualism of the Other; or, The Prosthesis of Origin*, trans. Patrick Mensah (Stanford: Stanford University Press, 1998).

15. Derrida, *Monolingualism of the Other*, p. 46.

16. Derrida, *Monolingualism of the Other*, p. 48.

17. Norman Page, *Muriel Spark* (London: Macmillan, 1990), p. 83.

18. Page, *Muriel Spark*, p. 85.

19. Page, *Muriel Spark*, p. 81.

20. Malcolm Bradbury, 'Muriel Spark's Fingernails', *Critical Quarterly* 14, 3 (1972), p. 245.

21. Page, *Muriel Spark*, p. 87.

22. Page, *Muriel Spark*, p. 96.

23. Bradbury, 'Muriel Spark's Fingernails', p. 242.

24. Bradbury, 'Muriel Spark's Fingernails', p. 250.

25. Parrinder, 'Muriel Spark and Her Critics', p. 24.

26. Derek Attridge, "'This Strange Institution Called Literature': An Interview with Jacques Derrida', in Attridge (ed.), *Acts of Literature: Jacques Derrida* (London: Routledge, 1992), p. 51.

27. Parrinder, 'Muriel Spark and Her Critics', p. 26.

28. In several letters, O'Connor refers to her reading of Spark's novels, including 'a very lively one called *Memento Mori*'. (Sally Fitzgerald, *Flannery O'Connor: The Habit of Being, Letters* edited and with an Introduction by Sally Fitzgerald (New York: Farrar Strauss Giroux, 1979), p. 331.) Elsewhere, O'Connor remarked 'I've got all of Muriel Spark ...'. On 21 March 1964, writing to Father John McCown, a Catholic priest who had asked her about writers who shared her faith, she listed Spark alongside other 'English' authors: 'The English are Waugh & Greene and Spark (Muriel)'. (p. 570.) On 15 May 1964, O'Connor thanks a friend for '*The Girls of Slender Means*, which came at 12 o'clock noon and I finished before I went to bed. I really did like it, better than the others. Some of hers settle in the middle, but that one humps right along'. (p. 577.)

29. Parrinder, 'Muriel Spark and Her Critics', p. 31.

30. Sinfield, '*Macbeth*: History, Ideology and Intellectuals', p. 63.

31. Sinfield, '*Macbeth*: History, Ideology and Intellectuals', p. 63.

32. Derrida, *Monolingualism of the Other*.

33. See my 'Swearing Blind: Kelman and the Curse of the Working Classes', *The*

Edinburgh Review 95 (1996), pp. 105–12, and 'Subversion and Squirrility in Irvine Welsh's Shorter Fiction', in Dermot Cavanagh and Tim Kirk (eds), *Subversion and Scurrility: Popular Discourse in Europe from 1500 to the Present* (Aldershot: Ashgate Press, 2000), pp. 191–205.

34. See Jacques Derrida, ''But Beyond . . . (Open Letter to Anne McClintock and Rob Nixon)', trans. P. Kamuf, in Henry Louis Gates, Jr, *'Race', Writing, and Difference* (University of Chicago Press: Chicago, 1986), pp. 354–69.

35. For this revised and enlarged concept of violence see Jacques Derrida, 'Violence and Metaphysics: An Essay on the Thought of Emmanuel Levinas', in *Writing and Difference*, trans. Alan Bass (London: Routledge, 1978), p. 313, n. 21.

36. Jacques Derrida, 'A 'Madness' Must Watch Over Thinking', trans. Peggy Kamuf, in Elisabeth Weber (ed.), *Points. . . Interviews, 1974–1994: Jacques Derrida* (Stanford: Stanford University Press, 1995), p. 352.

37. Jacques Derrida, 'Afterword', *Limited Inc*, trans. Samuel Weber and Jeffrey Mehlman, edited Gerald Graff (Evanston, Ill.: Northwestern University Press, 1988), p. 136.

38. Hynes, *Critical Essays on Muriel Spark* , p. 242.

39. Allan Massie, *Muriel Spark* (Edinburgh: Ramsay Head Press, 1979), p. 76.

40. Peter Kemp, *Muriel Spark* (London: Paul Elek, 1974), p. 130, p. 131.

41. Cited Kemp, *Muriel Spark*, p. 141.

42. Jacques Derrida, 'The Time is out of Joint', in Anselm Haverkamp (ed.), *Deconstruction is/in America: A New Sense of the Political* (New York and London: New York University Press, 1995), p. 25.

43. Kemp, *Muriel Spark*, p. 135.

44. Jacques Derrida, 'Force of Law: The "Mystical Foundation of Authority"', in Drucilla Cornell, Michel Rosenfeld, and David Gray (eds), *Deconstruction and the Possibility of Justice* (New York and London: Routledge, 1992), pp. 3–67.

45. Derrida, *Limited Inc*, pp. 135–6.

46. Jacques Derrida, 'Some Questions and Responses', in Nigel Fabb, Derek Attridge, Alan Durant, and Colin MacCabe (eds), *The Linguistics of Writing: Arguments Between Language and Literature* (Manchester: Manchester University Press, 1987), p. 256.

11
Memento Mori

Nicholas Royle

Feel secure
Don't like receiving calls from callers who withhold their
number? Anonymous Call Rejection is for you! It blocks
incoming calls where numbers have been withheld for just
£9.99 per quarter. For further information call 150.

(*BT Update*, April 2000)

The telephone rings. You think about answering it.

There is a moment in Elizabeth Bowen's *The House in Paris* (1935)
where a woman exclaims with incredulity: 'Reason? You might as
well say, what *reason* has one to answer the telephone?'[1] One answers
the phone, even if it makes no sense. It is without reason, if not
rhyme.

In English, and therefore in some sense perhaps untranslatably, the
phone's ring is rhymed, mimed, answered in its answering. Why does
one speak of answering a ring, of someone ringing or ringing off? (This
last connection cannot be made transatlantically, in so far as American
English speaks of calling, not ringing, someone.) In what ways,
according to what circuitry, does the ring ring true, or not?

What if you cannot answer it? What if the telephone were to be ringing and you never answer it, even though you spend your entire life trying to reach it? Why would literature, and in particular narrative fiction, have a privileged place in the context of trying to think about such questions?

I have said this before, a while ago now: the question of the telephone cannot be dissociated from that of telepathy. You understood then, even if now you're feeling completely disconnected.

> Dame Lettie Colston refilled her fountain-pen and continued her letter:
>
>> One of these days I hope you will write as brilliantly on a happier theme. In these days of cold war I *do* feel we should soar above the murk & smog & get into the clear crystal.
>
> The telephone rang. She lifted the receiver. As she had feared, the man spoke before she could say a word. When he had spoken the familiar sentence she said, 'Who is that speaking, who is it?'
> But the voice, as on eight previous occasions, had rung off.
> Dame Lettie telephoned to the Assistant Inspector as she had been requested to do. 'It has occurred again,' she said.
>
> (MM, p. 9)

So, one might loosely say, begins Muriel Spark's novel, *Memento Mori* (1959). But the novel begins, as one also says in Latin, *in medias res*, into the midst of things, already in the ghostly thick of telemedia. Dame Lettie Colston is refilling her fountain-pen; she is in the midst of writing, and writing about writing ('One of these days I hope you will write as brilliantly on a happier theme'). She is writing to Eric about his novel, and compares his work to that of his novelist mother, Charmian Piper. As she tells her husband Godfrey: '[Eric] has something of his mother's former brilliance, but it did seem to me that the subject-matter lacked the joy and hope which was the mark of a good novel in those days' (MM, p. 12). *Memento Mori* is packed with references to Charmian's once-fashionable novels and her novelistic reputation (there's repeated allusion to what is playfully called her novelistic 'revival': see for example MM, pp. 97, 123, 155, 184, 198), as well as with other examples of people pursuing writing projects – notably, Alec Warner with his absurd pseudonymous case histories of other characters (see MM, p. 61); Guy Leet with his memoirs; and Percy Mannering with his poetry (including the many versions and revisions of a sonnet entitled 'Memento Mori': see MM, p. 194).

The critical convention has been to put all this under the rubric of Spark's 'metafiction'. No longer a fashionable word, perhaps 'metafiction' needs to be *revived*, but with new heart. Take a standard definition, such as Patricia Waugh's, from her 1983 book, *Metafiction: The Theory and Practice of Self-Conscious Fiction*:

> *Metafiction* is a term given to fictional writing which self-consciously and systematically draws attention to its status as an artefact in order to pose questions about the relationship between fiction and reality. In providing a critique of their own methods of construction, such writings not only examine the fundamental structures of narrative fiction, they also explore the possible fictionality of the world outside the literary fictional text.[2]

There is something troubling about this seemingly easy deployment of 'fiction' and 'reality' as a binary opposition, about the idea of the literary work as a 'systematic', method-determined 'artefact' whose purpose is to 'provide a critique' of its own 'construction'. It recalls the foggy days of literary-critical-structuralism-as-science. Above all, perhaps, there is a problem with the notion of self-consciousness, a term that besets and muddles Waugh's project, starting from the title of her book. She claims that 'If metafiction is to be seen as a positive stage in the development of the novel, then its relevance and sensitivity to the increasing and diverse manifestations of self-consciousness in the culture as a whole have to be established' (p. 28). I lack telepathic insight into what Waugh means by 'a positive stage in the development of the novel', but I think her focus on self-consciousness perhaps elides what is most historically significant about the emergence of so-called metafiction, namely a new sense of how circumscribed, displaced, aporetic and spectralized the notion of self-consciousness becomes in the course of the twentieth century, the century summed up by Jacques Derrida as 'that of the techno-scientific and effective decentring of the earth, of geopolitics, of the *anthropos* in its onto-theological identity or its genetic properties, of the *ego cogito* – and of the very concept of narcissism'.[3] What is distinctive about 'metafiction' is a logic not so much of self-consciousness (as Waugh's study suggests) but of self-referring. Fiction cannot but refer to the fact that it is fiction (it cannot 'live' without this ghostly self-referring), but this self-referring remains irrevocably a moment *within* that fiction. The moment of self-referring at once belongs and does not belong to the fiction. The historical emergence of 'metafiction' in the 1960s is bound up with a new foregrounding of this strange logic (what has elsewhere been called 'participation without belonging'[4]): even if there is no fiction that is not in some respects metafictional, a dislocation of the sovereignty and authority of the figure of the author and of authorial self-consciousness is hooked up to that foregrounding. In this context, one might try to read Spark's novel, for example starting with its title, with a view to a new, spectrally 'revived' sense of 'metafiction'. The phrase *memento mori* would sound, like a telephone, without self-consciousness.

The novel begins with a scene of writing that has already begun, caught up in the scene of another telemedium, a telephone call that has happened before. It's as if Dame Lettie knows who it is going to be, or rather as if she knows it's going to be *that* voice again or knows at least what *words* she is going to hear, 'the familiar sentence'. She's experienced this before, 'on eight previous occasions': she does 'as she had been requested to do. "It has occurred again," she said.' Spark's text explores the notion of presentiment, the feeling that you know in advance who is going to be at the other end of the phone, it's déjà vu, déjà entendu, telepathy. In the case of each of these terms ('presentiment', 'déjà vu', 'déjà entendu', 'telepathy') what is at issue is something that will have interrupted every presentism, something that Derrida would call a 'structure of experience rather than a religion'[5], something tapping into thought in its imminence, the coming of the threat or promise, a telephone call to come.

Spark's work is pervaded by the telepathic. This is evident not just at the level of character and plot, where people seem to be reading each other's minds, picking up their words or thoughts, or feeling that their words or thoughts are being picked up by others: in *Memento Mori*, for example, we may think of the inaugural phone call itself, of various characters inexplicably picking up and using the phrase 'wonderful form' (MM, pp. 19–20), or of the moment when Miss Jean Taylor finishes one of Dame Lettie's thoughts for her:

> 'Being over seventy [said Miss Taylor] is like being engaged in a war. All our friends are going or gone and we survive amongst the dead and the dying as on a battlefield.'
> She is wandering in her mind and becoming morbid, thought Dame Lettie.
> 'Or suffering from war nerves,' said Miss Taylor.
>
> (MM, p. 37)

Such cases of mind-reading or the uncanny transmission of thoughts are bound up with the very nature of fictional narration. What happens under the rubric of 'metafiction' is indissociable from the question of telepathy. This is evident everywhere in Spark, starting with her first novel, *The Comforters* (1957), where the protagonist Caroline is unable to receive a certain telephone call from Sussex:

> Caroline thought, 'Well, he will ring in the morning.' She lay on her divan staring out at the night sky beyond her balcony, too tired to draw the curtains. She was warmed by the knowledge that Laurence was near to hand, wanting to speak to her. She could rely on him to take her side, should there be any difficulty with Helena over her rapid departure from St Philumena's. On the whole she did not think there would be any difficulty with Helena.
> Just then she heard the sound of a typewriter. It seemed to come through the wall on her left. It stopped, and was immediately followed by a voice remarking her own thoughts. It said: *On the whole she did not think there would be any difficulty with Helena.*
>
> (CO, p. 42)

Telephony, telepathy and narrative discourse share a party-line in Spark. A third person fictional narrative like *Memento Mori* is based on the fiction of a narrator who is able to inhabit the bodies, thoughts and feelings of different characters: this is what is sometimes, and quite misleadingly, referred to as 'omniscient narration'. At moments

Spark's novel makes metafictional fun of omniscience, for instance in its figuration of the Criminal Investigation Department as 'God, understanding all mysteries and all knowledge' (MM, p. 153), or the mental patient in Folkestone who 'thought he was God' (MM, p. 218). Saying so may run against the grain of Spark's declared religious beliefs and against the grain of the novel's religious construal of death, but omniscience in the context of literary narrative is itself a fiction. Metafiction might be said to entail a making explicit of this fiction-ality and a new sense of the possibilities of thinking about literary narration as telepathic rather than omniscient.

'Rubric of metafiction', did I say?

> **Rubric:** *n* a heading, guiding rule, entry or liturgical direction, *orig* one in red ink; a flourish after a signature; a thing definitely settled (*Chambers*).

'Rubric' can appear in Spark's work in a specifically liturgical context, for example in that description, near the start of *The Prime of Miss Jean Brodie*, of 'the lectern which ... held an open Bible with the text underlined in red ink, "O where shall I find a virtuous woman, for her price is above rubies"' (p. 6). Much red ink might be devoted to demonstrating how the rubric, the rubric of 'rubric', trembles, spills over: the rubric as 'a thing definitely settled' yet at the same time calling for other readings, unset-tled of its own, their own, 'telephone accords'; 'rubric' as what comes after (added on to a text, for instance as 'a flourish after a signature'), but also before ('a heading' or 'guiding entry').

That, in a sense, is the only thing I am interested in spilling here. But why is Spark's work so bloodless? Is this what the text means by 'cold war'? For a novel so full of death and corpses and people dying, there is curiously little blood in *Memento Mori*: there is occasional talk of 'blood pressure' (for instance MM, pp. 49 and 219); Granny Trotsky dies 'as the result of the bursting of a small blood-vessel in her brain' (MM, p. 51); Granny Roberts, another of those lined up to die in one of the geriatric beds on the Maud Long Ward, may wonder if the whole thing is just 'a bloody circus' (MM, p. 118); but the closest the novel comes to bloodiness is in the death of Dame Lettie herself when, without the mention of spilling a drop of blood, a burglar is described as having 'wrenched the stick from the old woman's hand and, with the blunt end of it, battered her to death' (p. 179). Such a long way – but in only twenty years – from Muriel Spark's *Memento Mori* to Angela Carter's *The Bloody Chamber* (1979): elsewhere, some day, I would like to write a history of blood in literature, a critical discourse like a measuring device that would assess and analyze figurations of blood and blood-levels. So much red, to be read. The rubric I am interested in spilling here, in showing to be spilt or split already, before the rubric, the rubric of rubric, is that of the title of this novel. The title-phrase constitutes the rubric of Spark's text. 'Memento mori' is what one must live up to, in other words first of all it is what one must read. *Memento legere.* The title comes at the beginning, at the head of the text, accompanied by various other peritextual material, including three epigraphs (from W. B. Yeats, Thomas Traherne and *The Penny Catechism*) and a dedication ('For Teresa Walshe with love'). But 'memento mori' is also a sort of flourish, linked to the signature, coming in a sense *after* the novel, the rubric that sums it up, encapsulates and capitalizes it. We talk as if we know what a title is, as if we know *when* it is, as if we know what 'memento mori' means.

The *OED* gives two meanings:

> **memento mori** [L. = 'remember that you have to die'.] **a.** A warning of death. **b.** *concr.* A reminder of death, such as a skull or other symbolical object.

I love that '*concr.*': it must be an abbreviation for 'concrete' (ah, the mad vocabulary of lexicography: will we ever know our way about the hallucinatorily concrete precincts of concrete adjectives, nouns and verbs?) Under the *OED* entry for 'concrete', I have just discovered the following note:

> In this Dictionary, *concr.* is prefixed to those senses in which substantives originally abstract come to be used as names of 'things' [why must the editors put 'things' in quotation marks here? What does this 'concretize', do you think?]; e.g. *crossing* vbl. n., i.e. abstract n. of action, *concr. a crossing* in a street, on a railway, etc.

What is buried in this *'concr.'*? The 'concrete' is 'symbolical'. How can what is concrete be a symbol? 'Memento mori' is firstly 'a warning of death', says the *OED*, but secondly *and concretely* 'a reminder ... such as a skull or other symbolical object'. Sense **a** has to do with the future ('a warning'), sense **b** with the past ('a reminder'): how is 'memento mori' split, spilt in this way between warning and reminder? Fissured between future and past, to what time would 'memento mori' belong? The fault here is not the *OED*'s, but a fault in sense, a fault we cannot not repeat. This strange temporality is also at work in the word 'memento' itself, that little word that thus becomes, for Derrida, a sort of synonym (without 'meaning') for 'deconstruction'.[6] In sense 2 the *OED* states:

> Memento: **2. a.** A reminder, warning, or hint as to conduct or with regard to future events. ? *Obs.* **b.** *concr.* An object serving to remind or warn in this way.

As the earliest example of sense **2. a** we are given: '1582 STANYHURST Æneis I. (Arb.) 22 Bee sure, this practise wil I nick in a freendlye memento.'

Something funny, I was saying, going on in the *OED*'s 'a reminder ... such as a skull or other symbolical object'. What is the status of the 'or' here? In what way is a skull a 'symbolical object' and in what ways would it be 'merely' an example? What other examples might be considered comparable? In *1 Henry IV* Bardolph complains to Falstaff: 'Why, Sir John, my face does you no harm.' Falstaff retorts: 'No, I'll be sworn, I make as good use of it as many a man doth of a death's-head or a *memento mori*. I never see thy face but I think upon hell-fire' (III, iii, 28–31). In Falstaff's vivifying trope, the so-called living face becomes a *memento mori*. Falstaff 's 'or' will have anticipated a more general hesitation: it would seem as if 'a death's-head' is not a *memento mori*, or at least as if there is something about the figure of *memento mori* that is not at one with itself, that calls for a supplement of itself, that carries a strange 'or' within itself.

Can one experience a 'memento mori'? Can one read the phrase, the title and rubric of Spark's novel? Will it be possible to move beyond this title-phrase, or even reach it, let alone respond to it? It is perhaps the most darkly sparkling thing about this novel, not only in or for itself but also with respect to what it suggests about titles and naming more generally. The title plays across the text, from beginning to end, before the beginning and beyond the end. 'Memento mori' is the title of the text, but the text is itself a 'memento mori'. As always with the logic of the example, it goes beyond itself, suggesting a way of thinking about the genre of the novel as *memento mori*. A character (first of all Dame Lettie but in due course most of the other named characters) receives a telephone call and hears a voice that says: '*Remember you must die*' (MM, p. 10). What is going on in the unspoken, tacit translation from the so-called dead language of Latin ('memento mori') to the so-called living language of English ('remember you must die')? The Latin phrase does not occur in the text itself until near the end (MM, p. 168); but as title, the Latin phrase lends an ironic decorum and cryptic power, serving to generate what might be called a memento-monumentality. Think if Spark's novel were titled in English, *Remember You Must Die*. 'Spark out': that's a slang term, if I remember correctly, for 'die'.

Remember correctly? The strange time of 'memento mori' (warning as regards the future, reminder as regards the past) is also audible in the English translation, 'remember you must die', 'remember that you have to die': why 'remember'? Doubtless it evokes its conventional opposite, forgetfulness: 'remember you must die' may seem to presume that you have forgotten you must die. So much is, perhaps, obvious. As Freud observes: 'It is true that the statement "All men are mortal" is paraded in text-books of logic as an example of a general proposition; but no human being really grasps it, and our unconscious has as little use now as it ever had for the idea of its own mortality'.[7] But the strangeness of the phrase remains, even in its most apparently legible and superficial form: how can you remember what has not happened and indeed never will be something that you could verify as having happened to you? As if it would be possible to say: Look, I have died! It's a good job I remembered.

☎

Spark's text at moments seems to subscribe to this notion of impossible memory:

> [Charmian] had reached the first half-landing when the telephone rang. She did not hurry, but it was still ringing when she reached it ...
>   'Charmian Piper – that's right, isn't it?'
>   'Yes. Are you a reporter?'
>   'Remember,' he said, 'you must die.'
>   'Oh, as to that,' she said, 'for the past thirty years and more I have thought of it from time to time. My memory is failing in certain respects. I am gone eighty-six. But somehow I do not forget my death, whenever that will be.'
>   'Delighted to hear it,' he said. 'Good-bye for now.'
>   'Good-bye,' she said. 'What paper do you represent?'
>   But he had rung off.
>
> (MM, p. 127)

Gone eighty-six, memory failing, Charmian does not forget her death, we are invited to suppose. But can anyone do this? And who could bear witness, even within oneself, in all so-called 'self-consciousness'? Can anyone not forget what is impossible to imagine, at least in the sense that Freud has in mind when he says: 'It is indeed impossible to imagine our own death; and whenever we attempt to do so we can perceive that we are in fact still present as spectators'?[8] Doubtless the novel's proclivity towards claiming to 'remember' is bound up with its religious, and specifically Christian, dimensions. The epigraph from *The Penny Catechism* that precedes the narrative comes back in the final words of the novel (MM, p. 220): 'The four last things to be ever remembered are Death, Judgement, Hell, and Heaven.' Spark seeks to impose a Christian framework elsewhere in the text as well, for instance in the account of Granny Trotsky's death: 'In the course of the night Granny Trotsky died as the result of the bursting of a small blood-vessel in her brain, and her spirit returned to God who gave it' (MM, p. 51). There is something faintly absurd about this, as though you could point at a telephone and say: This is a Christian telephone; it only takes Christian calls.

Mind out: ABYSS AHEAD. I love that phrase, 'mind out'. As Mrs Pettigrew tells Godfrey as he drives her towards Sloane Square: 'Watch where you're going, we'll have an accident. Mind out ...' (MM, p. 163).

'Remember you must die' is the abyssal refrain of the novel (see, for instance, MM, pp. 10, 38–9, 52, 100, 120, 124, 127, 137–8, 141–2, 147–9, 150, 150–1, 153, 165, 168, 175, 184, 192–3, 194, 207–8). Please forgive that line of numbers bedded down here: after all, numbers are the stuff of Spark's text – it loves to tell us how old everyone is, everyone seems to go about with a ghostly number (an age, though never a telephone number) attached to them. It is like a bizarre textual supermarket in which all characters are required to have an age-tag like a price and sell-by date. Consider the 'check out' of the final pages:

> Charmian died one morning in the following spring, at the age of eighty-seven.
> Godfrey died the same year ...
> Guy Leet died at the age of seventy-eight ...
> Ronald Sidebottome is allowed up in the afternoons but is not expected to last another winter.
> Janet Sidebottome died of a stroke following an increase in blood pressure, at the age of seventy-seven ...
> Chief Inspector Mortimer died suddenly of heart-failure at the age of seventy-three, while boarding his yacht *The Dragonfly*.
>
> (MM, pp. 218–19)

This final section of *Memento Mori* operates as a sort of memento, a kind of warning or foreshadowing of – and hinting towards – the eerie structure of *The Prime of Miss Jean Brodie* (1961). In this novel, too, notions of age, in particular youth and prime, are subjected to strange displacements. The final section of *Memento Mori* performs a time-skip and lets us know, in a comically but disquietingly cursory manner, how and when the various remaining characters in the story died. In *The Prime of Miss Jean Brodie* these death-divulging time-skips punctuate the narrative throughout. Thus of Mary Macgregor we read:

Back and forth along the corridors ran Mary Macgregor, through the thickening smoke. She ran one way; then, turning, the other way; and at either end the blast furnace of the fire met her. She heard no screams, for the roar of the fire drowned the screams; she gave no scream, for the smoke was choking her. She ran into somebody on her third turn, stumbled and died. But at the beginning of the nineteen-thirties, when Mary Macgregor was ten, there she was sitting blankly among Miss Brodie's pupils. 'Who has spilled ink on the floor – was it you, Mary?'

(P, p. 15)

The Prime of Miss Jean Brodie is another *memento mori*, at once about the concept (if it is one) of 'memento mori', and itself a *memento mori*. The earlier novel rings and resonates across it.

This business about putting an age-tag on characters is no doubt a way of dating the novel. Why does it become conventional, with what presuppositions and effects, for novels to issue these age-tags? It becomes established in the course of the nineteenth century: one associates it with Henry James, for example, but not Jane Austen. *Memento Mori* takes it to a comical extreme. This is in keeping with the novel's playfulness as an exploration of old age. On the one hand there is the 'absurdity' of 'decrepit age' (to recall the terms of Spark's opening epigraph, from W. B. Yeats's 'The Tower'). On the other, there is the sense of old age as 'venerable', ecstatic, sublime. The latter is linked to Spark's second epigraph, from an astonishing Christian messianic, expectation-talking passage in the Third Century of Traherne's *Meditations* (c.1668–71), in which the world is recalled from the perspective of being 'a little child again':

O what venerable and reverend creatures did the aged seem! Immortal cherubims! ... Boys and girls tumbling in the street, and playing, were moving jewels. I knew not that they were born or should die. But all things abided eternally as they were in their proper places. Eternity was manifest in the light of the day, and something infinite behind everything appeared: which talked with my expectation and moved my desire.[9]

Gerontophobia has a history: indeed, it does not appear in the 1989 edition of the *OED*, though it figures in the 1998 edition of *Chambers*, defined there as 'an irrational fear of old people and old age'. In this sense, it is an invention of the second half of the twentieth century. In a book called *Aging and Its Discontents*, Kathleen Woodward argues that psychoanalysis has played an important, negative role in the emergence of this phenomenon: 'Freudian psychoanalysis is complicit with our culture's repression of aging ... [T]he profound gerontophobia in our culture should be extirpated, and one of the ways to begin that process is to examine critically our representations of aging and to work to produce new ones'.[10] *Memento Mori* explores old age in ways at once productive and comical: if Freud's is (in Woodward's words) 'a powerful discourse of subjectivity and generational relations ... firmly anchored in infancy and early childhood' (p. 9), Spark's novel suggests new perspectives based on an anchoring in old age. The originality of *Memento Mori* partly lies here – as an inaugural text in a genre one might call gerontophobic satire.

Memento vivere: this phrase perhaps first occurs in Edmund Blunden's great memento-work about the First World War, *Undertones of War* (1928), in a chapter entitled 'Trench Education', where he recalls: 'One night while Doogan was sitting in the headquarters dugout with *La Vie Parisienne* as a *memento vivere*, a shot arrived in the earth wall just above him by way of *memento mori*'.[11] The phrase should not be taken simply as an opposition to 'memento mori': one would haunt the other. Remember to live, mind out you do, learn to do it, as well as you can. The entire oeuvre of Jacques Derrida might be summarized in these two words: *memento vivere*. As he puts it at the start of *Specters of Marx*, it is a matter of a 'strange watchword' (p. xvii), *learn to live*:

> It is ethics itself: to learn to live – alone, from oneself, by oneself ... This is, therefore, a strange commitment, both impossible and necessary, for a living being supposed to be alive ... If it – learning to live – remains to be done, it can only happen between life and death. Neither in life nor in death *alone*. The time of the 'learning to live', a time without tutelary present, would amount to this ...: to learn to live *with* ghosts, in the upkeep, the conversation, the company or companionship ... of ghosts.
>
> (p. xviii)

The history of the novel is inseparable from that of teleculture and telecommunications. In a postcard dated 23 June 1979, Derrida scribbled a warning (another memento) that literature may not be able to survive 'a certain technological regime of telecommunications'.[12] Such a memento also speaks of literature's conditions and chances. The future of the novel is inseparable from a new thinking of spectrality, telepathy and telephony that can be traced in this 1959 novel, *Memento Mori*. The messianic in Derrida's terms, as the 'structure of an experience rather than a religion', is inscribed in the telephone of this text. Parodying and resisting the logic of a whodunnit, Spark's novel does not reveal the source or identity of the caller: it ends, as it begins, in a suspension and dissemination of the identification of the source of the words 'memento mori'. The telephone calls that structure the narrative are 'anonymous' (MM, p. 175). Their 'author' may be figured as the Christian God, Muriel Spark, hallucination (MM, p. 136–7), 'mass hysteria' (MM, p. 152), 'Death' (MM, p. 153, 175), male or female (MM, p. 153), young or old (MM, p. 148), a 'reporter' (MM, p. 124), 'a man of the Orient' (MM, p. 149) or someone in 'the shape of a telephone receiver' (MM, p. 184). No answer is given. Likewise the identity of the recipient or addressee. It may be one or other character in the novel. It may be the reader, any reader, you or me, alive or dead, alive *and* dead. And of course it may also be the novel addressing itself, addressing the genre of the novel itself, metafiction (a word first used only in 1960, according to the *OED*) already in a dead language: *memento mori*.

The telephone rings.

Notes

1. Elizabeth Bowen, (1935), *The House in Paris* (London: Penguin, 1976), p. 161.
2. Patricia Waugh, *Metafiction: The Theory and Practice of Self-Conscious Fiction* (London: Methuen, 1984), p. 2.
3. Jacques Derrida, *Specters of Marx: The State of the Debt, the Work of Mourning, and the New International*, trans. Peggy Kamuf (New York: Routledge, 1994), p. 98.
4. See Jacques Derrida, 'The Law of Genre', trans. Avital Ronell, in *Acts of*

Literature, ed. Derek Attridge (London and New York: Routledge, 1992), p. 227.

5. Derrida, *Specters of Marx*, p. 168.

6. See Jacques Derrida, *Mémoires: for Paul de Man*, trans. Cecile Lindsay, Jonathan Culler and Eduardo Cadava (New York: Columbia University Press, 1986), pp. 113–14.

7. Sigmund Freud, 'The "Uncanny"' (1919), in *Art and Literature*, Pelican Freud Library vol. 14, trans. James Strachey, ed. Albert Dickson (London: Penguin, 1985), p. 364.

8. Sigmund Freud, 'Thoughts for the Times on War and Death' (1915), in *Civilization, Society and Religion, Group Psychology, Civilization and Its Discontents and Other Works*, Pelican Freud Library, vol. 12, trans. James Strachey, ed. Albert Dickson (London: Penguin, 1985), p. 77.

9. Thomas Traherne, *Selected Poems and Prose*, ed. Alan Bradford (London: Penguin, 1991), p. 226–7.

10. Kathleen Woodward, *Aging and Its Discontents: Freud and Other Fictions* (Bloomington: Indiana University Press, 1991), p. 193.

11. Edmund Blunden, (1928) *Undertones of War* (London: Penguin, 1936), p. 29.

12. Jacques Derrida, *The Post Card: From Socrates to Freud and Beyond*, trans. Alan Bass (Chicago: Chicago University Press, 1987), p. 197.

12

Grimacing Catholicism: Muriel Spark's Macabre Farce (1)

and

Muriel Spark's Latest Novel: *The Public Image* (2)

Hélène Cixous

(1) Grimacing Catholicism

In a series of short, scathing novels written after her conversion to catholicism (in 1954), Muriel Spark has carved out the devil's share in English society today: her evil spirit gambols invisibly, or in the guise of someone with horns or cloven hooves, within tight circles infected with deadly sins shared by a whole category of individuals: old people, single people, pubescent schoolgirls, workers at a factory, or young women at a charitable institution are the toys of Spark's rightly famous satiric verve, which haunts, harasses, judges, and scatters them.

Editor's note. These texts first appeared as book reviews in *Le Monde*, 1968 ('La Farce Macabre de Muriel Spark: Un Catholicisme Grimacant', *Le Monde* 7157 (17 January): viia, 'Le Monde des Livres'; 'Le Dernier Roman de Muriel Spark: '*L'Image Publique*', *Le Monde* 7410 (9 November): viiia, 'Le Monde des Livres'). They are journalism but of a superior kind: dismissive of a purely religious reading of Spark, suspicious of the supposed theological content of Spark's novels. While these short pieces cannot be compared to Cixous' mature consideration of *l'écriture féminine* (*La jeune née*, with Catherine Clement, was not written until 1975) they are nevertheless of interest and might be considered an early attempt to 'theorize' Muriel Spark. In 1969 Cixous won the Prix Medicis for her novel *Dedans* (the jury included Michel Butor, Marguerite Duras, Claude Mauriac, Alain Robbe-Grillet and Claude Simon). It is interesting to note that in the preceding year, when Cixous had been writing her novel, she had also been a reader of Spark.

Among writers today whose work aims to assess the existence of evil in the world, Muriel Spark is the only one who does not turn it into a subject of mourning, tragedy, or pessimism. Whereas someone like William Golding despairs of fallen and godless mankind; while misfortune, hypocrisy, and weakness beset Graham Greene at the outer edge of the civilized world; and Evelyn Waugh's Catholicism is the reactionary expression of a nostalgic longing for a noble and pure era, Muriel Spark makes evil her province and hell her everyday concern.

Unlike her coreligionists, whose view of the world reflects their attachment to traditional humanist values and their distance from a world they deem decadent, Spark underscores the irreparable duplicity of the universe, where ordinary things coexist with supernatural ones in hideous harmony. Life is like a story told by a devil who likes to make chance pucker and ensnare people in their vices as they give themselves over to them with the innocent shamelessness of those who do not realize they are being watched. In the face of this violent and vulgar world, laughter bursts out, cruelty finds its justification: a girl burns to death in a hotel fire but her stupid agitation makes people laugh; a missionary is lynched in Haiti or Tahiti (hard to tell them apart): 'How marvelous it is,' and 'Besides, he talked too much.' A macabre cheerfulness springs up from the complete absence of values: things happen, deaths occur one after the other, but the author always presents them and contents herself with faithfully recounting the action. She is omniscient and detached, and she refrains from moralizing. Her faith is so ingrained that it has simply become an intellectual catalyst: the human theater reveals the inhumanity of individuals. If there is satire it is without bitterness, neutralized by the unspoken yet determining notion that the only world that counts is the other world. Iris Murdoch would have found material for a melodrama in the places where Spark remains cold and impassible, hardened like a priest war-worn by confessions. Indeed, nothing should come as a surprise in a time when souls are possessed by war, money, and sex.

A metaphor for hell

The disturbing charm of her tales arises from the contrast between the plainness and false innocence of the tone, and the savagery of aworld the concrete presence of which admirably simulates realist art: all her novels seem to belong to the social romance genre, with humor as an added ingredient. But, in fact, they are all transfigured thanks to a subtle reversal of the signifier and the signified: reality is nothing but a mask of death, and the world is a metaphor for hell. Under the cover of insignificant words lurks a great, infernal supernaturalness. Spark makes use of the imagery of hell and all of its attributes (spirits, ghosts, fire), and yet she pretends to take them as literary references while hell gapes beneath her transparent language.

The play of evil is comically modern: it proceeds mechanically and anonymously, often by telephone or threatening letters. A number of characters are its unknowing accomplices for, in the lot, there is always some Judas who stands above the average thanks to his intelligence and who exerts occult powers, either by blackmail, or profession (if he is a medium), or a gift for second sight. In *Memento Mori*, direct communication with the beyond is set up in telephone messages to those who are over seventy years old: 'Remember that you shall die.' The victims of this joke will never find out what the wise old police inspector has guessed: it is death in person who is calling.

Muriel Spark's moral aim, in fact, is to remind the reader brutally that one should ever forget the four final ends: death, judgment-day, hell, paradise. Thus, the imagination takes on a catechistic tone in which dramatic irony is both a comic ploy and a form of prophecy that operates by a play of tenses. Told in the past tense, the story is continually interrupted and commented in advance from the vantage of a future which the author knows but the concerned parties do not. Everything is heavy with the weight of destiny, and not of daily life, and the beings caught in this total time, which they can perceive only partially, are always ridiculous. Nothing is lasting or unchangeable.

God in the service of the Devil

There is no room for pity as there is none for traditional noble sentiments, for this comedy is a triumph of the opposite of noble sentiments: in place of love, sexual perversion sneaks in; heroism disguised as fascism; gluttonous greed cancels charity; those who are not evil are stupid; those who are intelligent are unscrupulous. And finally chance takes the place of grace, and all downhill roads lead to Rome: dubious motives induce spectacular conversions. Religion is smeared with hypocrisy because nothing is sacred that is not also bound for sacrilege: a father takes his paralyzed son to the Holy Land, but the pilgrimage is a cover for trafficking and the two scoundrels bring back diamonds housed in various statuettes and relics. And so God is in the service of the devil. Yet ... miracles will occur. There are rewards for the bad as well as the good, and, paradoxically, they deserve them for it is the sudden vision of evil that may bring about a conversion, and not the spectacle of goodness. That is the theme of *Girls of Slender Means*, in which a young immoralist poet, an untalented anarchist, has a revelation and finds his vocation when he witnesses 'an act of such savagery that he cannot help but cross himself '; during a fire at a boarding school, slender, Selina heroically slips into the blaze to save ... her Schiaparelli gown, while huge and pure Joanna, dressed in a simple jumper and a threadbare skirt, allows the flames to devour her so that she can quickly go to heaven.

The tragic is comical in Spark's tales. Flamboyant sadism cleanses man to the bone, and the joy of a purifying destruction are felt. Here Muriel Spark moves away from catholic literature and joins the tradition of Edwardian cynics like Max Beerbohm, whom the world does not deceive because they expect nothing from it.

(2) Muriel Spark's Latest Novel: *The Public Image*

Here at first is a detestable book, which becomes fascinating, and in the end is almost pleasing: the characters, the plot, the construction of this short novel are repellent, at first, in their platitude, mediocrity, and selfishness. Except for money, the only value, which is an obsession, everything in it is light. Because they move about in the world of movies; because they are spied on, photographed, discussed; because they are part of a myth that newspapers feed to the good public; because they are stars made into examples, these two-dimensional beings are subjected to the will of an impresario or a film director who bestows monstrous powers upon them. Annabel Christopher's talent as an actress consists in posing in front of the camera, and she knows that it is not necessary to be intelligent, that existing and being there are enough. An Italian producer cleverly exploits this availability, and he transforms the wan little Englishwoman with fear in her eyes into an ambivalent type, a femme fatale whose insular serenity in the daytime parallels her voluptuous sexuality at night, all that much more exciting for the viewer's imagination that this 'English tigress' is the wife of a gentleman seducer who is cold and gallant with her. The complicity is troubling, the publicity is titillating, and soon the couple is promoted to the rank of 'the couple you would like to be'. Actually Frederick, a failed actor and scriptwriter, tumbles into a psychotic hell of castration, while Annabel climbs the path leading to the Oscars, and their marriage deteriorates. Unwittingly Annabel becomes what she appears to be: a tigress in everything except in love, an unscrupulous businesswoman, a machine making movies with few pretensions, as long as her career proceeds upward. In the end Frederick commits suicide: a scandal, headlines, blackmail, an upheaval, down with stars! etc. Nothing there is new. But this is Spark; therefore what is banal turns into an Italian *opéra comique*.

The art of hollowness

The Romans' sentimental explosions underscore the deadly coldness of British emotions. Two forms of national cynicism confront each other. Rome wants Annabel to be a heartbroken wife, a tearful mother, a dignified widow who hands out tokens of forgiveness to imaginary Bacchantes after they supposedly have torn her charming husband to shreds. Annabel does not wish to disclose the hatred and self-interest that had been boiling under the public image. At this point fate triggers a retaliatory device: the image must turn into a reality. Annabel must play her part in life as she was doing it in films; she makes obvious her inability to experience any feelings unless a film script dictated them. While obstacles pile up because the truth is intent on ripping up the image, Annabel discovers that whoever just exists in front of a camera ceases to exist. For a long time she has believed that one's personality is nothing but the impression one has on other people. But now these other people view her in a different light, and she is threatened with changes, even with extinction.

All there is left for her to be is herself, but who? Without a part, she stops being anything; without Frederick, she no longer has her husband's failures to buttress her cruel triumph all the time. And now at long last she has a great problem. It is precious as she holds it tightly to her chest like her miracle baby, fathered by Frederick, who is making her so proud because he exists apart from any image. Who should she be? There is no script left to guide her, no drama for her to perform, since life has become a drama in which everybody is playing except for her. While good and bad advisers are struggling to save this image that has cost millions and may still yield some, Annabel suddenly escapes in the first plane, with her baby on one arm and a bag on the other.

It is an immoral tale; virtue finds no rewards; blind female vitality wins a game against male sensitivity; Annabel is an ice-cold little vampire; around bitter Frederick's corpse grotesquerie kicks up a dance; and the reader, craving justice, turns away in disgust from the triumphs of that instinct of aggression and conservation. What energy in such a small woman! And so much art! But it is an art of the hollow, intentionally light and easy so that it will tell how light and easy it is to live as an image and without a heart; everything moves very well and fast as always, more or less; virtually, good and evil are represented by the same image, and any judgment becomes an absurdity.

Translated Christine Irizzary

Christine Irizzary is a translator living and working in Nashville and Washington. She is currently translating *Le Touche, Jean-Luc Nancy* by Jacques Derrida.

13
'The Same Informed Air': An Interview with Muriel Spark*

Critical Spark

Martin McQuillan: This interview presupposes a contract, whereby I'm not going to ask about your biography but rather ask questions that come out of reading the books. Instead of collecting a book of criticism in which the author doesn't do anything (writing about some*body*). The author can intervene here and respond to the issues that are raised by the criticism. So, if we start with the topic of criticism itself and with critical writing about you. What do you think of your own critical reception?

Muriel Spark: Well I did a lot of critical research myself before I became a novelist; I was a critic. I always thought the classic idea was to analyse and compare. To analyse is easy to a shrewd mind, to compare is not so easy, because you have to have a good background of reading. So I read as much as I could to have a field of comparison. I was really enjoying criticism when I realised I wanted to write novels. I had an opportunity to write a novel and I found that was really my *métier*, but I was enjoying criticism and biography which is next door to it.

MMcQ: But you never wanted to go back to criticism?

MS: Well I often have since writing novels. I've often done reviews or written essays. Penelope Jardine at the moment is putting together a book of my non-fiction prose. It's essays and criticism and all sorts,

*Arezzo, Italy: November 1998.

under different headings. She's got it under religion, philosophy, literature etc. I've written a lot, an enormous amount, mostly for journals and magazines, but sometimes just spontaneously.

MMcQ: What is the difference between criticism and fiction?

MS: Criticism is dealing with facts, actual facts; it doesn't go into the realm of invention. You invent characters, absolutely, but fiction embraces criticism. At the same time as one is writing, the mind is working on a critical level; you must know that this will appeal to the reader, you're writing for a reader. You want to be understood, you're critical the whole time, and you make changes accordingly. It's a critical process at the same time as it's inventive.

MMcQ: You've written a good deal about *The Book of Job*, the articles in *The Spectator* but also something like *The Only Problem* – would that qualify as a piece of criticism?

MS: Yes, as well as a novel. What I wanted to bring out there was that in *The Book of Job* Job has these so-called comforters, the elders of Judaism who come and tell him that he must have sinned or he wouldn't be suffering like this. They're identified only by name and they're all really saying the same thing, even towards the end when a young man comes out of the whirlwind, 'Job you must have done something wrong'. He keeps on saying 'No, God is not like that. I did nothing wrong, I did everything right. What I did was right and I'm not going to admit that I did anything wrong, it's only that I'm suffering.' He then says to God to come out and reason with him and tell him why, what's the reason for his suffering. God comes out of the whirlwind and doesn't give any reason whatsoever. 'I did this and I did that': that was all; most unsatisfactory. Quite a lot of writers like Shelley and Virginia Woolf thought it a most unsatisfactory argument on God's part. However, the active appearance of God and his poetical description of his Creation did have a therapeutic effect on Job. Now, all that came into the novel. What I wanted to show was that this author, who was writing on *The Book of Job*, went through a period of police interrogation, and they come in one after the other asking the same question trying to break him down. It struck me that in the bible these interpreters of Job's suffering interpreted always in the same way and they interrogate him. They're interrogators; they really are Fascist interrogators and Job just rebels against it and throws them off.

MMcQ: Which is the more satisfying way of talking about *Job*, doing it through the novel or writing the essays?

MS: Well I had more fun, I enjoyed it better and I had more scope through the novel, because it deals with suffering. The problem of *The Book of Job* is that he suffers the problem of argument as much as he argues the problem of suffering. The problem of argument, that he's in such a situation. Look, you can't argue, what has the problem of argument to do with? Consider for instance, Nicaragua and Honduras wiped out like that, hundreds of thousands of people wiped out [Floods in Central America had recently caused widespread devastation, November 1998] and you know you've got to ask God, what did they do to deserve it? You know they didn't. So this is an argument beyond arguments; you can't argue it. There are no two sides, there's no dialogue. There's just nothing and it's no use pretending there is. I did enjoy writing the book from that point of view.

MMcQ: The books of criticism that you have written, on the Brontës, Mary Shelley and John Masefield. Why the Brontës? What interested you?

MS: Well, I was always very interested in the Brontës. I think they were a remarkable set of people and very non-Victorian. They came straight out of the eighteenth century and into the twentieth century, or almost. They were extremely advanced. A little group of people in Howarth in the North, with only the old father to bring them up. Really they brought themselves up. He was a very interesting man, the father, the minister of the Parish. He let them have a lot of leeway and he had an Irish turn of thought. He was very much a radical, and they were radical. They were free-spoken for young women of the time, very advanced and the books are charming. *Jane Eyre* is an absolutely lovely book, full of improbabilities and 'dragged-in' coincidences. I thought that Emily Brontë's book was marvellous too. Then their letters were also very interesting, because I thought they were more or less biographical. Put them together and you have a biography of the Brontës. In fact, I've done just that in my book *The Essence of the Brontës*.

MMcQ: What is your opinion of *Villette*?

MS: I like *Villette* very much. I think it's very good; I like it even better than *Jane Eyre*. Full of realism, haunted, various scenes where she has taken too much opium, or laudanum. She's sick, she's alone in the holidays and she goes out into the carnival crowd and sees everyone looking hideous. Its amazingly vivid, the scenes are very good. *Villette* is really the superior book; also *Villette* has a touch of the French. She must have been reading some French novels; she's escaped from the more parochial type there.

MMcQ: Mary Shelley – you were the first person ever to write a proper critical book on Mary Shelley.

MS: Yes there was another one I think, but I did a critical study. She had a temperament very different from mine. She got into a state of deep depression after Shelley's death. She had been greatly dependent on him. She always felt herself to be Shelley's widow which was a pity: she was more than that. As a girl writing *Frankenstein* she was much more independent. I think too she was a victim of her age; everyone was expecting her to be the mother of Percy Shelley the son. I think that she was very depressed and depressing, pessimistic; she had a touch of never happy unless she was miserable. But of course I think she had a very good mind; I admire her tremendously.

MMcQ: When you are writing are you conscious of an academic audience reading you and teaching you?

MS: No. I don't know what I'm conscious of; an audience, yes, but people like myself, perhaps. I have an academic audience. I do know that what I write is not necessarily appreciated by the majority of fiction readers. They don't really get the subtleties and the ironies, but I can't help that. I don't know who I'm writing for; probably I'm writing for the original Miss Brodie or somebody like that. I don't have a precise idea in my head. It's got to satisfy me though. I talk to myself: it's a dialogue with myself largely.

MMcQ: Do you think that the way *Jean Brodie* has been received – made into a play, a film, the play revived – has limited the ways in which you are read?

MS: Yes, in a way. It has increased my readership, because people see the film and then buy the books they wouldn't normally have read. I've got a wider public generally, because of Miss Brodie and its success on the stage and film, than I would have had if it hadn't happened that way. But in fact, it's affected the way people read my work and I can't tell you how bored I am with Miss Brodie. Thomas Hardy used to talk about *Tess of the D'Urbervilles* as 'Tess my old milch cow' because she brought him a lot of money, and I really feel the same about Miss Brodie.

Background Spark

MMcQ: It's clear from the novels that your work and background are very complicated.

MS: I haven't written about birth certificates or anything like that [referring to the media rumpus surrounding Spark's 'Jewishness' and Bryan Cheyette's essay in this volume]. What I wrote about was my experiences as a child and you can't take that away from me. I went to a Presbyterian school, I never went to a Jewish school. I adored my father; he was a Jew. There was a mixture of things and those are the facts. My mother put her grandfather's name, after her father's name, on her marriage certificate. When Martin [Stannard, Spark's biographer] was trying to get the truth out of them – the offices of the Jewish Congregation in London, their central office of information – he had terrible trouble with them. They kept covering up things. In the end he just got on the train and went to Somerset House, who had the information about my grandmother's wedding in a church (St. Bartholemew's, Bethnal Green). I thought we'd ring up the church where my grandfather and grandmother were married, to see where the records were (actually the church is now turned into an AIDS centre; not a church). We spoke to the Reverend John Wier. He gave me a lot of information about the city churches. My grandmother, this might interest you from a literary point of view, was a friend of Emmeline Pankhurst and she marched with the Suffragettes. She didn't tie herself to railings or anything, but she ran the Watford chapter of the suffragettes. Her mother was not a Jew. She married Philip Hyams, a Jew. There is no Jewish descendence on the maternal side in our family. My father, a full Jew, was aware that my mother was not born Jewish, but had one Jewish grandfather. My brother is of the opinion that my mother falsified her marriage certificate because she wanted to pass for a Jew. 'She wanted to marry Dad' are my brother's words. My own writings are the most accurate guide to my background but the question is not of great material interest to me: I am a Roman Catholic.

MMcQ: *The Mandelbaum Gate* strikes me as an interesting book in that respect.

MS: Yes, that was how I thought of the book. There were so many half-Jews that I knew and I thought this is a whole way of looking at life, a whole consideration worth writing about. That's what I wrote about, and I went to the Eichmann trial for *The Observer*.

MMcQ: It seems to me a very pivotal book in terms of your career, because before that there are the first seven novels which are all very similar in terms of plot and characters then *The Mandelbaum Gate* is a different sort of book, a much longer work.

MS: I objectified everything much more after that. I didn't write 'the English novel' so much after *The Mandelbaum Gate*. I wrote books more like *Not to Disturb* and *The Driver's Seat* and was very much more influenced by the French writers of the *nouveau roman*.

MMcQ: How did you feel about *The Mandelbaum Gate* once you had finished it? It's so different from most of what you've written.

MS: Yes, I took a long time to do that book, I took two years. After writing two books a year, one book in two years was a long time. It's a long book. I did it in the form of short stories: each chapter was a short story with a different point of view. They published most of it in *The New Yorker*. How did I feel afterwards? I was very exhausted. I was not sure that I wanted to do anything more like that; I felt I had done my *Passage to India*. I felt I'd got out of myself what I wanted to say, but I certainly didn't want to go in for more sociological books.

MMcQ: After that there is the fabulous period of *Not to Disturb*, *The Abbess of Crewe*, and *The Driver's Seat*. These have very thin, sparse prose; were they also a response to the size of that book? Do you think *The Mandelbaum Gate* got out of hand?

MS: I prefer those books; they're nearer to poetry, more my sort of thing.

MMcQ: The novels after *The Mandlebaum Gate*, you suggested, were influenced by the *nouveau roman*. Do you think that you were influenced by the *nouveau roman*, or, that by living in Europe at the time, you were thinking in the same way as they were thinking?

MS: I was thinking the same thoughts that they were thinking, people like Robbe-Grillet. We were influenced by the same, breathing the same informed air. So, I naturally would have a bent towards the *nouveau roman* but in fact I was very influenced by Robbe-Grillet.

MMcQ: Marguerite Duras?

MS: Yes, very very impressed by her. I would think influenced because I was so attracted. What I loved about Robbe-Grillet – I tried it of course in *The Ballad of Peckham Rye* and I think it came off – he would write a book without once saying 'he or she thought' or 'he or she felt'. Thoughts and feelings not mentioned but they are there: he mentioned only what they said and did. In fact Simenon does it a bit. It has a strange atmospheric effect. With *The Ballad of Peckham Rye* I never once mention thoughts and feelings, only what people say and do.

MMcQ: Would you say you were a modernist writer?

MS: Maybe Post-modernist; I don't know about Modernist. I think so, probably. They say postmodernist, mostly, whatever that means.

MMcQ: Do you know what it means?

MS: Well I think that it means that there is another dimension which is a bit creepy, supernatural ... not supernatural but not necessarily, consequential. I always think that causality is not chronology. I go on that; one thing doesn't necessarily lead to another inevitable thing, although it does lead to something else in actual fact.

MMcQ: Do you think your own novels have influenced the shape of the novel in English?

MS: I think so, I hope so. I think it was getting very dull around the time of the Angry Young Men. I think that something had to shake it up, in the way of another dimension. I was hoping to do that. Whether I did or not, I don't know. I consciously set about doing that. I was enough of a critic to know what I wanted to do for the novel. It wasn't by chance.

MMcQ: Perhaps people like Jeanette Winterson, Martin Amis, Ian

McEwan, etc. are possible, all of their novels are possible, because of what you did.

MS: Well, yes, it would follow on. They might have done it without me, but anyway, it follows on, it's certainly a break from the past.

MMcQ: You were talking a minute ago about the complexity of your background. One of the things I find distressing about much 'Spark criticism' is the way it tries to pigeon-hole you as a Catholic writer. It says 'Muriel Spark, Catholic writer'. If you understand the penny Catechism, you understand everything in Muriel Spark. However, the novels are always exploring the complexities and contradictions of Catholicism.

MS: I am a Catholic and I'm a believing Catholic. I do adhere to the Catholic doctrines although not the practices, the trimmings and all that. They are bound to colour my narrative, inform my narrative approach. What I think and how I express it is, I think, inevitable. Although I don't set out to be a Catholic apologist in any form.

MMcQ: Yours is certainly an unorthodox Catholicism. For example, *The Comforters*, if you take the first novel, is all about how awful Catholics are.

MS: Yes, I'd just become a Catholic and was mixing with them at Aylesford Priory. I thought I might as well write about what I felt like and what I saw. Although Catholics wouldn't put me off being a Catholic, the people there were really awful.

MMcQ: You've talked a lot before about Catholicism as a fixed point. You've said that 'I cannot help but believe' – what is it that you cannot help but believe?

MS: It's as simple as this: I hold by the creed. I would find it difficult to say that this is a load of rubbish, although I can't explain every-thing. I probably can't explain anything. But it does seem to me to be the culmination of western, Mediterranean civilization. I don't want to knock the Oriental religions or anything, but as far as doing some-thing for each other and getting the world revived and getting on with things, I don't think you can beat Western religion. Because we don't live up to it isn't to say we ought not to. We should live up to what we can do; our possibilities are great. All these religions round the Mediterranean, the Judeo–Christian tradition, seems to me to a have a better set of values altogether, politically and in every way.

MMcQ: Malcolm Bradbury famously described you in an essay, 'Muriel Spark's Fingernails', after the figure in Joyce as a Catholic novelist paring her fingernails, looking down on the world. Are you happy with that description?

MS: No! I hadn't thought of it actually. I would say that's more of a Buddhist tradition, that you distance yourself and look down. No, no I don't think so. I don't think I like that very much. However, perhaps that's the impression I give. Bradbury is a very intelligent fellow.

MMcQ: That figure comes from Joyce but the other figure that comes from Joyce is JewGreek, Leopold Bloom immanent within the situation, anarchic, moving about … not distanced, not *sub specie aeternitatis*.

MS: Yes, that's a lovely idea I agree.

MMcQ: In *Symposium* you refer to the philosophy of *'les autres'*. I wonder if you can maybe just talk about that; what did you mean by it?

MS: Well, it depends who's talking … that was in the mouth of Margaret's husband. I think it just means a philosophy of recognizing the existence of others and really trying to see what other people are thinking. It's very very difficult; we're all very much aware of ourselves, self-conscious. It's not a bad thing because then we can express ourselves and meet other people through words, music, art. But to be really sort of 'under the skin' of others is a very big exercise.

MMcQ: When I was reading it I was thinking of Freud, of otherness within.

MS: I don't know anything about Freud very much. I've read a bit of Freud, but I'm really not very well versed in Freud. Did he have a theory of otherness?

MMcQ: One of the problems of recognizing and taking account of other people is the otherness within the self of the contradictions within the self.

MS: That's very true.

MMcQ: I was thinking of all the different complexities within yourself, having this complex Jewish background in Edinburgh, having been brought up Christian with a Jewish heritage, being British in Africa, being a Scot in London, being a Catholic in Edinburgh.

MS: English-speaking people take each other very naturally. But in the case of conflict one resolves it. The act of writing is a wonderful resolver of conflict, especially writing novels, because it is possible to have dialogue and create characters to represent ways of thinking.

MMcQ: Like the Abbess of Crewe, are you homesick for your own kind?

MS: For my own kind? Yes. I very much like that line.

MMcQ: Who are your own kind?

MS: My own kind would be really intelligent people, more or less intellectuals. I'm weary for them if I'm cut off for too long.

The Spark continent

MMcQ: I was interested in the fact that you wrote your stories about Africa in the 50s and the 60s while you were living in London after decolonization. Was there anything in that historical moment that affected your writing about the 20s and 30s?

MS: I met a lot of people who didn't understand what life had been like in the 30s and 40s in the old colonial days. Or, I met a lot of people who had a crude idea that the British were there being absolutely ghastly and behaving badly, which they weren't. Some behaved badly and the whole idea wasn't a good one. It wasn't our country (none of these countries were ours) but at the same time not all our behaviour was bad. The only people who were doing anything to add something to the country, as if they wanted to improve it, were the missionaries. If not, why go there? There was no need to improve it. They had their witch doctor system, they died early, they had pneumonia ... They had a lot of things that were put right by us, because most of the good work was done by missionaries: much maligned. They had schools, they had hospitals for the blacks. They did help them and they did teach them skills and various things. But the ordinary white settler did nothing, just employed them. All right, serve in the shop or do something, but they never did anything to start a school or a club or a football match, anything, nothing. We could have shown them how these things came about. You had plenty of blacks working away keeping the football pitch bright, or the cricket pitch neat, but they didn't play cricket or football and that I found was really wanting. When I looked round there were the Germans, the French and the Belgians in Africa at that time (apart from the South Africans who were unspeakable) they were doing even less than us, than the British. We should have been doing far more. The only people who were doing anything for the Africans were the missionaries. At the same time we were showing them a way of life that they obviously aspired to. We had motor cars but all they could get was a bicycle, which they had never had before. A bicycle, a pair of shoes – maybe that was some advance. It should have really been a much better show in our colonial effort. I think that the same thing happened in India. I went to India for a while, only for a few weeks, and I found the same sort of thing had happened. We'd been there, shown them a better way of life, but not made them participate in any form at all. They didn't even have a vote, nothing. They had their own police force, which I suppose was a step up.

MMcQ: The short-stories 'The Go Away Bird' and 'The Curtain Blown by the Breeze' seem particularly interesting regarding the position of women in Empire and the role that women play. Women go out to Empire, and the purpose of being there is to marry, they are there to breed. They are therefore an intrinsic part of the colonial set-up.

MS: Yes, but also on the women's side in Africa, there was always the question of interbreeding. Some of them had black blood, they inter-bred a bit. Men had been on these lonely outposts and of course had had children. These had become part of the white family and there was always that social teetering, not quite acceptable and yet accepted. A totally different thing from anything we know now. At the same time it was against the law to say that someone had black blood, if they had crinkly hair or some feature. Actually a crime, you weren't allowed to say it, which I found boring.

MMcQ: In these stories, women go to the colonies to escape domestic duties in Britain and find that they're even more restrained in what they can do.

MS: Oh yes very much. I didn't like it in Africa. I couldn't get back for many years because of the war. But I found it fascinating from the point of view of an experience. I knew I ought to take it in as an experience and write about it later.

MMcQ: Are the short stories just a reflection of your experiences there or do you think that they are also a political comment?

MS: They are a political comment, but they were short stories. I really felt I wanted to write these stories; I had them in me. I had prototypes in my mind for all the characters. Like in 'The Portobello Road' and 'The Seraph and the Zambesi', which was the first short story I wrote. It was the first bit of fiction I wrote really for publication.

Political Spark

MMcQ: You've said before that you are not political, in the way that, say, Doris Lessing, is political.

MS: Not party political.

MMcQ: Would it be fair to say that whilst you are not interested in Politics, *the political* interests you very much.

MS: Oh yes, you have to live in this world. You can't be non-political, not unless you are really empty-headed.

MMcQ: This is something you discuss a lot in the novels. For example, in *The Only Problem* you write about the Red Brigades, in *The Driver's Seat* there is a moment where Lise is going around in the car, she takes a wrong turning and there's a student riot. It's just in the corner of the field of vision but seems to inform the whole of the novel.

MS: Oh yes, it's there; you can't ignore it.

MMcQ: There's other things like *Not to Disturb*, told from the servant's point of view.

MS: That's quite a political novel I would say, although it's at a supernatural level. It's quite politically orientated, but it's supposed to be a satire. I think you can't get out of politics, you can't get away from philosophy and religion so easily. It comes into everything, everyday life. Its the air we breathe, what we breathe. I don't write political novels. No one could say I write a political novel; even Graham Greene's novels are more political than mine, I think. I just don't write political novels any more than religious novels. Maybe *Memento Mori* is a religious novel, one about old age.

MMcQ: You don't write political novels, but certainly the political that you're writing about is always there and is always influential. But something like 'The Desegregation of Art', that very important essay, the way you speak about politics in that essay is very different from the way you deal with them in your novels.

MS: Really?

MMcQ: I think so. In that essay you certainly thematize it a lot more. You say that ridicule is the only weapon left to us to effect some kind of change.

MS: Yes, well, I mean that. Ridicule is the only respectable weapon we have. In a way, I think it's probably the most deadly.

MMcQ: In that sense, is the novel there to effect social change? Do you think that's what the novel can do?

MS: A novel can do it. I think it just depends on the time and the circumstances, if it does do it. I think if you set out to do it, that's another type of novel; its really an *Uncle Tom's Cabin* type novel. You set out to right a wrong. I haven't ever done that. I haven't a message just like that. I would hope that everything I write changes something, opens windows in people's minds, something. I do want to do *that*, to clarify.

MMcQ: Can I ask you about two passages from two different novels? One of them is from the latest novel, *Reality and Dreams*, when you say 'the century is very old', and you quote T. S. Eliot's phrase 'the desperate exercise of failing power'.

MS: 'The desperate exercise of failing power' means that old people over-reach themselves because they're frustrated or exasperated by their physical limitations and often by impotency, especially in men. They over-reach themselves in power, clamp down with more show of power than they've actually got.

MMcQ: I'm interested in *Reality and Dreams* because one of the issues that you treat in that novel is redundancy.

MS: I wanted to write about redundancy very much because this is an issue that people have. They have to make up their mind how important it is to be useful because there are a lot of people who are not useful; machines have taken their place. They are redundant because there are just too many of them and one person can do the work of forty. It leads to a crisis, a frightful emotional crisis. Old women feel this dreadfully. I remember my mother got old and I said to the doctor, 'Look, I've got to get her some more help'. 'Oh', he said, 'don't do that. Let her potter, it will be terrible if she has too much help'. That was quite right. The thing is you've got to feel useful. The issue is to have a whole new philosophy of life where usefulness is questioned. Do we have to be so useful we can't accept the fact that we might be in the world to enjoy ourselves? It's quite possible we can enjoy ourselves. A lot of people do without having the problem of whether they're useful or not. If it's an economic problem, it can be solved by the rest of society being arranged in such a way that there's enough for everybody. What one does with one's time is said to be important because of this puritanical thing about having to work to be useful. It is true that one should be useful when there are plenty of jobs to be done, which are not done because the trade unions won't let you work or you don't want to or something like that. But I don't see the point of being discredited as a human being just because you're unemployed. I never thought of it that way, but people do. That's one of the things that I wanted to bring out in the book, this frustration people have about redundancy. There's this awful girl, Marigold, a sort of social welfare worker, working up this feeling at the same time. Maybe I don't bring that out enough in the novel. I don't want to plug away at an idea too much, to hammer home things, it's better to let them diffuse.

MMcQ: The other passage I have is from *The Takeover*. It's remarkable because there's nothing like it in the rest of the novel, and nothing like it in any of your other novels. When the characters are all sitting down to lunch and the narrator goes off at a tangent to say, 'It was not in their minds at this time, that at this last quarter of the year at the end of 1973 was in fact the beginning of something new in the world, a change in the meaning of property and money' and so forth ... It goes on to refer to 'a sea change in the nature of reality as could not be envisaged by Karl Marx or Sigmund Freud'. What did you mean by that?

MS: Well, I meant exactly what was going on then. I think there was a big change, an enormous change in things. Certainly in the idea of the hierarchies, which were all breaking down just then. Money was becoming very much more of a shaky thing. There had been lots of black Mondays or Fridays or whatever they are called, and I just thought there had been a change. There was a total change that hadn't been envisaged and that was the beginning of a lot of technology which put people out of work. I think the consequences of that change are still with us. I think there is a lot of hysteria and people haven't learnt to cope. I think our ideals and standards are wrong. I think we should have another philosophy of life that comprises enjoyment. We should enjoy life. I don't mean hilariously but I mean enjoy life, while we have it, treasure it, share life with people, in a simple way. There are simple ways of enjoying life: sunshine, walks, seaside, reading, playing the piano, watching television if it's good. I really don't see any harm in people doing nothing if they're not making other people suffer. But I don't see why they should lose face. That's all wrong. I don't care if they do nothing as long a they are not miserable or guilty. In 1973, the 'winds of change' in the Communist world began to be felt, you know. There was a loosening at the end of the Vietnam War, a limited arms agreement between Breshnev and Nixon, and finally the great oil embargo on the part of the Arabs, when fuel prices rose precipitously.

MMcQ: One of the topics you've written about quite a lot is terrorism. Why?

MS: I see it happening – in families – terrorism and blackmail. It spreads out. I see that all through life: terroristic actions and intentions. It goes along with a certain type of blackmail. A lot of life goes on at that level. The terrorism in the novels is symbolic of everything that goes on like that, which is wrong. There's lots of blackmail in my work and unspoken blackmail. I see it and I suffer from it. I don't wear it. I always call people's bluff. I can't stand it.

MMcQ: *The Abbess of Crewe*, your Watergate satire, involves blackmail and terrorism of various kinds. You said before that the whole thing was just like nuns squabbling over a thimble.

MS: I still think that. I think that at the moment [during the Lewinsky affair] they're mad, these Americans. They are the most powerful nation on Earth, on the face of it, and educated people. They titter, titter, titter over the president having an affair with a secretary. Everything skyrockets! The dollar goes down, or up, just because of this. It's absolutely absurd. Clinton has been doing a lot of good for the country. I don't know what he's like as a person, but the people know it. They don't want to send him away just because he's a woman-izer. I don't think his private life has got anything to do with anybody. But this was the same with Watergate; it was a lark, breaking and entering. It was the dirty tricks department. But everybody knows that they're mad. Even the Americans themselves know that they're mad but they don't know how to stop.

MMcQ: I thought the comparison of Nixon to nuns fighting over a thimble had a resonance with Effie stealing a Mars bar in *The Only Problem* – in which acts of terrorism against huge multi-nationals, which can't possibly be effected in any way, are just like stealing a Mars bar.

MS: Yes, that's it yes. How I took it though, was that Harvey her husband, the one who was writing a book on *The Book of Job*, felt it was the last straw *for him*. They weren't suited at all in their outlook on life and this stealing of the chocolate was the last straw – as if it was some-thing very tremendous.

MMcQ: This is something that happens a lot in the later novels. Characters will get married three times within the novel, there's partner swapping within the groups, for example in *The Takeover* or in *Reality and Dreams*. What sort of characterization are you trying to suggest through that?

MS: Well, I suppose I'm trying to suggest a society in flux, not stable. We're not living in stable times. I don't know if instability has come about through television; it might have. One forgets that behind all these programmes are the programme makers, who are by no means divinely inspired. They are by no means settled people and are awfully unstable themselves, and that's what we're getting.

MMcQ: Is it also to do with escaping the family?

MS: It might be that; there's a lot about escaping the family in contemporary novels. I think it's a very important theme in modern life, escaping the family. It happens in my life a lot. I'm always on the run from my family. [Laughs] Not so much now, when I don't need to be, but it is a basic.

MMcQ: In *The Public Image* you have the whole question of disorientation and flux brought about by a media culture. There you have Annabel, who runs away from the family again. That's also the only novel, I think I'm correct, where you talk about motherhood as well.

MS: There's a mother and son in *Memento Mori*, but it doesn't come in very much. But I think that's right: I haven't got much time for family. This isn't personal because I think people are dependent on their families. I quite like to see happy families but I'm not a family person myself. I enjoyed my mother and father's presence when I was younger, and my brother when he was younger, but I'm not really very good at it. Its not quite my thing. I've always felt that people you choose are much better than people you don't choose. It's very difficult unless you've got a lot of intellectuals in the family: you can meet on that level. I can't, in my case. Not that I'm an outright intellectual but I've got intellectual ideas.

MMcQ: Perhaps, we could discuss your Scottish identity.

MS: Yes, I'm Scottish as far as I can claim to be anything. My father was a Scot; he was born in Edinburgh and went to school in Edinburgh. I was born in Edinburgh and went to school in Edinburgh. My mother was English but lived most of her life in Edinburgh – she married as a girl and lived the rest of her life in Edinburgh. I was brought up as Scottish as anyone else around.

MMcQ: But you don't have time for Scottish nationalism?

MS: I never liked it, I don't like nationalism as an idea. It was going on in the thirties when everyone was going international. I really don't like nationalism as a phenomenon. There is a place for folklore, and every village likes its own type of dancing, cooking etc. and that's very charming, but to make a national creed of it seems rather pathetic. I don't like it, at all. It shuts too many doors, far more doors than it ever opens. The Nationalists are shutting themselves off from a great many wonderful things in the world. In Europe, Scotland would only be accepted as part of Britain. Europeans regard it as a province of Britain. The Scottish law has always been apart but it's not so very different. I don't know if the non-proven verdict is still in force. If it is, that is different. But there's no Nationalist foreign policy as far as I can see. I don't know what their economic policy is. I think devolution might work, but Nationalism makes Scotland into the Caledonian Society of Life, you know, that's all. Devolution is a way towards independence isn't it? I think they're both largely the same. I really do think that the Scots have a point in that they've been neglected by the English parliament, who really don't take Scottish affairs seriously enough. On the other hand, Scottish affairs have not been so very serious. There's nothing really they have to offer except tourism, which is a very big thing, but it's inclined to mess up Scotland a great deal. Edinburgh is a lovely city but then it becomes a theme park with all these jazzed up slums.

MMcQ: One of the things that has happened in Scottish Literature departments is an attempt to reclaim your writing as distinctly Scottish.

MS: Yes it's true, unfortunately, in a sense. Nobody can get my novels in Edinburgh, because when they ask for my novels they are filed under Scottish Literature. Readers never think of asking for me under Scottish novels. I don't mind that because I consider myself a Scot. I can't consider myself anything else. I've got foreign blood of many types but sooner or later you become a Scot. The language I speak is English. I quite like Scottish turns of phrase, if they're good in sound. But this is a matter for your literary ear, you can't nail that down.

Writing Spark

MMcQ: You have written a good deal about the episode at the house of Louis MacNeice, which formed the short story 'The House of the Famous Poet'.

MS: I wrote a piece about it, a short story, and a piece about writing the short story. It was very strange: I just found myself in Louis MacNeice's house. This girl had asked me. I was on a train, the bombs were coming down thick and fast, so she said come back with her. Nobody was there and I found myself just by looking at the books: 'To Louis from Wynstan' and things like that. I said, 'Is this Professor's MacNeice's house, that famous poet?', and she said yes. I was amazed; I went round touching everything to see, you know, that it was true.

MMcQ: Do you think origins in that sense are important for a writer?

MS: Yes I think it stuck in my mind, encouraged me to write really. I was almost afraid to stay there. I had never envisaged what a writer's house would be like. Actually being there . . . it suddenly could be mine eventually. A writer's life was concrete. I could live like this too. I knew I was going to write. It helped a great deal; it was an amazing fetish-like experience.

MMcQ: Can I ask about writing the autobiography, what's the difference between writing an autobiography and writing a novel?

MS: Oh, such a difference, they're the very opposite. As a matter of fact I found autobiography very difficult. I decided not to trust my memory, to put down everything I remembered, because I have crowded memories, but to check every single thing against either a document or a living person. I made one mistake. I remembered a couple of small boys I used to play with as a child. I thought they were half-Indian and they wrote to me very amused. 'We loved reading about ourselves in your autobiography, but we're not Indian, we're Scots'. I wrote back and said 'I'll change it in the next edition'.

MMcQ: Were there any similarities with writing a novel, in terms of telling the story?

MS: Not really. I found it difficult. My pen didn't run away with me as it does when I'm writing a novel. If I come to a difficulty in a novel, I leave a big space and then go on and pick it up; I have a sense of structure. With this, it had its own structure. I decided to stop at the point where I started writing novels because in a sense they tell their own story. I still had plenty more to say but I wanted to get my childhood and girlhood down as much as I could without bothering people who were still alive. There was a lot I left out which I've thought of since. In a novel the narrative runs away with you while you're writing. I have general principles or ideas, a sense of censorship almost, but it does flow.

MMcQ: I'm interested in the idea that you no longer need the autobiography once you've got the novels.

MS: The autobiography I found easier when I came to descriptive things. I don't write very emotional novels but in describing emotions I tried to get across the pleasures of childhood especially, and this extraordinary school I went to. It was progressive before I knew anything about progressive schools. I didn't realize it, none of us did. We've since talked to other girls who've been there. They've said 'Really!' We didn't know, looking round now, how very advanced it was.

MMcQ: The final question, of the ones that you've written, what's your favourite novel?

MS: *The Driver's Seat.* I think it's the best written and constructed, it's the most interesting. It's got interesting characters. All the characters have something; there are no subsidiary nonentities. There's always something about them one way or another. I think it's probably my best novel to date and it's the creepiest. I have a special weakness, too, for my new novel *Aiding and Abetting*. It's about the notorious Lord Lucan, among other characters.

A Muriel Spark Bibliography

1. Texts by Muriel Spark

Novels

Spark, M., *The Comforters* (London: Macmillan, 1957).
——, *Robinson* (London: Macmillan, 1958).
——, *Memento Mori* (London: Macmillan, 1959).
——, *The Bachelors* (London: Macmillan, 1960).
——, *The Ballad of Peckham Rye* (London; Macmillan, 1960).
——, *The Prime of Miss Jean Brodie* (London: Macmillan, 1961).
——, *The Girls of Slender Means* (London: Macmillan, 1963).
——, *The Mandlebaum Gate* (London: Macmillan, 1965).
——, *The Public Image* (London: Macmillan, 1968).
——, *The Driver's Seat* (London: Macmillan, 1970).
——, *Not to Disturb* (London: Macmillan, 1971).
——, *The Hothouse by the East River* (London: Macmillan, 1973).
——, *The Abbess of Crewe* (London: Macmillan, 1974).
——, *The Takeover* (London: Macmillan, 1976).
——, *Territorial Rights* (London: Macmillan, 1979).
——, *Loitering with Intent* (London: Macmillan, 1981).
——, *The Only Problem* (London: Bodley Head, 1984).
——, *A Far Cry from Kensington* (London: Macmillan, 1988).
——, *Symposium* (London: Macmillan, 1990).
——, *Reality and Dreams* (London: Constable, 1996).
——, *Aiding and Abetting* (London: Constable, 2000).

Autobiography

——, *Curriculum Vitae* (London: Constable, 1992).

Drama

——, *Voices at Play* (London: Macmillan, 1961), includes radio drama.
——, *Doctors of Philosophy* (London: Macmillan, 1963).

Stories

——, *The Go-Away Bird and Other Stories* (London: Macmillan, 1958).
——, *Voices at Play* (London: Macmillan, 1961), includes short stories.
——, *Collected Stories I* (London: Macmillan, 1967)
——, *The Stories of Muriel Spark* (London: Macmillan, 1987).
——, *Bang-Bang You're Dead and Other Stories* (St Albans: Granada, 1982).
——, *Collected Short Stories* (London: Macmillan, 1995).
——, *Madam X* (London: Colophon Press, 1996).

——, *Harper and Wilton* (London: Colophon Press, 1996).
——, *Open to the Public: New and Collected Stories* (London: New Directions Books, 1997).
——, *The Quest for Lavishes Ghost* (London: The Cuckoo Press, 1998).
——, *The Young Man Who Discovered the Secret of Life and Other Stories* (London: Travelman Publishing, 1999).

Un-anthologized short stories include:
——, 'Ladies and Gentlemen', *Chance* 3, April–June 1953.
——, 'The End of Summer Time', *London Mystery Magazine* 37, June 1958.
——, 'Going Up and Coming Down', *The Daily Telegraph* 6, August 1994, Section 2, p. 11.

Children's literature

——, *The Very Fine Clock* (London: Macmillan, 1968)
——, *The Small Telephone* (London: Colophon Press, 1983).
——, *The French Window* (London: Colophon Press, 1993).

Poetry

——, *The Fanfarlo and Other Verse* (Adlington: The Hand and Flower Press, 1952).
——, *Collected Poems I* (London: Macmillan, 1967).
——, *Going Up to Sotheby's* (St Albans: Granada, 1982).

Other published poetry includes:
——, 'Snowflakes', *Gillespie's School Magazine* July 1929, p. 31.
——, 'Starshine', 'Other Worlds' and 'The Door of Youth', *Gillespie's School Magazine*, July 1931, pp. 37–8, 50–1.
——, 'Pan's Pipes' and 'Says Beetle', *Gillespie's School Magazine*, July 1932, pp. 22–3.
——, 'Shell Tales', 'A Dog-Day Dream – in School', 'Out of a Book', and 'Seagulls in the Links', *Gillespie's School Magazine*, July 1933, pp. 28–9, 36–7, 44.
——, 'Dust', *Gillespie's School Magazine*, July 1934, p. 16.
——, 'The Idiot', *School: The Annual of the Rhodesia Teacher's Association* 2(1), 1941, p. 39.
——, 'The Victoria Falls', *Poetry Review* 37 (4), August–September, 1946, p. 285.
——, 'Frantic a Child Ran' and 'Three Thoughts in Africa', *Poetry of To-Day* 1(72), 1946, pp. 80–2.
——, 'Poem for a Pianist', 'They Sigh for Old Dreams' and 'I Have a Lovely Meadow Land', *Poetry of To-Day* 3(74), 1946, pp. 10–2.
——, 'The Well', *Poetry Review* 38 (1), January–February, 1947, pp. 82–6.
——, 'Leaning Over an Old Wall' and 'Autumn', *Poetry Review* 38(2), March–April 1947, p. 106, 155–6.
——, 'The Robe and the Song', *Poetry Review* 38(4), May–June 1947, pp. 192–3.
——, 'Birthday', *Poetry Review* 38(4), July–August 1947, p. 270.
——, 'The Bells at Bray' and 'Cadmus', *Poetry Review* 38(5), September–October 1947, pp. 353, 379.
——, 'Omega', *Poetry Review* 38 (6), December 1947, pp. 519.

——, 'Song', *Outposts* 9, Winter 1947, p. 10.

——, 'You, Dreamer', *Canadian Poetry Magazine*, 11(3), March 1948, p. 23.

——, 'Invocation to a Child', *Poetry Quarterly* 10(1), Spring 1948, p. 22.

——, 'Poem', *Prospect* 2(10), Summer 1948, p. 5.

——, 'Song of the Divided Lover', *Poetry Commonwealth* 1, Summer 1948, p. 5.

——, 'Standing in Dusk', *Variegation* 3(3), Summer 1948, p. 3.

——, 'Lost Lover', *Outposts* 11, Autumn 1948, p. 3.

——, 'Anniversary', *Variegation* 3(4), Autumn 1948, p. 17.

——, 'A Letter to Howard', *Poetry Quarterly* 10(3), Autumn 1948, p. 152.

——, 'Tracing the Landscape . . .', *Poetry Commonwealth* 2, Autumn 1948, p. 5.

——, 'Sin', *Punch* 215(5628), 27 October 1948.

——, 'She Wore His Luck on Her Breast', *Outposts* 12, Winter 1948, pp. 10, 19–20.

—— and Howard Sergeant, *Reassessment: Poetry Pamphlet No.1* (London: G. Nicholls and Co, 1948).

——, 'Reassessment', *Women's Review*, 4 January 1949, pp. 18–9.

——, 'Magdalen', *Geminin* 1, May 1949, p. 3.

——, 'The Beads', *Poetry Quarterly*, 11(3), Autumn 1949, pp. 144–5, 162–8.

——, 'Indian Feathers', *Variegation*, 4(4), Autumn 1949, p. 4.

——, 'This Plato', *Arena* 21, 1949, pp. 12–13.

——, 'The Voice of One Lost Sings its Gain', *Poetry Quarterly* 11(4), Winter 1949–50, p. 221.

——, 'Invocation in a Churchyard on All Hallow's Eve', *Gemini 3*, January 1950.

——, 'The Dancers', *World Review* 12 February 1950, p. 3.

——, 'Elegy in a Kensington Churchyard', *Fortnightly* September, 1950.

——, 'Kindness or Weakness?', *Public Opinion* 4643, 17 November 1950, p. 24.

—— and Derek Stanford, translation of 'Poem XVII' from *Shadows of my Love*, Guillaume Apollinaire, *Poetry Quarterly* 12(3), 1950.

——, 'Snow-fall', *Public Opinion* 16 March 1951, p. 28.

——, 'No Need for Shouting', *Poetry Quarterly* 13(1) Spring 1951, p. 24.

——, 'A Sleep of Prisoners', *Spectator* 6413, 25 May 1951, p. 688.

——, 'Birthday Acrostic', *Poetry Quarterly* 13(2) Summer 1951, p. 68.

——, 'Portrait', *Recurrence*, 2(2) Autumn 1951, p. 7.

——, 'Conundrum' and 'The Miners', *Chanticleer* 1(1), Autumn 1952, p. 10.

——, 'A Letter at Christmas', *Outposts* 20, 1952, pp. 5–6.

——, 'Eyes and Noses', *The Observer* 18 January 1953.

——, 'Pearl Miners', *Poetry* (Chicago), September 1953.

——, 'Domestic Dawn', *Saturday Review* 13 April 1957.

——, 'Faith and Works', *Aylesford Review* 2(2), Winter 1957–8.

——, 'The Card Party', *The New Yorker* 28 December 1963, p. 30.

——, 'Canaan', *The New Yorker* 16 April 1966, p. 48.

——, 'The She-Wolf', *The New Yorker* 4 February 1967, p. 40.

——, 'The Messengers', *The New Yorker* 16 September 1967, p. 44.

Criticism and biography

—— and Derek Stanford, eds, *Tribute to Wordsworth* (London: Wingate, 1950).

——, *Child of Light: A Reassessment of Mary Wollstonecraft Shelley* (Hadleigh, Essex: Tower Bridge Publications, 1951).

——, *A Selection of Poems by Emily Brontë* (London: Grey Walls Press, 1952).

—— and Derek Stanford, eds, *My Best Mary: Selected Letters of Mary Shelley* (London: Wingate, 1953).

——, *John Masefield* (London: Peter Nevill, 1953) republished with new introduction (London: Hutchinson, 1991).

—— and Derek Stanford, eds, *Emily Brontë: Her life and Work* (London: Peter Owen, 1953).

——, *The Brontë Letters* (London: Peter Nevill, 1954).

—— and Derek Stanford, eds, *Letters of John Henry Newman* (London: Peter Owen, 1957).

——, *Mary Shelley* (London: Penguin, 1987).

——, *The Essence of the Brontës* (London: Peter Owen, 1993).

Critical essays and journalism

——, 'The Catholic View' *Poetry Review* 38 (6), December 1947, pp. 402–5.

——, 'Criticism, Effects and Morals', *Poetry Review* 39(1), February 1948, pp. 3–6.

——, 'Reassessment', *Poetry Review* 39(2), April–May 1948, pp. 103–4.

——, 'Reassessment – II', *Poetry Review* 39(3), August–September 1948, p. 234.

——, 'A pamphlet from the U.S.', *Poetry Review*, 39(4), October–November 1948, p. 318.

——, 'Poetry and Politics', *Parliamentary Affairs* 1(4), Autumn 1948, pp. 12–23.

——, 'Review Article', *Outposts* 12, Winter 1948, pp. 10, 19–20.

——, 'Poetry and the Other Arts', *Poetry Review* 39(5), December 1948–January 1949, p. 390.

——, 'The Dramatic Works of T.S. Eliot', *Women's Review* 5, March–April 1949, pp. 2–4.

——, 'African Handouts', *The New English Weekly* 35(3), 28 April 1949, pp. 32–3.

——, 'The Poetry of Anne Brontë', *The New English Weekly* 26 May 1949.

——, 'Introduction', *Forum* 1(1), Summer 1949, p. 1.

——, 'The Poet in Mr Eliot's Ideal State', *Outposts* 14, Summer 1949, pp. 26–8.

——, 'Cecil Day Lewis', *Poetry Quarterly* 11(3), Autumn 1949, pp. 162–8.

——, 'Poetry and the American Government', *Parliamentary Affairs* 3(1), Winter 1949, pp. 260–72.

——, 'The Dramatic Work of T.S. Eliot', *Women's Review* 5, 1949.

——, 'Introduction', *Forum* 1(2), 1949, pp. 25–6.

——, 'Mary Shelley: A Prophetic Novelist', *Listener* 22 February 1951.

——, 'Passionate Humbugs, Book Review', *Public Opinion* 4567, 23 February 1951.

——, 'The Complete Frost, Book Review', *Public Opinion* 4662, 30 March 1951.

——, 'Two-way', *Church of England Newspaper* 25 May 1951.

——, 'Psychology and Criticism', *Times Literary Supplement* 25 May 1951.

——, 'In Defence of the Highbrow', *Public Opinion* 4672, 8 June 1951, p. 28.

——, 'Does Celibacy Affect Judgement?', *Church of England Newspaper* 16 November 1951, p. 10.

——, 'Civilised Humour', *The Journal of the Scottish Secondary Teachers' Association* 7(1), October 1952, pp. 30–2.

——, 'Talks in Moscow', *The Church of England Newspaper* 31 October 1952.

——, 'Ex-pagan Reader', *Church of England Newspaper* 19 December 1952, p. 10.

——, 'All Laugh Together?', *The English Speaking World* 35(2), March 1953, pp. 32–6.

——, 'R.E. Williams 'Punch Replies', *The English Speaking World* 35(3), May 1953, pp. 24–8.

——, 'If I were "Punch" ...' *The English Speaking World* 35(4), June 1953, pp. 23–5.

——, 'Edinburgh Festival Diary: A Prophet's Married Life', *The Church of England Newspaper*, 3115, 4 September 1953, p. 5.

——, 'Edinburgh Festival Diary: The Wisdom of T.S. Eliot', *The Church of England Newspaper* 3116, 11 September 1953, p. 5.

——, 'The Religion of an Agnostic: A Sacramental View of the World in the Writings of Proust', *The Church of England Newspaper* November 27, 1953.

——, 'Review of John Masefield', *The Journal of the Scottish Secondary Teachers' Association* 8(2), February 1954, p. 58.

——, 'Aylesford Priory', *The Tablet* 12 February 1955, p. 154.

——, 'The Mystery of Job's Suffering: Jung's New Interpretation Examined', *The Church of England Newspaper* April 15, 1955.

——, 'St. Monica', *The Canadian Messenger of the Sacred Heart* 67(5) May 1957, pp. 318–25. Reprinted in *The Month* New Series 17(5), May 1957, pp. 309–20, and *Saints and Ourselves*, ed. p. Carman (London: Hollis & Carter, 1958).

——, 'How I Became a Novelist', *John O'London's Magazine* 1 December 1960, p. 683. Reprinted in *Books and Bookmen* 7(2), November 1961, p. 9.

——, 'The Poet's House', *The Critic* (Chicago), 19(4), Febuary–March 1961. Reprinted in *Encounter* 30, May 1968, pp. 48–50.

——, 'My Conversion', *Twentieth Century* 170, Autumn 1961, pp. 58–63.

——, 'Edinburgh-born', *New Statesman* 64 (1639), 10 August 1962, p. 180. Reprinted as 'What Images Return', *Memoirs of a Modern Scotland*, ed. Karl Miller (London: Faber and Faber, 1970), p. 153–5.

——, 'On the Lack of Sleep', *The New Yorker* 7 December 1963, p. 58.

——, 'The Sermons of Newman', *The Critic* 22(6), June–July 1964, pp. 531–4.

——, 'The Brontës as Teachers', *The New Yorker* 22 January 1966. Reprinted in *The Journal of the Scottish Secondary Teachers' Association* 6(2), pp. 28–31.

——, 'Exotic Departures', *The New Yorker* 28 January 1967, pp. 31–2.

——, 'The Desegregation of Art', The Annual Blashfield Foundation Address, Proceedings of the American Academy of Arts and Letters and the National Institute of Arts and Letters, 2nd ser., 21 (New York: Spiral Press, 1971), pp. 21–7.

——, 'When Israel Went to the Vatican', *The Tablet* 227, 24 March 1973, pp. 277–8.

——, 'Three Champagnes', *The Tablet* 229, 11 January 1975.

——, 'Heinrich Boll', *New York Times Book Review* 4 December 1977, pp. 66,70.

——, 'Created and Abandoned', *The New Yorker* 12 November 1979, p. 60.

——, 'The Books that Made Writers', *New York Times Book Review* 25 November 1979, p. 7.

——, 'Conversation Piece', *The New Yorker*, 23 November 1981, p. 54.

——, 'I Would Like to Have Written', *New York Times Book Review* 1981, 86(49), p. 7.

——, 'My Most Obnoxious Writer', *New York Times Book Review* 1982, 87(35), p. 7.

——, 'The Pleasures of Rereading', *New York Times Book Review* 1983, 88(24), p. 14.

——, 'Pitch Dark: Review of Renata Adler', *New York Times Book Review* 1983, 88(51), p. 1.

——, 'My Rome', *New York Times Magazine* 13 March 1983, pp. 36, 39, 70–72.

——, 'On Love', *Partisan Review* 1984, 51(4), pp. 780–83.

——, 'Abroad', *New York Times Magazine* 10 March 1984.

——, 'Side Roads of Tuscany', *New York Times Magazine* 7 October 1984, pp. 28–9, 72–9.

——, 'Spirit and Substance', *Vanity Fair* 12 (47), December 1984, pp. 102–3.

——, 'Footnote to a Poet's House', *Architectural Digest* 42 (11), 1985.

——, 'Echoes of Shelley in Italy', *Architectural Digest* 1986, 43(6), p. 262.

——, 'Ravenna's Jewelled Churches', *New York Times Magazine* 4 October 1987, pp. 50–1, 68–71.

——, 'Plotting an Alpine Cliffhanger: The Baggatti-Valsecchi Villa above Lake Como', *Architectural Digest* 1987, 44(2), p. 124.

——, 'A Winterson Tale: Review of Jeanette Winterson's *The Passion*', *Vanity Fair* May 1988.

——, 'Manzu Giacomo: Triumphs of Matter and Spirit in Bronze', *Architectural Digest* 1988, 45(5), p. 40.

——, 'Whose Europe is it Anyway?', *New Statesman and Society* 106(3), 22 June 1990, p. 12.

——, 'Home Thoughts: Muriel Spark on How to Write a Letter', *The Independent Magazine* 102, 18 August 1990, p. 16.

——, 'The Ravenna Mosaics', *Antique and New Art* Winter 1990, pp. 122–5.

——, 'Highland Flings', *The Sunday Times* (Section 7, Books), 23 June 1996, p. 1.

Texts by Muriel Spark also appear in *Argentor, The Fortnightly, Recurrence, World Review, The Norseman, European Affairs, Courier, Botteghe Oscure, The Glasgow Herald*, and *The Observer* (television reviews).

2. Critical texts on Muriel Spark

Adler, R., 'Muriel Spark', in Kostelanetz, R., ed., *On Contemporary Literature* (New York: Avon Books, 1969).

Ashworth, A., 'The Betrayal of the Mentor in *The Prime of Miss Jean Brodie*', *Journal of Evolutionary Psychology* 16(1), March 1995, pp. 37–46.

Auerbach, N., 'One Big Miss Brodie', in *Communities of Women: An Idea in Fiction* (Cambridge, Mass: Harvard University Press, 1978).

Baldanza, F., 'Muriel Spark and the Occult', *Wisconsin Studies in Contemporary Literature* 6, 1965, pp. 190–203.

Barber, L., 'An Interview with Muriel Spark', *Mostly Men* pp. 273–83.

Barreca, R., 'The Ancestral Laughter of the Streets: Humor in Muriel Spark's Earlier Works', in Barreca, R., ed., *New Perspectives on Women and Comedy* (Philadelphia, PA: Gordon & Breach, 1992), pp. 223–40.

Berthoff, W., 'Fortunes of the Novel: Muriel Spark and Iris Murdoch', *Massachusetts Review* 8, 1967, pp. 301–32.

Blodgett, H., 'Desegregated Art by Muriel Spark', *International Fiction Review* 3, 1976, pp. 25–9.

Bold, A., *Muriel Spark*, (London: Methuen, 1986).

Bold, A., ed., *Muriel Spark: An Odd Capacity for Vision* (London: Vision Press, 1984).

Bower, A. L., 'The Narrative Structure of Muriel Spark's The Prime of Miss Jean Brodie', *Mid West Quarterly* 31(4), 1990, pp. 488–98.

Bower, A. L., 'Tyranny, Telling, Learning: Teaching the Female Student', *West Virginia University Philological Papers* 36, 1990, pp. 38–45.

Bradbury, M., 'Dark Spark', *New Society* 24 September 1970.

Bradbury, M., 'Muriel Spark's Fingernails', in *Possibilities: Essays on the State of the Novel*, (London: Oxford University Press, 1973).

Brooke-Rose, C., 'Le Roman Experimental en Angleterre', *Les Langues Modernes* 63, 1969, pp. 158–68.

Button, M. D., 'On Her Way Rejoicing: The Artist and Her Craft in the Works of Muriel Spark', *The Nassau Review* 5(4), 1988, pp. 6–14.

Calder, A., 'Miss Jean Brodie and the Kaledonian Klan', in *Revolving Culture: Notes from the Scottish Republic* (London: I.B Tauris, 1994).

Carruthers, G., 'The Remarkable Fictions of Muriel Spark', in Gifford-Douglas and McMillan-Dorothy eds, *A History of Scottish Women's Writing* (Edinburgh: Edinburgh University Press, 1997).

Cheyette, B., *Muriel Spark* (Plymouth: Northcote House, 2000).

Cixous, H., 'La Farce Macabre de Muriel Spark: Un Catholicisme Grimaçant', *Le Monde* (January 17, 1968), 7157, p. viia.

Cixous, H., 'Le Dernier Roman de Muriel Spark: L'Image Publique', in *Le Monde* (November 9, 1968), 7410, p. viiia.

Codaccioni, M-J., 'La Recherche du Pouvoir chez Muriel Spark ou l'Art de Manipuler Autrui', in Rigaud, N. J., ed., *Le Pouvoir dans la Litterature et la Pensée Anglaises* (Aix en Provence: Centre Aixois de Recherches Anglaises, Université de Provence Aix, 1981), pp. 111–22.

Codaccioni, M-J., 'L'Échange dans *The Towers of Trebizond* et *The Mandelbaum Gate*' in *Échanges: Actes du Congres de Strasbourg de Sociétedes Anglicistes de l'Enseignement Supérieur*, (Paris: Didier, 1982), pp. 271–9.

Coe, J., 'Conversions', *London Review of Books* London, 12(17), 13 Sept 1990, pp. 15–6.

De Reuck, J. A., 'A New Voice in Narrative: Muriel Spark's "You Should Have Seen the Mess"', *Journal of Literary Studies Tydskrif Vir Literaturwetenskap* 2(2), 1986, pp. 41–56.

Devoize, J. and Valette, p. , 'An Interview with Muriel Spark', *Journal of the Short Story in English* 13, Autumn 1989, pp. 11–22.

Dobie, A. B., '*The Prime of Miss Jean Brodie*: Muriel Spark Bridges the Credibility Gap', *Arizona Quarterly* 25, 1969, pp. 217–28.

Dobie, A. B., 'Muriel Spark's Definition of Reality', *Critique: Studies in Modern Fiction*, 12(1), 1970, pp. 20–7.

Dobie, A. B., and Wooton, C., 'Spark and Waugh: Similarities by Coincidence', *Midwest Quarterly: A Journal of Contemporary Thought* 13, 1972, pp. 423–34.

Edgecombe, R. S., *Vocation and Identity in Muriel Spark* (London: University of Missouri Press, 1990).

Edgecombe, R. S., 'Muriel Spark, Cardinal Newman and an Aphorism in Memento Mori', *Notes on Contemporary Literature* 24(1), Jan 1994, p. 12.

Fay, B., 'Muriel Spark en sa Fleur', *Nouvelle Revue Française* 75341, 14 Feb 1966, pp. 307–15.

Felton, S., 'Portraits of the Artists as Young Defiers: James Joyce and Muriel Spark', *Tennessee Philological Bulletin* 33, 1966, pp. 4–33.

Frankel, S., 'An Interview with Muriel Spark', *Partisan Review* 54(3), 1987, pp. 443–57.

Galvin, J., 'Muriel Spark's Unknowing Fiction', *Women's Studies: An Interdisciplinary Journal* 15(1–3), 1988, pp. 221–41.

Gilliatt, p. , 'The Dashing Novellas of Muriel Spark', *Grand-Street* 8(4), Summer, pp. 139–46.

Greene, G., 'Du Cote de Chez Disaster: The Novels of Muriel Spark', *Papers on Language and Literature* 16, 1980, pp. 295–315.

Grosskurth, p. , 'The World of Muriel Spark: Spirits or Spooks?', *Tamarack Review* 39, 1966, pp. 62–7.

Halio, J. L., 'Muriel Spark: The Novelist's Sense of Wonder', in Biles, J.I., ed., *British Novelists since 1900* (New York: AMS, 1987), pp. 267–77.

Harrison, B., 'Muriel Spark and Jane Austen', in Josipovici, G., ed., *The Modern English Novel: The Reader, the Writer, and the Work* (New York: Barnes & Noble, 1976), pp. 225–51.

Hart, F. R., 'Region, Character and Identity in Recent Scottish Fiction' *Virginia Quarterly Review* 43, 1967, pp. 597–613.

Hart, F. R., *The Scottish Novel: From Smollett to Spark* (Cambridge, Mass.: Harvard University Press, 1978).

Hendry, D., 'Spooky Spark: On Muriel Spark and the Post-war Poetry Society', *Poetry Review* 1992, 823, pp. 70–1.

Holloway, J., 'Narrative Structure and Text Structure: Isherwood's *A Meeting by the River* and Muriel Spark's *The Prime of Miss Jean Brodie*', *Critical Inquiry* 1, 1975, pp. 581–604.

Hosmer, R. E., Jr., 'The Book of Job: The Novel of Harvey', *Renascence: Essays on Value in Literature* 39(3), Spring 1987, pp. 442–9.

Hoyt, C. A., 'Muriel Spark: The Surrealist Jane Austen', in Shapiro, C., ed., *Contemporary British Novelists* (Carbondale and Edwardsville: Southern Illinois University Press, 1965), pp. 125–43.

Hynes, J., 'After Marabar: Reading Forster, Robbe-Grillet, Spark', *The Iowa Review* 5(1), 1974, pp. 120–6.

Hynes, J., *The Art of the Real: Muriel Spark's Novels* (London: Dickson University Press, 1988).

Hynes, J., 'Muriel Spark and the Oxymoronic Vision', in Hosmer, R.E. Jr, ed., *Contemporary British Women Writers: Narrative Strategies* (New York: St Martin's, 1993), pp. 161–87.

Hynes, J., ed., *Critical Essays on Muriel Spark* (Oxford: Maxwell Macmillan International, 1992).

Hynes, S., 'The Prime of Muriel Spark', *Commonweal* 75, 23 February 1962, pp. 562–3, 567–8.

Jacobsen, J., 'A Catholic Quartet', *Christian Scholar* 47, 1964, pp. 139–54.

Jordis, C., 'Muriel Spark', *Nouvelle Revue Française* 406, 1986, pp. 60–70.

Josipovici, G., 'On the Side of Job', *Times Literary Supplement* 4249(989), 7 Sept 1984.

Kane, R., *Iris Murdoch, Muriel Spark and John Fowles: Didactic Demons in Modern Fiction* (London: Farleigh Dickinson University Press, 1988).

Kane, R. C., 'Didactic Demons in Contemporary British Fiction', *University of*

Mississippi Studies in English 8, 1990, pp. 36–57.

Kelleher, V.M.K., 'The Religious Artistry of Muriel Spark', *The Critical Review* 18, 1976, pp. 79–92.

Kemp, p. , *Muriel Spark* (London: Elek Books, 1974).

Kennedy, A., 'Cannibals, Okapis and Self-Slaughter in the Novels of Muriel Spark', in *The Protean Self: Dramatic Action in Contemporary Fiction* (New York: Columbia University Press, 1974).

Kermode, F., 'The House of Fiction: Interviews with Seven English Novelists', *Partisan Review* Spring, 1963, pp. 79–82.

Kermode, F., 'The Prime of Miss Muriel Spark', *New Statesman* 27 September 1963.

Kermode, F., 'God's Plots', *The Listener* 78, 7 December 1967, pp. 759–60.

Kermode, F., 'To The Girls of Slender Means', 'The Public Image', 'The Novel as Jerusalem', in *Modern Essays* (London: Fontana, 1971), pp. 267–83.

Kermode, F., 'Foreseeing the Unforeseen', *The Listener* 86, 11 December 1971, pp. 657–8.

Kermode, F., 'Diana of the Crossroads', *New Statesman* 91, 4 June 1976, pp. 746–7.

Kermode, F., 'Judgement in Venice', *The Listener* 101, 26 April 1979, pp. 584–5.

Keyser, B., 'Muriel Spark, Watergate, and the Mass Media', *Arizona Quarterly* 32(1), 1976, pp. 146–53.

Kimball, R., 'The First Half of Muriel Spark', *The New Criterion* 11(8), April 1993 pp. 9–16

Kimball, S. L., 'Intentional Garble: Irony in the Communication of Muriel Spark', *West Virginia University Philological Papers* 33, 1987, pp. 86–91.

Laffin, G. S., 'Muriel Spark's Portrait of the Artist as a Young Girl', *Renascence: Essays on Value in Literature* 24, 1972, pp. 213–23.

Leonard, J., 'Muriel Spark's Parables: The Religious Limits of Her Art', in Apczynski, J.V., ed., *Foundations of Religious Literacy* (Chico, CA: Scholars, 1983), pp. 153–64.

Leonard, J., 'Loitering with Intent: Muriel Spark's Parabolic Technique', *Studies in the Literary Imagination* 18(1), Spring 1985, pp. 65–77.

Little, J., *Comedy and the Woman Writer: Woolf, Spark, and Feminism* (London: University of Nebraska Press, 1983).

Little, J., 'Endless Different Ways: Muriel Spark's Re-Visions of the Spinster', in Doan, L.L., ed., *Old Maids to Radical Spinsters: Unmarried Women in the Twentieth-Century Novel* (Urbana: University of Illinois Press, 1991), pp. 19–35.

Little, J., 'Muriel Spark's Grammars of Assent', in Acheson, J., ed., *The British and Irish Novel Since 1960* (New York: St Martin's, 1991), pp. 1–16.

Litvack, L. B., 'The Road to Rome: Muriel Spark, Newman and the "Nevertheless Principle"', in Bevan, David, ed., *Literature and the Bible* (Amsterdam: Rodopi, 1993), pp. 29–46.

Litvack, L., '"We All Have Something to Hide": Muriel Spark, Autobiography, and the Influence of Newman on the Career of a Novelist', *Durham University Journal* 86:55 (2), July 1994, pp. 281–89.

Lodge, D., 'The Uses and Abuses of Omniscience: Method and Meaning in Muriel Spark's *The Prime of Miss Jean Brodie*', in *The Novelist at the Crossroads* (London: Kegan Paul, 1971).

Lodge, D., 'Time-Shift', *The Art of Fiction* (Hammondsworth: Penguin, 1992).

McBrien, W., 'Muriel Spark: The Novelist as Dandy', in Staley, T.F., ed., *Twentieth Century Women Novelists* (Totowa, NJ: Barnes & Noble, 1982), pp. 153–78.

MacLachlan, C., 'Muriel Spark and Gothic', in Hagemann, S., ed., *Studies in Scottish Fiction: 1945 to the Present* (Frankfurt: Peter Lang, 1996), pp. 125–44.

Malin, I., 'The Deceptions of Muriel Spark', in Friedman, M. J., ed., *The Vision Obscured: Perceptions of Some Twentieth Century Catholic Novelists* (New York: Fordham University Press, 1970), pp. 95–107.

Malkoff, K., *Muriel Spark* (New York: Columbia University Press, 1968).

Malkoff, K., 'Demonology and Dualism: The Supernatural in Isaac Singer and Muriel Spark', in Malin, I., ed., *Critical Views of Isaac Bashevis Singer* (New York: New York University Press, 1969), pp. 149–68.

Manning, G. F., 'Sunsets and Sunrises: Nursing Home as Microcosm in *Memento Mori* and *Mr. Scobie's Riddle*', *ARIEL* 18(2), April 1987, pp. 27–43.

Massie, A., *Muriel Spark* (Edinburgh: Ramsey Head Press, 1979).

Mayne, R., 'Fiery Particle: On Muriel Spark', *Encounter* 25, December 1965, pp. 61–8.

Mendelsohn, J., 'The Devil in Miss Spark: Muriel's Wicked, Wicked Ways', *Village Voice Literary Supplement* 91, Dec 1990, pp. 25–6.

Mengham, R., '1973 The End of History: Cultural Change According to Muriel Spark', in Mengham, R., ed., *An Introduction to Contemporary Fiction: International Writing in English since 1970* (Cambridge: Polity, 1999).

Monterrey, T., 'Old and New Elements in Muriel Spark's *Symposium*', *Studies in Scottish Literature* Columbia, 27, 1992, pp. 175–88.

Montgomery, B., 'Spark and Newman: Jean Brodie Reconsidered', *Twentieth Century Literature* 43(1), Spring 1997, pp. 94–106.

Murphy, C., 'A Spark of the Supernatural', *Approach*, Summer 1966.

Nordhjem, B., *What Fiction Means* (Copenhagen: Atheneum Distributor, 1987).

Ohmann, C. B., 'Muriel Spark's *Robinson*', *Critique: Studies in Modern Fiction* 8(1), 1965, pp. 70–84.

Page, N., *Muriel Spark* (London: Macmillan, 1990).

Parrinder, P., 'Muriel Spark and her Critics', *Critical Quarterly* 25(2), 1983, pp. 23–31.

Paul, A., 'Muriel Spark and *The Prime of Miss Jean Brodie*', *Dutch Quarterly Review of Anglo American Letters* 7, 1977, pp. 170–83.

Pearlman, M., 'The Element of the Fantastic and the Artist Figure in the Novels of Muriel Spark', in Langford, M.K., ed., *Contours of the Fantastic: Selected Essays from the Eighth International Conference on the Fantastic in the Arts* (New York: Greenwood, 1994), pp. 149–61.

Poitou, M., 'Les Ironies de Venise: Roman et Decor dans *Territorial Rights* de Muriel Spark', *Cycnos* 1, 1984, pp. 15–24.

Poitou, M., 'La Rage d'Être Autre: *The Mandelbaum Gate* de Muriel Spark', *Cycnos* 2, Winter 1985–86, pp. 17–25.

Potter, N.A.J., 'Muriel Spark: Transformer of the Commonplace', *Renascence: Essays on Value in Literature* 17, 1965, pp. 115–20.

Pyper, H., 'The Reader in Pain: Job as Text and Pretext', *Literature and Theology:An International Journal of Theory, Criticism and Culture* 7(2), June 1993, pp. 111–29.

Randsi, J. L., *On Her Way Rejoicing: the Fiction of Muriel Spark* (Washington DC: The Catholic University of America Press, 1991) .

Rankin, I., 'Surface and Structure: Reading Muriel Spark's *The Driver's Seat*', *Journal of Narrative Technique*, 15(2), 1985, pp. 146–55.

Ray, P. E. 'Jean Brodie and Edinburgh: Personality and Place in Murial Spark's *The Prime of Miss Jean Brodie*', *Studies in Scottish Literature* Columbia, 13, 1978, pp. 24–31.

Rees, D., *Muriel Spark, William Trevor, Ian McEwan: A Bibliography of their First Editions* (London: Colophon Press, 1992).

Richmond, V. B., 'The Darkening Vision of Muriel Spark', *Critique: Studies in Modern Fiction* 15(1), 1973, pp. 71–85.

Richmond, V. B., *Muriel Spark* (New York: Ungar, 1985).

Richmond, V. B., 'Chaucer's Religiosity and a Twentieth-Century Analogue, Muriel Spark', *Modern Language Quarterly* 51(3), Sept 1990, pp. 427–45.

Robb, D. S., 'Muriel Spark's *The Prime of Miss Jean Brodie*' (Aberdeen: Association. for Scottish Literary Studies, 1992).

Rowe, M. M., 'Muriel Spark and the Angel of the Body', *Critique: Studies in Modern Fiction* 28(3), 1987, pp. 167–76.

Schiff, S., 'Muriel Spark Between the Lines', *The New Yorker* 24 May 1993, pp. 36–43.

Schneider, H.W., 'A Writer in Her Prime: The Fiction of Muriel Spark', *Critique* 15, 1973, pp. 28–45.

Schneider, M.W., 'The Double Life in Muriel Spark's *The Prime of Miss Jean Brodie*' *Midwest Quarterly: A Journal of Contemporary Thought* 18, 1977, pp. 418–31.

Shaw,V., 'Muriel Spark', in Craig, C. ed., *The History of Scottish Literature, IV: Twentieth Century* (Aberdeen: Aberdeen University Press, 1987), pp. 277–90.

Snow, L., 'Muriel Spark and the Uses of Mythology', *Research Studies* 45, 1977, pp. 38–44.

Sproxton, J., *The Women of Muriel Spark* (London: Constable, 1992).

Stanford, D., 'The Work of Muriel Spark: An Essay on her Fictional Method', *Month*, August 1962.

Stanford, D., *Muriel Spark: A Biographical and Critical Study* (London: Centaur Press, 1963).

Stanford, D., *Inside the Forties: Literary Memoirs 1937–1957* (Essex: Anchor Press, 1977).

Stannard, M., 'The Letter Killeth', *The Spectator* 6 June 1998, pp. 36–7.

Stannard, M., *Muriel Spark: A Biography* (London: Weidenfeld and Nicolson General, 2001).

Stevenson, S., '"Poetry Deleted": Parody Added: Watergate, Spark's Style, and Bakhtin's Stylistics', *ARIEL* 24(4), 1993, pp. 71–85.

Stubbs, p. , *Muriel Spark* (Harlow: Longman, 1973).

Stubbs, p. , 'Two Contemporary Views on Fiction: Iris Murdoch and Muriel Spark', *English* 23, 1974, pp. 102–10.

Todd, R., 'The Crystalline Novels of Muriel Spark', in Bock, H. and Wertheim, A., eds, *Essays on the Contemporary British Novel* (Munich: Max Hueber, 1986), pp. 175–92.

Updike, J., 'Creatures of the Air', *The New Yorker* 37, 30 September 1961, pp. 161–6.

Updike, J., 'Between a Wedding and a Funeral', *The New Yorker* 39, 14 September 1963, pp. 192–4.

Updike, J., 'A Romp with Job', *The New Yorker* 50, 6 January 1985, pp. 104–7.

Updike, J., 'Topnotch Witcheries', *The New Yorker* 50, 6 January 1975, pp. 76–81.

Updike, J., 'Seeresses', *The New Yorker* 52, 29 November 1976, pp. 164–74.

Updike, J., 'Fresh from the Forties', *The New Yorker* 57, 8 June 1981, pp. 148–56.

Walker, D., *Muriel Spark* (Boston: Twayne Publishers, 1988).

Wallace, G., 'The Deliberate Cunning of Muriel Spark', in Wallace, G. and Stevenson, R., eds, *The Scottish Novel since the Seventies: New Visions, Old Dreams* (Edinburgh: Edinburgh University Press, 1993), pp. 41–53.

Waugh, E., 'Something Fresh: *The Comforters*', *The Spectator* 22 February 1957, p. 256.

Waugh, E., 'Threatened Genius: Difficult Saint', *The Spectator* 7 July 1961.

Whiteley, P. J., 'The Social Framework of Knowledge: Muriel Spark's *The Prime of Miss Jean Brodie*', *Mosaic* 29(4), Dec 1996, pp. 79–100

Whittaker, R., 'Angels Dining at the Ritz: The Faith and Fiction of Muriel Spark', in Bradbury, M. and Palmer, D., eds, *The Contemporary English Novel* (New York: Holmes & Meier, 1979), pp. 157–79.

Whittaker, R., *The Faith and Fiction of Muriel Spark* (London: Macmillan, 1982)

Wildman, J. H., 'Translated by Muriel Spark', in Stanford, D. E., ed., *Nine Essays in Modern Literature* (Baton Rouge: Louisiana State University Press, 1965), pp. 129–44.

Index

.